"What a remarkable display of insightful revelation, historical narrative, personal evolution, and creative vision! With the beautiful language of a poet and the humility of an enlightened spirit guide, Erving Polster gives readers the gift of a wisdom nearly a century in the making. Reading, no *savoring*, this book provided an extraordinary opportunity to get to know the man and share his passion for catalyzing personal growth. Polster is one of this field's greatest treasures, and when you read *Enchantment and Gestalt Therapy* you'll know why."

Michael D. Yapko, *clinical psychologist, author of* Trancework (5th ed.)

"From his earliest writings, Polster has argued that psychotherapy, more explicitly the Gestalt approach, is too important to be confined to 'patients' and the psychotherapist's office. In this delightful, thought provoking, and wonderfully written book, he contends that it is the telling of ordinary stories in group settings that is essential to forming cohesive societies. Using Gestalt principles and drawing from the fields of religion, music, poetry and literature, Polster deconstructs and elucidates the mysterious process of generating communal intimacy. As with his other books, this one will enchant you."

Joseph Melnick, *Founding Editor,* Gestalt Review

"Erving Polster re-conceives psychotherapy not just as a cure for symptoms or a return to normality, but as a path to a life of absorbing fascination and fulfillment. No one makes better use of Gestalt therapy's teaching that a sharpened awareness of one's present situation is the key to wellbeing. Polster thoroughly persuades us through a mix of theory, example, and memoir how such awareness, especially in relationships with others, can amplify even the most ordinary passing moment into 'a stepping-stone to enchantment.'"

Michael Vincent Miller, *author of* Intimate Terrorism: The Crisis of Love in an Age of Disillusion *and* Teaching a Paranoid to Flirt: The Poetics of Gestalt Therapy

Enchantment and Gestalt Therapy

Enchantment and Gestalt Therapy is a personal exploration of Erving Polster's remarkable career, the value of the Gestalt approach, and the power of enchantment in psychotherapy.

Polster points ahead to a vision of a psychotherapy that includes the population as a whole rather than focusing on individuals, highlights common aspects of living, and focuses on creating an ethos for a shared understanding. The book outlines the six Gestalt therapy concepts that have formed the basis of Polster's work and describes Life Focus Groups, with an emphasis on the communal relationship between tellers and listeners. Polster also describes the phenomenon of enchantment in psychotherapy in detail, with reference to his own experiences.

This unique work is essential reading for Gestalt therapists, other professionals interested in Gestalt approaches, and readers looking for a deeper insight into community and connection.

Erving Polster is a veteran teacher of Gestalt therapy and the author of several books. His major interests have long been the transformation of psychotherapy as a curative process into psychotherapy as a communal source of orientation and guidance.

Gestalt Therapy Book Series

The Istituto di Gestalt series of Gestalt therapy books emerges from the ground of a growing interest in theory, research and clinical practice in the Gestalt community. The members of the Scientific and Editorial Boards have been committed for many years to the process of supporting research and publications in our field: through this series we want to offer our colleagues internationally the richness of the current trends in Gestalt therapy theory and practice, underpinned by research. The goal of this series is to develop the original principles in hermeneutic terms: to articulate a relational perspective, namely a phenomenological, aesthetic, field-oriented approach to psychotherapy. It is also intended to help professions and to support a solid development and dialogue of Gestalt therapy with other psychotherapeutic methods.

The series includes original books specifically created for it, as well as translations of volumes originally published in other languages. We hope that our editorial effort will support the growth of the Gestalt therapy community; a dialogue with other modalities and disciplines; and new developments in research, clinics and other fields where Gestalt therapy theory can be applied (e.g., organizations, education, political and social critique and movements).

We would like to dedicate this Gestalt Therapy Book Series to all our masters and colleagues who have sown fruitful seeds in our minds and hearts.

Scientific Board
Vincent Béja, Dan Bloom, Bernd Bocian, Phil Brownell, Pietro A. Cavaleri, Scott Churchill, Michael Clemmens, Peter Cole, Susan L. Fischer, Madeleine Fogarty, Ruella Frank, Pablo Herrera Salinas, Lynne Jacobs, Natasha Kedrova, Timothy Leung, Alan Meara, Joseph Melnick, Myriam Muñoz Polit, Antonio Narzisi, Leanne O'Shea, Malcolm Parlett, Peter Philippson, Erving Polster, Jean-Marie Robine, Jan Roubal, Adriana Schnake, Peter Schulthess, Christine Stevens, Daan van Baalen, Carmen Vázquez Bandín, Gordon Wheeler, Gary Yontef

Editorial Board
Rafael Salgado, Billy Desmond, Fabiola Maggio, Max Mishchenko, Georg Pernter, Silvia Tosi, Jay Tropianskaia, Andy Williams, Jelena Zeleskov Djoric

Coordinators
Jeff Allison and Stefania Benini

Editorial Assistant
Serena Iacono Isidoro

General Editor
Margherita Spagnuolo Lobb

Series Editor **Margherita Spagnuolo Lobb**

Gestalt Therapy Book Series

Series editor: Margherita Spagnuolo Lobb

Enchantment and Gestalt Therapy
Partners in Exploring Life
Erving Polster

Sexuality, Masculinity and Culture in Gestalt Therapy
An Autoethnographic Approach
Adam Kincel

Human Interaction and Emotional Awareness in Gestalt Therapy
Exploring the Phenomenology of Contacting and Feeling
Peter H. Dreitzel

For more information on the titles in this series, please visit www.routledge.com/Gestalt-Therapy/book-series/GESTHE and www.gestaltitaly.com

Enchantment and Gestalt Therapy

Partners in Exploring Life

Erving Polster

LONDON AND NEW YORK

First published 2021
by Routledge
2 Park Square, Milton Park, Abingdon, Oxon OX14 4RN

and by Routledge
52 Vanderbilt Avenue, New York, NY 10017

Routledge is an imprint of the Taylor & Francis Group, an informa business

© 2021 Erving Polster

The right of Erving Polster to be identified as author of this work has been asserted by him in accordance with sections 77 and 78 of the Copyright, Designs and Patents Act 1988.

All rights reserved. No part of this book may be reprinted or reproduced or utilised in any form or by any electronic, mechanical, or other means, now known or hereafter invented, including photocopying and recording, or in any information storage or retrieval system, without permission in writing from the publishers.

Trademark notice: Product or corporate names may be trademarks or registered trademarks, and are used only for identification and explanation without intent to infringe.

British Library Cataloguing-in-Publication Data
A catalogue record for this book is available from the British Library

Library of Congress Cataloging-in-Publication Data
A catalog record for this book has been requested

ISBN: 978-0-367-61271-9 (hbk)
ISBN: 978-0-367-61273-3 (pbk)
ISBN: 978-1-003-10493-3 (ebk)

Typeset in Times New Roman
by MPS Limited, Dehradun

Contents

	Foreword by Scott D. Churchill	*x*
	Gratitude	*xiv*
	Introduction	*xviii*
1	My beginnings: Stolen by gypsies	1
2	Concentration: Fundamentals	11
3	Concentration: Enchantment	23
4	Figure/ground relationship: Basic process	35
5	Figure/ground: Here and now/there and then	45
6	Figure/ground: Life focus groups	56
7	Figure/ground: Belonging	68
8	Awareness: Fundamentals	80
9	Contact boundary: Fundamentals	93
10	Contact boundary: Morality	104
11	Polarities: Self-formation	115
12	Resistance	129
13	Public trust	141
	Author's note	152
	Bibliography	153
	Afterword by Margherita Spagnuolo Lobb	155
	Index	163

Foreword

Scott D. Churchill[1]

At once a memoir, a grand revisiting of a lifetime's work, and an intellectually robust revisioning of a movement that he has helped to nurture over many decades, Erving Polster's reflections comprise a welcome contribution to the ever-evolving field of Gestalt Therapy. In these pages he observes how "each person's stories contribute singularly to a communal conversational vitality, a stretch beyond the self" (p. 46). It is to his credit that the author weaves into his reflections not only his own personal experiences, but insights that have developed out of his always relational interest in contact, contemplation, and amplification within therapeutic work.

I first encountered Erving Polster's work over four decades ago at Duquesne University, in Anthony Barton's doctoral class on Gestalt Therapy. The book that Erving had coauthored with his wife Miriam Polster—*Gestalt Therapy Integrated* (Vintage, 1973)—was required reading, along with recent works by Joseph Zinker, Walter Kempler, Joen Fagan, and Irma Lee Shepherd, and of course, the "bible" of the field, *Gestalt Therapy: Excitement and Growth in the Human Personality* (two volumes in one book) penned by Frederick Perls, Ralph Hefferline, and Paul Goodman (1951). I loved Polster's writing as a doctoral student. So it was a very humbling experience to be asked to write the foreword for a book by such an esteemed Gestalt mentor figure!

As I learned in my existential phenomenological education, the meaning of the term *Gestalt* was never meant to be applied to something "over there" that we might presumably view from our own center "over here"—a step removed, as it were, from a reality existing "outside" of us. For Gestalt therapists, as well as for the original Gestalt psychologists, this term embraces both the "subject" and the "object" of perception. Therapist and patient *together* constitute a vital gestalt, joined in conversational as well as gestural communality. With rich examples drawn from his own practice, Dr. Polster demonstrates the essential features of a therapeutic modality that continues to grow and to mellow with age. A perusal of his reflections here reveals a man writing while still at the top of his game.

In this work, a master therapist takes us from Gestalt Therapy's earliest forays into human consciousness (such as the contact boundary, awareness, concentrated fascination, experiment, figure/ground relationships and their reversals) to new horizons in therapeutic practice that bring us into contact with what Polster calls "the accessibly hidden." The French philosopher Merleau-Ponty once commented that phenomenology and psychoanalysis are aiming at the "same latencies" in our experience: something initially "invisible" that lies within a depth that is nonetheless accessible through the visible. Polster's current ventures into the accessibly hidden are at once a bringing into focus of our *methods of access* themselves. Access in therapy requires not just any quality of contact, but rather a genuine *encountering* of the other. He writes:

> A further exploration of the relationship of surface to depth is the phenomenon of tight therapeutic sequences. The fluidity of our moment-to-moment experience is easily overlooked, because it's going on all the time, even when it feels choppy. What stands out most clearly, even more than the continuity, are the **events** that populate our sequences. (p. 138)

Polster teaches us to not just look "inside" the person whom we are trying to help. "Needs" as originally conceptualized by Perls (in dialogue with and contradistinction from psychoanalysis) are developed by Polster as emanating out of the "accessibly hidden" dimensions of our co-experiencing and beckoned forth by a living phenomenology of co-created contact. If for classical psychoanalysis our relationality could be viewed against the backdrop of our drives, for Polster's gestalt psychology it is our desires that must be seen and understood—and modified—from within the context of relationality. The move toward accessing the hidden comes with a shift in our focus from what is "inside" to what is "outside," from the invisible to the visible, and thus from inner needs to observable events. Polster offers us his more relational and even reflexive view of contact making, where contact becomes a form of co-creation. In his treatment of awareness and meaning, he tells us:

> Meaning can be achieved in two ways: horizontally and vertically. The horizontal dimension of meaning is reached through a continuum of awarenesses, as they unfold into a realization of the connections between what has preceded and what follows any particular awareness. Meaning evolves through a step-by-step process of experiences, never by isolated experience. Each step leads, gradually,

to a new understanding of the context of our experience. The vertical dimension of meaning is plumbed by interpretation and insight.

This metaphor of the horizontal and the vertical, of perceptual breadth and reflective depth, allows the reader to bring Polster's latest refinement of Gestalt Therapy into dialogue with recent developments in both phenomenology and depth psychology. He writes: "*Since holism is crucial to gestalt therapy's figure/ground concept, we must re-examine the theory's love affair with the experience of here and now. Theories always need freshening up.*" (p. 77). Thus Polster finds meaningful gestalts to exist not only in the horizontal world of perception, but also in the vertical world of our personal history.

In his poetic style of languaging the "here and now" of ordinary experience, Polster shows us how the Life Focus Group can bring us to "*a euphoric appreciation of the extreme beauty of each person's perceptual possibilities*" (p. 49). This, he admits, is a very ambitious expectation. The human person is bound to flow and change throughout life; and throughout this work, Polster celebrates the plasticity and resilience that makes us capable of becoming more than we are at any given moment in time.

Along the way, he weaves a variety of figures into his narrative: not only illustrations of therapists with their patients, but also the voices of an array of muses: Kierkegaard, Sartre, Proust, Kafka, Joyce, Faulkner—even The Buddha. More contemporary references to Loren Eisely and Mihaly Csikszentmihaly will be found in these pages as well—but always returning to the founding principles of Gestalt Therapy.

Circling us back through figure/ground relationships, the tyranny of the should, tight boundaries, longing for contact, and curiosity in the face of what lies beneath, Polster refreshes our acquaintance with the immediate experiences that inform and motivate our work. For him, what is important to gestalt therapists is not simply the flow, but rather what he calls the "fluidity"—the changeability, the adaptability—that the therapist can help to engender and release within the individual. He refers to this capacity for change as "a perpetually operative figure/ground relationship."

> This fluidity reminds us that at any moment, that which is figural may recede into the ground and something else moves to the foreground. ... Innocent flow is only part of the story. Studies show that the perceiver ... [actively] harmonizes his figural perceptions with his background of inner needs. (p. 61)

It is in this harmonizing of figure and ground that Polster points toward an equilibrium that becomes one of the central aims of the therapeutic enterprise.

Written with an inspiring sense of openness and guided by his profound humility, Polster's *Enchantment and Gestalt Therapy* represents a sweeping embrace of lessons learned throughout the course of an illustrious career.

Note

1 President-elect of division 24 of APA, Society for Theoretical and Philosophical Psychology, Professor at Dallas University, Editor of the Journal *The Humanistic Psychotherapist*.

Gratitude

One image of writing a book is that it is a lonely work. The fact, however, is that it is also an opportunity to connect with people who join in checking out what I have written. This heightens, brightens, and clarifies an otherwise private experience. Serving that purpose for me has been my conversations with those who read segments of this manuscript and told me their thoughts. They are Michael Yapko, Diane Yapko, Joseph Barber, Joseph Melnick, Eva Gold, Steve Zahm, Peter Cole, and Joan Cole. When they talk, I like to listen.

I also feel much gratitude to Jeffrey Zeig, who has created the most exciting and integrative psychotherapy conferences ever: The Evolution of Psychotherapy. His invitations since 1985 to be a faculty member, have provided me with a most stimulating atmosphere, one which included presentations by pioneers in the development of a number of therapy theories. This offered me an opportunity to present my work to broad audiences and advanced my wish to write about my perspectives.

Joined with this stimulation has been the everyday relationship with my wife, Rose Lee, who was not only available for discussion, but also contributed a most discerning editorial sensibility, rescuing me from an excess of professionalized lingo. I welcomed her conceptual savvy and clarity. Not only does she provide her insights but also a loving partnership, living in a home together that has been a highlight of my later years. When she smiles, my heart is warmed and I feel the pleasure of the primary familiarity that I have described in this book. Furthermore, in our everyday living, she helps me in so many ways to face the limitations of my advanced age, without which writing might be an empty fantasy.

Prior to my marriage to Rose Lee, I was married 52 years to my beloved Miriam. Together we formed the Gestalt Training Center-San Diego, and we were deeply intertwined with each other in our teaching and writing experiences. I recall one time when a student observing the closeness of our union said in identifying us as Erv and Miriam that we could just as well be called Merv and Iriam. Together we taught in our own international training program in San Diego, CA, and traveled to many other places around the world teaching Gestalt therapy. I learned so much from the range of people with whom I engaged, a part of life, which in earlier years would have felt like a fray tale. Miriam died in 2001, and I am a very lucky person to have lived so much of my life with her.

Also important to me have been the conversational insights I have had with a number of friends who have kept my mind percolating about many social realities, quickening my interest at an age when I might otherwise not care. These conversations have unidentifiably made their way into my professional perspectives on everyday concerns and the nature of good living. Jean and Milt Richlin have been like lovable family to me for a very long time, we laugh, we gab, and we conjecture. Our conversations are always so absorbing that they make me feel like the things we tell each other *matter*. John Reis has been unbelievably generous in making the old adage real: that a friend in need is a friend indeed. He drives me places, and he supervises my financial needs. He and David Garmon, whom I also love, have had lunch with me every week for many years, covering so many themes and keeping me tuned into the world we live in. Sharon Grodner is another reminder of zestful living. She is a wonder of scintillation, and I never come away without feeling this is a pretty good world.

I have already named Michael and Diane Yapko as people who have provided observations about this book, but they live in San Diego so they are part of my day-to-day community. Diane is a person who it is so easy to laugh with, a bright spirit whose wisdom is down to earth. Michael, who is much younger than I am, is like an older brother, who knows the ropes about anything I want to check out with him. Cathy Conheim is a person with whom I have had robust and illuminating conversations for about 40 years. I ponder and she races; yet our thoughts fit together, and we have had a lot of laughter and meeting of our minds.

Then there is Joseph Barber. In addition to his conversational attention to what I have written, he also has provided me with a special gift. He wrote the abstracts for each of these chapters as called for by my publisher. What a blessing that was.

Preceding and following it all, there is my son Adam, a foundational part of me, only less so than my eyes and legs. When he says the word "Dad," he affirms the intimacy that is so old and so new. While he has cerebral palsy, he has transcended the handicaps and lived a life of inestimable courage, laughter, and love. He married Kathy about 20 years ago, introducing me to a new loving relationship. Kathy has been a devoted person with great zest, and she has created an impactful and humanitarian career, counseling and guiding the lives of so many people in need. Adam and Kathy have a daughter, Mariah. She is a talented dancer and is blessed with a radiance that refreshes me whenever I see her.

My beloved daughter Sarah died in 2001 when her daughter, Anna was only 4 years old. Anna is now a grown, loving, young woman, with acute sensibility. It is always heartwarming to hear her voice on the phone. She has now started on her college career, and it would not surprise me if she were to become a psychologist. Her development has been strongly influenced by the parenting of Jeff and Marny Voorhees. They are the kindest and brightest people one could hope for and have played a key role in Anna's recent life. Jeff and I have wonderful conversations on the phone, and I feel blessed for him and Marny to be in my life.

A further gift came with my wife Rose Lee's family. They have been so much more than the incidental addition to my life that they might have been. They have welcomed me into their world with generosity and love, which makes visits to them like holidays. They are Paul and Lisa Woodworth and their children: Sarah, Hanna, and Mathew. They combine a sparkling intelligence with a simple humanity; thus they can talk about either ordinary happenings or novel understandings, as though it's just folks getting together.

In addition to these engagements with people who are part of my ongoing world, I'm also thankful for the chance to have had a long, long background with Margherita Spagnuolo Lobb. So much nostalgia goes with it. She has been a colleague of mine for approximately 40 years and has recently become a publisher of books. She is now publishing this book, and I have been delighted to be engaged with her in a personal way where I feel that the professional joins so inseparably with the friendship.

I also had highly sensitive and thorough professional editorial help given by Arnie Kotler as the primary editor and Arial Adams as the copyeditor. They were a pleasure to work with. They had a clear understanding of what I was trying to say and opened me to communication gaps, which I would not otherwise have noticed. We had some good laughs, and they always guided me with a comradely coordination.

While I save this statement of gratitude for last, it is the one that has been most directly instrumental in the writing of this book. I am referring to the secretarial help I got from Kristin Green and Kathryn Conklin, who guided me through the workings of my office. They have full time jobs as licensed marriage and family therapists. Yet, they each work with me a few mornings a week. They make my office a happy place. Kristin is a bright spirit, who guided my search for segments of my previous writings and made them accessible to me. She also served as a trial reader providing me with her reactions as a person not oriented to Gestalt therapy.

Kathryn has a long history with me. She has been my secretary for 30 years, becoming a licensed psychotherapist during this time. She was indivisible from me in the editorial phase of this book. Because my vision is extremely limited, I can't read, and she painstakingly read every editorial suggestion to me. But she did more. She joined me with her sensitive reactions to certain words and phrases, serving me almost as an alternate brain. Without her I might still be thinking about finishing this book.

Introduction

I was introduced to Frederick Perls and Gestalt Therapy in 1953 and am possibly the earliest of Gestalt therapists still living. The theory and method were eye-openers for me. Now, at 97, I want to take stock of some foundational concepts, showing how they are reflected in my writings, teaching, and therapeutic work, and accentuating what they promise for the future.

When I first heard of Gestalt therapy, I had the mistaken impression it was based on exercises that could be the source of a self-therapy. That prospect intrigued me, as it pointed ahead to a future that would target the population at large rather than only those with psychological disturbance. While I was dreaming wrongly about exercises for self-therapy, in my first Gestalt Therapy Workshop I found two interwoven shifts in therapeutic attitude that made the theory hospitable to the populist perspective that I was seeking. One was the emphasis on simple experiences about what people want, feel, and do, the stuff of which everyday living is made. The other was the workshop format for learning, where concepts were interwoven with the actual personal experiences of the participants. The workshop format was composed of demonstrations of therapy, not with patients but with workshop participants. In those days, people simply didn't reveal personal experiences in a public setting, even as part of an educational process, so this was a more novel approach then than it would be now.

A prime principle of Gestalt therapy was that whatever is happening at the moment is center stage, rather than a search for large and meaningful discoveries about why what was happening happened. This was an empowering pathway, one that highlighted ordinary, personal experience recognizable as it actually happened to people every day rather than searching for hidden, and seemingly inaccessible, meaning. This emphasis was normally not considered deep enough, but the method of enhanced attention to immediate personal experience gave it considerable consequentiality. It focused us toward appreciating life as it is, rather than searching for more romantic insights. This not only helped enhance the value of easily identifiable experience but, surprisingly, opened people to the potential for revelations that came with an organically hospitable process. What started out as mundane became enlarged by the sweep of one thing following another, revealing a meaningful, charged, and personal storyline. Thus we proceeded from easily identifiable experiences to appreciating the power of fluidity, the moment-to-moment trip to assimilable conclusions. This concept proposed that if you stay with the awareness of each moment, you will get to where you want to go.

The rapt attention of the group is also a powerful agent in accentuating the importance of what is happening in the group. Further, the group has microcosmic implications as we recognize the universality of each person's experience. Such universality of concerns guides participants into telling stories resonant with common experiences of people at large. The group becomes a transformer of ordinary experience onto a larger stage, providing commentary on the inherent depth in all of life's realities.

The process, it turned out, was a stepping stone to enchantment, commonly seen when large numbers of people are moved by union with others, all pointing toward a common human experience. We see this enchantment in the theater when the curtain rises, at athletic events where the attention of multitudes is focused simultaneously, and at musical events, political rallies, weddings, and other gatherings when large groups of people zero in on the same object. Although this union of minds is normal at celebrations, it is a phenomenon not widely recognized in psychotherapy circles. Perhaps this lack of recognition is based on a professional perfectionism wary of undue influence. Of course, there is risk of enchantment serving nefarious purposes; there is no way to ensure purity. The mysterious process of forging a communal judgment is crucial in discerning whether an enchantment is legitimate. So, while enchantment is risky, there is no way out of its major role in influencing human beings. This crucial communal vibrancy thus merits inclusion into a psychological social repertoire that advances personal affirmation and inspires people at large.

Psychotherapists can take a lesson from religion, without having to copy it, regarding the role of enchantment in the exploration of the basics of being human. While religion may focus on the supernatural and on authority to direct communal behavior, it is also evident that enchantment has a strong influence on the mix. This is recognizable in biblical stories, religious music, grand architecture, wise poetry, congregation-inspiring commentary, and personal instruction. The stories of Abraham, Moses, Job, parting of the sea, wandering in the desert, and the crucifixion of Christ all create a communal enchantment.

Psychotherapy is also filled with enchanting stories, examples of which are reported in this book. These may not have as obvious a universal message, but they were extremely absorbing to the participants as reflections of the lives they are living. Tellers and listeners joined, and this union inspired a generosity of stories and an accompanying communal elaboration that were not just personal, because they had a resonance that connected people with each other. They were not just casual events, but poignant for their shared reality. They were messengers announcing the arrival of a world of depth and a personal accessibility to the wonders of our sensibilities.

This union of minds loosened the need for privacy and opened the group to a wide membership, ushering in the freedom to trust the evolving storyline, replacing shame and confession. New light is thus cast on painful memories, such as having cruelly teased a disabled person, or running away from a fight, or lying to a teacher to cover up one's own guilt when others were falsely accused. As long as the subject was immersed in immediacy, shame took a back seat, allowing a greater freedom to address whatever was most relevant.

Loosening the need for privacy brought about increased openness to exploring group interests. First among my communal explorations was the formation of "encounter" sessions in a coffee house in Cleveland. Themes important to the participants were discussed and played out. After that I designed freshman orientation encounters at local universities and a series of meetings at The Gestalt Institute of Cleveland for people exploring not just personal problems but the larger realm of what mattered in their lives.

I also met with religious groups where the liturgy was transformed into personal messages. Whatever was said during the public worship was elaborated by personal experiences of gratitude, obedience, and moral responsiveness—all about everyday human activity. Over the years, I also conducted demonstrations of Gestalt therapy sessions in front of large audiences, and, to my surprise, the presence of an audience did not prove to be a barrier to the work. Rather, the presence of the audience was an invigorating force and a source of inspiration for the unfolding of genuine inner work. These benign and supportive audiences amplified the humanity of the therapy engagement with a recognition that we were all in the same boat, and our union with each other strengthened the union with the wider world. Privacy still was operative in the sense that people did not reveal experiences they did not want to, but most were emboldened by the sweep of freedom, a sense of togetherness, and the power of the communal support they felt, which honored their own free choices.

These and other explorations into communal extensions of private therapy showed that the whole of its story is larger than its enhancement of individuals and their personal freedom. It also incorporates a broad perspective on the nature of living and the interest in the eternally elusive mysteries.

In this book, which includes both new material and segments excerpted from my previous writings, I name six Gestalt therapy concepts that have formed the basis of my own evolution. These concepts and their social promise are the core of a communally oriented application of these principles. This writing is thus an homage to communally minded perspectives and a call to recognize the transformation of psychotherapy from a curative modality to a vehicle for public awakening. The Life Focus Groups I describe in this book are one example of a design for large groups that honor the lifelong need we have to come together and examine how we feel, what is true for us, and how we want to live our lives.

This communal orientation and the accompanying guidance is a departure from the western religions in its understandings about life, its techniques for personal enlightenment, and its development of a new morality. It will take a shared awareness of this need and a coalescence of the many forces already advancing us, for the psychotherapy profession to co-create a new stage for people at large to witness and create their own lives. This will require transforming psychotherapy's emphatic individualism to a communal belonging and enlightenment.

The mission of this book is to advance the powers of a life focus practice toward a broad understanding of a psychotherapeutic social perspective: a step beyond curative inner work and even the teachings of religion. As a beneficiary of the lessons of religion, psychotherapy explores age-old human concerns and provides new answers and new partners and new modalities.

Chapter 1

My beginnings
Stolen by gypsies

When I was four, my mother, who was transplanted from Czechoslovakia, used to tell me stories about gypsies[1] who steal children. Standing head-high to her ironing board in unblinking absorption, I heard about children with fairy names, such as Jobbela-Bobbela. They were always transcendentally dear to their parents. The gypsies stole these children just because they loved them and had no inhibitions about stealing. They reared them as princes. The children, nevertheless, always longed to find their lost homes where their primal familiarity would be restored. Mother got to me, filling my psyche with her homing message. Even now, I still weave in and out in the struggle between a love for what is familiar and a search for the novel, as will become evident in this integration of Gestalt therapy.

What I am calling *primal familiarity* is a feeling I would, even now, have difficulty defining. One of its characteristics is that it is raw, an unschooled sense of life as it is. It says, "Yes, yes, yes." We may feel it when our child enters the room, when a breeze blows across our faces, when a beloved friend calls us on the phone, or when we glance at the azaleas in front of our house in the springtime. This feeling can happen every day with hardly a notice, or it may be the cause of celebration. In any case, it's a resting place for happenings, a contrast and companion to novelty. It is dependable, a support that fertilizes future unknowns. I received this message while listening to my mother without even knowing it, except now in retrospect.

Such a feeling of the simple rightness of experience is enabling, serving as the foundation for accommodating life's unfoldings. It is this constancy that helps me feel the same agelessness at 97 as I did at nine. I am recurrently mystified by the fact that my age keeps changing, and yet I remain the same in my native awareness, not counting the aches and pains. It's true that I experience myself differently now, but not so much in my primal quality as in the content of what I do day to day, like listening to novels instead of reading them—and I surely would not have been typing these words when I was nine. I would have been throwing a ball at the point of our front steps, trying to catch the rebound and counting how many times I could do it in a row. The inner striving, attentiveness, and even adventure is quite the same, though.

The details of what I'm doing are important only because I can no longer get that old sensation of throwing a ball against the steps, except perhaps in a moment of nostalgia.

As an adult, I've recognized a huge range of experiences that give me this basic sense of familiarity, and paradoxically the more novel the experience is, the more likely it is that a primal familiarity will be part of it. I may feel this while it's happening, but often I feel it in retrospect, fleshing out the pleasure of experience with the sense of being at home with life. I may get it with a stranger on an airplane. It may appear in awesome physical settings, such as the place where the Mediterranean Sea meets the Alps. It happened when I broke into second wind while swimming. I felt it when I was making butter in kindergarten, on the roller coaster, and in the ball yard, during a holiday in the synagogue, when I first touched a girl's breast, meeting my brother in Little Rock, seeing my sister married, driving to the hospital knowing my mother had just died, seeing my wife rolled out of the delivery room or even just seeing her as I walked into the house, the birth of our two children and the death at birth of another, coming down from altitude after a bombing mission, a beer after sweating, a surprise meeting with an old friend, an ice cream cone. Then, of course, there are the experiences that happen every day, like sitting with my feet under me, smiling at a light word, or remembering something that builds on another person's story.

The differences between my parents and me were givens, hardly worth noticing even though the split was a crucial one. For one thing, my parents knew next to nothing about most of the events of my life. Though this seemed okay, like breathing, it unconsciously accented the novelty of the world out there. Whereas we all grow up spellbound by new *experiences*, for me these were transformed into new *worlds*, accentuating not only the spell, as new experiences naturally would, but also emphasizing my own awkwardness and nonbelonging. When I first saw Santa Claus, and later when I first played basketball in a Christian church, or hitchhiked, or heard stories about marijuana, or talked to kids who had been to reform school, I was not only growing up, I was entering new worlds. When I would occasionally over the years relate "American" experiences to my parents or guests at home, they would smile at the incongruity or sometimes laugh hilariously, tickled by the ludicrous unreality, as though the stuff of movies had entered right into the house. Consequently, although I didn't verbalize it, even to myself, I always knew that I was on my own. This was underlined by the fact that I got my bachelor's degree, spent three years fighting in World War II, and was already in my second year in graduate school when my father talked to me for the first time about my future. He asked me what this psychology thing was about and whether I was going to be able to make a living at it. I reassured him that it was going to be all right, and he was satisfied, blessed with a strange faith in my own self-regulation. I wish I'd had as much faith as he did.

He was a self-possessed man who struggled to support us all and tightened every muscle to keep his body and soul together during the depression. He asked for no help, guidance, or sympathy from anyone, and he never gave me any either. There was a story about him, possibly apocryphal but probably literally true, that he was sent to a Polish regiment in World War 1. While living in the trenches, he would pull out his Jewish prayer phylacteries daily, binding them liturgically around himself, and pray. The fact that he did this among people, of whom some required only small arousal to slit the throat of a Jewish person, didn't prevent him from doing what was a simple indispensability to him. Life was as simple as that. He was never a greedy man. He worked hard, doing what he could, but never lusted for the world beyond, as I have. Even the most cunning gypsies could never tempt him.

My mother never had to venture into "America" as he did, nor did she ever try. She was at home in our familial home, in our extended family, and in our neighborhood. In the 34 years she lived in this country, she never went outside the neighborhood alone. Not that she felt deprived, because all she seemed to want existed within her familiar environment and she was not about to be shown new possibilities by any of us. At home, she cooked familiar foods; laughed like music; screamed from a transparent mind in panic, rage, or exasperation; and told stories in her soft, accented voice. She projected her inner nature reflexively and would sometimes rue the fact that, as she put it, what was on her lung was on her tongue. And all she ever had to do was say my name, and I could feel her love. But she never was at home in "America," right up to the day she died when she refused to accept the hospital's oxygen mask.

Somewhere along the borders of my awareness, I frequently felt a gnawing responsibility for my mother, and for my sister, too. My father wasn't around because he worked all the time. My little brother was a simple pleasure, always luminous. He would join in the games of us older boys. I would teach him athletics and just play with him. But I never needed to "do" anything for him. My mother and sister, though, wanted something from me, which I could never identify. I was impacted by my own feeling that women had a lousy fate in this world, and I felt sorry for them. They seemed hemmed in. But I copped out and went my own way. Later on, as an adult, I had some of my warmest conversations ever with my sister. But in those days there was always a lingering undertone that I should be more helpful, that I was defecting from an obligation. Maybe this was the psychotherapist budding in a corner of my life, waiting for its chance to be put into action. But what could I do then?

Grade school was my first other-world experience. During my years in grade school, I could not understand the contrast between my school behavior, on the one hand, and my behavior in my neighborhood or at home, on the other. At school I was quiet, daydreamed about saving girls from burning schools and similar exploits, and watched the clock interminably.

(I own a clock like that now, and it hangs beautifully in my kitchen.) School was boring. In our neighborhood and at home, there was always a lot of action, and I was organically involved, more quiet than most but fully absorbed and strangely serene. I excelled at nothing, yet because of some odd combination of incongruities in me, whenever there was a continuing grouping of people, like a ball team or a social club, I would find I was central, often elected captain or president. At school I was always a spot in the background, unnoticed and noncontributing, while in my home territory I would be in the clear foreground. Only in writing this now do I realize that I was making sure the gypsies couldn't catch me.

Not until graduate school at Case Western Reserve University in 1946 did I find a scholastic métier where I experienced the primal familiarity I needed. For the first time, not only in college but also in "America," I finally became a meaningful participant as well as an awed observer. Luck was with me. I was enrolled in a beautiful department led by Calvin Hall, the most brilliant and inclusive man I knew and the person who turned me on to psychology. My cup ranneth over when I was recognized and included in the workings of that department. I was offered a responsible and engaging assistantship, doing therapy with undergraduates, and later a fellowship. I also became part of a psychoanalytic repartee that blew my mind open as I discovered the knowability of persons. In that department, nothing was sacred, and I operated within an altogether new frame of mind, exploring the unconscious while broadening my view of life almost unassimilable. We, faculty and students alike, presumptuously applied our recognition of each other's deep characteristics, adventurously and incisively confronting each other. We only barely escaped from hideousness by the hilarity of our humor, an abiding affection that transcended specific remarks, and our hardiness. The image of my being affected by castration anxiety or wanting to screw my mother or growing through the psychosexual stages was simultaneously ludicrous and compelling. When someone remarked about how deeply hidden my homosexuality was, I was shocked. I almost swallowed the psychoanalytic message hook, line, and sinker, a risky business but worth it to me. Even though I no longer accept the psychoanalytic perspective, I owe a lot to my willingness to be innocently fascinated with it. Learning happens best for me when, through my intuition, I am willing to temporarily set aside my interferingly critical faculties and absorb messages as given—like mother's milk or a nursery rhyme. Discernment came later, of course, just as necessary. But my mind expanded by approaching psychoanalysis with an innocence that is native to me and by allowing my sophistication to develop organically. The new liturgy had a timely relevance and was far more exciting to me than the orthodox Jewish liturgy had been before I gave it up many years earlier.

Once at a family party, I explained to my uncle that I had been learning how we all pass through the oral, anal, phallic, and genital stages.

He, unschooled and a man of great earthy exuberance, laughed with wide-eyed bawdiness at this ineffable union of the forbidden and the advanced college education. It was as though I'd become wise in ways he couldn't understand, but which reflected upon my humanity favorably. We bridged the two-world quality, which is a major theme in my life.

The two-world notion is the natural view of a foreigner. Incongruities are not necessarily confusing, they are just difficult to hold simultaneously or to integrate. For me, this holding of incongruities was a move into the gypsy world. I naively wanted to go beyond professionalism and exercise my commentary on the world out there. I wanted my education to be relevant.

In spite of my new focus on "the world out there," I continued to live at home throughout graduate school. I was 24 before it occurred to me to live anyplace else. For one thing, I was dead broke. For another, I had just finished a stint in the Air Force, and after the bombing missions, it was a serene pleasure to be at home, where my movements were always my own. In spite of the vastly new experience I was soaking in at school and the new camaraderie with other graduate students, my lifelong friends, and family were still the core of my community. The psychological world was becoming more and more compelling, though, and in addition, at the end of graduate school I got married. Then I left Cleveland to take a job at the University of Iowa, and though I came back to Cleveland two years later to go into private practice, my two worlds never meshed well again. One could say I grew up, but I've often felt more like a renegade. Nevertheless, this was a natural life development for me.

I had married Miriam, who was lovely and added new dimension and texture to my life. She sang beautiful songs, made household lovelies, smiled like sunshine, told stories, and left me trails of funny notes and other endearments. I was spellbound when I was with her. The new home with her was as primally familiar to me as the old, only far more exciting. But Miriam did not have the same investment in my family or my old friends. Besides, I was up to my ears in new "professional" activities and I didn't have the extra energy to sustain my old life.

Gypsies

The giant step in my new direction came in 1953, two years after I began my practice. Fritz Perls gave a workshop in Gestalt therapy in Cleveland, and he was a revelation. He was an undulating mushroom of a man, with a large, transcendent head and lithe legs that wrapped themselves into the space he occupied. He was a breathing freedom, like a respirator, and he had a voice that made every word feel like the final accent with which life itself would be endowed. He had a radar sensitivity and a simple faith in the power of staying with people step by step as he worked with them. He could also be trusted in a clutch. I experienced that one day when I raged at him. He had inspired my rage with instructions that finally led to shouting and left me open to spasms of crying and a return deep inside myself to primal aloneness. In a moment, focused on the only light left, inside me, I felt his warm hand, and there he was as I opened my eyes, so tender. He said some soft words I can't remember, and I felt damp and lubricated all through me.

And he was a very tough man, Fritz, as many people have observed. He was widely known as a person who was cutting and rejecting whenever the spirit happened to move him. It is not as well known that he had a vast capacity for tenderness, and indeed it was this quality as well as his unparalleled imagination and sensitivity, that made his work go. One knew that he knew and delights of life. Once during a break in a workshop, he asked me why I was so silent. I told him I was afraid. He said he knew about that, too, that up to a few years earlier, he couldn't say a word publicly without reading from a paper, so shy did he feel. I was amazed and felt the gift he was giving me. Later, he named me "interferer" in a group, because I hadn't wanted to say things that might interfere with whatever process was going on. He instructed me to interfere at any point I wanted to. I did it without reservation, interrupting aloud over and over. Finally, he got angry with me. Someone in the group said, "But you told him to interfere," and Fritz said, "Yes, but I didn't tell him I would like it." I continued to interfere, though, and discovered that what had started out as "interference" became lively leadership, one of the more important lessons I have learned. Despite his great tenderness, though, Fritz could turn into a first-class bastard when he felt people trying to capture him or foist a sense of obligation on him. His own unwillingness to inhale environmental toxins communicated his vital message: we create our own lives.

Fritz was an eye-opener in Cleveland, as he later was throughout the country. Among us, he found the first place where he had a substantial breakthrough in teaching his method of therapy. He was counter intellectual and, as I now realize, he moved fast into primal familiarity. He described the nature of good contact and exercised it, stripped of amenities and professionalism. He showed how good contact joined with techniques for heightened awareness could provide new leverage into developing profound emotional experiences. The resulting emotionality was a rarity in those days. Even to cry in a group of 15 people was remarkable then and, in fact, quite suspect for the rest of the community, who saw his methods as dangerous and irresponsible. We got a lot of flak about what we were doing, but our new community had too much discovery and excitement in it for us to worry about being well liked.

What was new to me was entering into the *experience* of therapy rather than trying to *understand* it. This simple change in orientation seems old hat now, but at the time it presaged a core change in my professional existence. I gave up being merely professional and allowed myself to become as deeply absorbed as needed for the sense of primal familiarity. I moved from the periphery of others' lives. I moved out from behind my desk and began to allow myself the sense of people's native centrality. Whatever relationship developed, I no longer felt as a professional applique for a transferring patient. Rather, I was an actual person, responding with as much artistry as I could, joined in the creation of fulfilling drama. One of my first patients with whom my Gestalt flow became noticeable said to me, "It's not so lonely here anymore." I was teaching another patient how to bark, and I succeeded so well that the psychiatrist across the hallway teased me the next day about my patients bringing dogs to therapy. When I told him it was no dog, that it was me, he was shocked. Nothing more was said, and there is no telling what rumors followed. My patient learned more from barking than any stream of words could have taught him.

Perls was not the only eye-opener. Our Gestalt community in Cleveland was, too, as were the other teachers we invited from New York, including Paul Goodman, Paul Weisz, Laura Perls, and Isadore From. When I first saw Isadore From, he looked like a scholarly Arabian jockey—tiny, exotic, and elegant in his language and mind flow. Outside of Gestalt circles, he is hardly known because careerism was incidental to his life. He only accidentally fell off the psychotherapy tree, ripened by therapy with Fritz and Laura Perls and their wide knowledge of phenomenology. In spite of the great impact of all our teachers from New York, Isadore was the most important to us. The others came for the most fertile workshops four or five times a year, but Isadore stayed with us for six years, coming twice a month at first, then once a month. His visits were like holidays, not recreational but the kind of holiday that is a harvest of sensation that addresses itself to life's primary forces. In my private therapy with Isadore, I talked, cried, screamed, touched, whispered, walked, saw, heard, remembered, fantasized, and laughed. He had a remarkable knack for what was organic between us, never contriving an experiment and never resorting to theoretical fiat. I became a poetic patient, respectful of my inner flow, always moving from initial confusion and verbal constipation into the most heartfelt and eloquent statements I had ever been able to make. He was exquisitely tuned in to my character, and his learnedness and wisdom were the fulcrum around which my life grew for 10 years after I met him.

Our Gestalt community had weekly leaderless meetings for two years, at which time, in 1955, we formed the Gestalt Institute of Cleveland, an experiential precedent for the later encounter groups. We first set up training experiences for ourselves as a learning community, and as we grew, we took on the training of others who wanted to learn Gestalt therapy. I was central in this process, leading our first workshops, teaching our first courses, and being a prime mover in establishing our postgraduate training program. We carved out our own style of functioning, and my part in this has been a major radiance in my work life. This was a place in "America" where what I contributed and what I received were comparable. Being at home among these people was therefore another recycling of my early primal familiarity, joining the old feelings of familiarity and the new associations, restoring the old environment without imitating it. *Plus ça change, plus c'est la même chose; the more things change, the more they are the same.*

Present leaning into future

What I see happening now, which I will spell out later, is an expansion of the opportunities to join groups that stimulate and support people's attention to the lives they're living. Such groups are appearing all over the country, and it's now evident that psychotherapists and their brother and sister workers are now in the midst of developing *a populist psychotherapy* that moves beyond patients and offices to address the needs of people at large.

The traditional psychotherapist's view was the naïve one that with good therapeutic experience, we would all be enabled to manage the society we live in. Presumably the society had such range within it that anyone in sound psychological form could find their rightful place. Only those who were filled with distortion and obsession could fail to fulfill the requirements of their own directions. It's apparent now that these assumptions were pure Pollyanna. We wanted only to "cure" people until it became clear that sickness was an obviously inadequate word to describe most of the people we worked with. So the term *growth* came into popularity.

New people came on board, more than ever, seeking more fulfilling forms of living rather than a cure for acute problems. They were focused on self-improvement and personal discovery. Excitement became more central as a motivation, and the forms of interaction did induce great excitement, leading to experiences of primal familiarity.

A central factor in the inducing of this excitement has been what I have metaphorically called the "synaptic experience." This is the experience of personal unity and vibrancy brought on by conjoining an individual's awareness with his actions. Because we are all sensory-motor beings through neurological predetermination, we are most complete when our sensory and motor sides are both represented in our existence. There is a variable preference among individuals for the sensory side or the motor side, and under certain conditions, either may cover over the other, blocking our full sense of presence. The restoration of unity of awareness and action is one of the directions that growth-oriented groups take, calling attention to individuals' feelings, wants, values, and assessments. The accompanying actions—mostly talking but also including nonverbal acts—come as a result of knowing what is going on inside, such as dancing when we recognize our wish to dance. Or the other way around, the actions artfully developed may make us newly aware of what is going on inside, like feeling scintillated because one has danced. Whichever way the union happens, a heightening of personal presence develops with an accompanying sense of the primal familiarity involved in being in fresh union between awareness and action.

Another quality of growth groups is in the symbolic process, which through its power to heighten excitement reproduces primal familiarity. Symbolism is humans' way of creating brief but faithful representation of vast stretches of our experiences. Through symbolism, we express poetic as well as literal truth, achieving clarity and meaningfulness. For example, a person who is large and silent in a group might see himself poetically as an elephant. When he imagines it, he might get into a wrestling match where, in mindless aggression, he nearly injures his opponent vanquishing him with far greater force than necessary. He is now faced with the dismay, feeling what it's like, perhaps for the first time, to exercise the elephant in himself. Through this he can then fathom the fact that people are frequently frightened of him even though he doesn't usually do frightening things. The transition from a projected danger into what he actually imagined results in a whoosh of excitement, releasing the energy subsumed within the shorthand.

Given these conditions for fostering primal familiarity and for developing revolutionary effect, we come to the sociological step that moves not only beyond cure but also beyond growth and into the development of a *new climate*. Because none of us can escape the psychological pollution of our surroundings, until we create psychologically necessary changes in our communal climate, we in our groups or therapy continue a two-world existence. New ways of communicating; new values; new priorities; changing institutions, such as marriage, schools, and government; new vocational requirements; and new reward systems are all parts of a necessary change in the spiritual atmosphere of our society. In a society based on the irrepressibility of change, changes just naturally happen. In this time in history, psychotherapists and their kindred workers are feeding their perspectives and wishes into our sociological stream. They are currently having a great impact but are hardly assured at this point of having the most effective voices.

The greatest challenge comes as always from the materialistic primacy among people. We are absorbed with survival priorities, such as the needs for food, shelter, and medical treatment. These needs, of course, overshadow all other considerations, including such life concerns as confidence in doing a job, belonging among a community of friends, freedom to transcend outdated taboos, and the examination of the mysteries we live with. These needs often recede into the background. It is therefore from a position of limited leverage that we join the age-old arts and religion in creating a psychologically informed system of guidance. Yet we are doing it, and I believe we will continue to, without necessarily ignoring basic material needs. Perhaps a union of the psychological with material accomplishment has already begun through the extensive work of psychologists in industry and the growth of consultations with governments and other social institutions.

A leap forward in the struggle to integrate the personal and the communal became apparent in the 1960s. Many people developed a more fully holistic ambition, seeking to create a social climate in which people were not only whole within themselves but inseparable from the community. The loosening of taboos against certain individualistic perspectives was happening all around us. Boys had begun wearing long hair, young men and women lived in the same dormitories, black people appeared on TV commercials, communal living foreshadowed new forms of family life, peaceniks slowed down a war, nude people were seen on stage and screen, men's clothes had become a riotous delight, and so on. Psychotherapy had an important place in all these creations, having encouraged people to experience their actuality rather than to swallow the stereotypes and distortions that have always made deviations from the norm seem like pathology.

The messages continue. We can hardly keep up with emerging technologies. The *design* of the interactions that were introduced in open-ended small groups invites large group interactions that allow us to work with as many as a thousand people in a room and unlimited people on the internet. Groups commonly interact in conferences, growth centers, churches, housing projects, industry, universities, welfare agencies, town meetings, and other ordinary groupings of people. These promises for a new view of the lives we live face inevitable social complexities, but the progression of psychological contributions has its own momentum.

I believe that widespread innovations in humanist technology will move the society at large, further into the direction of people joining together to enhance their orientation about the experiences of a lifetime. For me, this entire movement, has been a communal home. It is my gypsy home, and I have been repeatedly fascinated in it. When I next visit my mother's grave, I should tell her about my gypsy experiences. She would have a harder time believing my story than I did hers. After all, what's a mother for, if not to come back to?

Note

1 In this context, the word "gypsies" is clearly not pejorative. Rather it is part of a fairy tale metaphor about the world at large, which must ultimately be integrated with the sense of home and its accompanying familiarity.

Chapter 2

Concentration
Fundamentals

Gestalt therapy was born with Frederick Perls' declaration that *concentration* was to be a core concept in his deviation from psychoanalysis. He said,

> It has long been realized that the essential element in every progress, in every success, is concentration. You may have all the talents, all the facilities in the world, but without concentration these are valueless.... Correct concentration is best described by the word *fascination*; here the object occupies the foreground without any effort, the rest of the world disappears, time and surroundings cease to exist; no internal conflict or protest against the concentration arises. Such concentration is easily found in children, and often in adults when engaged in some interesting work or hobby. As every part of the personality is temporarily coordinated and subordinated to one purpose only, it is not difficult to realize that such an attitude is the basis of every development. If, to quote Freud, compulsion changes into volition, the most important stepping stone to a healthy and successful life is laid. (Perls, 1947)

This was a transformative statement, enunciating psychotherapy's shift from the psychoanalytic search for the meaning of events, often a distraction from the immediate sensibility to *the events themselves*. The then-familiar therapeutic repertoire was an intellectual enterprise, addressing the person's deepest emotional history. That psychoanalytic enterprise was a wondrous exploration of the depths of personal experience. I loved the daring of it, reaching beyond the obvious into surprising understandings. However, this search, as fascinating as it was, often distracted both therapist and patient from the actuality of *what* the patient was saying, *how* they were saying it, and how they *felt* about it.

Gestalt therapy, in contrast, increases attention to the simple experience. It focuses on immediate events themselves. That is, the therapy is concerned with what the person is actually saying, what they want, what they feel, and what they imagine. The consequent step-by-step attention introduces a satori-like absorption, aroused by this continuously sharp focus on event after event, each moment adding importance to the events. Because of this escape from all the distracting complexity of a lifetime of feelings, purposes, and understandings, the gates are opened for fresh entry into the focused immediacy of what's actually happening. Without disabling contradictions, there are increases in clarity of perception and arousal to action, and the new testing out of one's fears. That is not to say that events and their meaning are unimportant. They are, indeed, profoundly important, but they must be integrated with the person's ability to pay attention freshly.

The simplicity that concentration fosters is as natural as breathing. One sees it everywhere: in the eyes of a baby entranced by everything she sees; in the sharp attention of a carpenter, for whom nothing exists but the wood he is sawing; in the baseball player who keeps his eyes on the ball. Those are ordinary experiences that have immediate attraction, and they are the major objects of therapeutic attention. There is probably no better example of pure continuity of concentration, deliberately created, than in the person who meditates, keeping his mind centered on a mantra or a stream of thoughts or just breathing. He is swept into union with the narrow object of attention, losing a sense of differentiation between the act of concentration and the object of concentration. He becomes deeply absorbed with this narrow world that is compelling his attention; a world that is unadorned, a world that is just as it is, right now.

Of course, such simplicity is not easily achieved. Even among meditators, the highest level of absorption is reserved for the masters; so one would expect such purity of concentration only in exceptional therapeutic moments. This is because a large range of happenings, and the contradictions created among these happenings, distract our personal attention. We don't even feel it, but that diversity is always going on. For example, one patient of mine was telling me about a friend's painful experience, but relating this upstaged her current happiness about the man she loves proposing marriage. How does a person handle such complexity with deep attention undiminished? There is a relational saving grace. We see it when the therapist drinks in his patient and everything she says, soaking in her purposes and conflicts, her words and movements, developing a resonance in the patient and a finely tuned responsiveness. For the therapist, one might say, the patient is the only person in the world who counts right then.

It is, therefore, a significant consequence of concentrated attention that the patient temporarily dims the debilitating *context* of her life. This context includes prohibitions against having opinions, inculcated goals, demeaning criticism, physical beatings, and a whole range of internal tyrants. Even when the patient does talk about contextual matters, including old, painful experiences, the fixed aspects of her life may loosen and she may speak of old wounds with a new freedom. The mutual concentration of therapist and patient is like opening the window in a room of stale air. They can experience the therapy room as a place where they can be as freshly attentive as they might be when totally absorbed in a movie, a conversation, or a physical exertion.

What is most intriguing about concentration is that in its generic form it has no more *content* than sunlight. That is a surprising statement to make when we recognize that concentration always has an object. We don't just concentrate; we concentrate on this or that. However, while the object is important, the concentration is grounded in a raw, contentless energy that drives it without prejudice about the nature of what's being observed. That is, a dual function exists, wherein the content of life is most apparent and most determinative of one's state of mind, but the raw energy that drives concentration goes on without prejudice. It represents a continuing aliveness, transcending life's happenings. Therefore, the idea one often hears after a death or another terrible event that "life goes on" says not only that events keep on happening but that there is a continuing pulsation, an incontrovertible reality of the often hidden power of life itself.

The source and nature of this energy is elusive and has been variously described. Historically it has been highly generalized as *élan vital*, libido, spirit, excitement, and will, as well as other more exotic terms that have been invented outside Western civilizations. Nowadays, there is much research on various forms of bodily energy, including neurotransmitters, adrenalin release, the throb of heart pulsations, a sense of peacefulness, and the rhythmic arcs of breathing. These are all ways of identifying the energy that underlies human experience. The fundamental sense of *presence* affirms being alive. That is, though this presence may be party to either pleasurable or painful consequences, it, itself, is psychologically neutral and enduring. It calls us to pay attention to whatever is happening, creating a connectedness with the world as it is.

Though this foundational force is an indivisible part of everything we do, it often takes a back seat in our awareness to the happenings to which it is wedded. These happenings serve as the agents of misery or happiness, success or failure, sickness or health, blessedness or cursedness. To make good or bad decisions at work, to have a fruitful or sterile marriage, even to go for a leisurely or invigorating walk are further examples of the content of ordinary consciousness. Concentration, as an instrument of this energy, is thus a vehicle for the underlying, ubiquitous layer of aliveness, submarining below events, providing supportive grounding in the face of the varieties of personal experience. In its highest realization, a person's concentration would remain inviolate to these discrete, everyday concerns, providing a sense of constant and dependable presence, the ticket to feeling alive that transcends momentary experiences of either distress or pleasure.

This inspiration for life does not require instruction from God. Nor does it assure an understanding of worldly phenomena, as science promises. It is, instead, a metaphorical approximation of a perpetually active force, like a pilot light, that powers our existence, keeping us perpetually animated.

While this energy is indivisible from the occurrences of life, it is itself a constant affirmation of a life beyond everyday happenings, irrespective of the particular perceptions or feelings that serve as more familiar messengers. While many people are in distress through depression, persecution, or dismay, it is important to know that being alive—in itself—is a value that is always in the background waiting for its moment to return into the mind. As Antonio Damasio (1999) has said in describing the screening process that hides the interiors of our experience:

> Like a veil thrown over the skin to secure its modesty, but not too well, the screen partially removes from the mind the inner states of the body, those that constitute the flow of life as it wanders in the journey of each day. When the veil is lifted, however, at the scale of understanding permitted to the human mind, I believe we can sense the origin of the construct we call self in the representation of the individual's life. (pp. 28–29)

A pivotal benefit of such sharpened focus is its simplicity. *Anybody* can just pay attention to their breathing or their sadness, a human-scale task that does not require the more complex integrations of insight. This simplicity overshadows the intermittent and often abstruse enlightenment of insight, offering a more innocent attunement to what is continually going on in one's life: large or small, intellectual or primitive, inferential or direct. Here's an example. In a psychology class, students were asked to pay attention to any concrete object that would normally *not* draw high focus. One student said:

> Today I concentrated on a friend's Cadillac, which he has owned and been tremendously proud of for over a year and which I have frequently ridden in. I had always been a trifle scornful of his great pride of ownership. For the first time I really noticed the beautiful lines and curves of its construction, and its magnificent functional capabilities. I received an esthetic emotion that I never would have expected a car would arouse. My pleasure from this was exceeded by my friend's when I made a sincere and spontaneous comment on the car's beauty. A small incident, perhaps, but I found it indicative of the new areas of experience that true awareness can open for me. (Perls, Hefferline, & Goodman, 1951)

We see here a simple though sharply pointed focus that offers both esthetic and relational pleasure. From this vantage point, he could see beauty where his routine vision passed it by. Equally important, he could join his friend in enthusiasm. He had thus expanded his vista from casual recognition of the car into a perceptual bonanza, surprised at its beauty, a step beyond the routine experience for which he would otherwise have settled. This included insight, in a way, but not as much about causation as about the *phenomena* of beauty and relationship.

While this brightened car emerged from an otherwise routine experience, it's important to see the effects of sharp focus also evident in a deeper and more complex emotionality. One illustration is the story told in a Life Focus Group by a woman whose 50-year-old son had been diagnosed with a life-threatening illness. There was no bromidic slippage from her feelings of desperation and helplessness in telling her story to these people. They were highly concentrated listeners, rapt in conversational resonance. It was as though the whole world resided in this conversation. The people in the group were not looking for a solution as they gave their attention to a necessary suffering, inextinguishable. The words they spoke accentuated them as a world of people who would continue to be available in intimacy and dependability. Nobody needed to exactly say that. The bonding permeated the group atmosphere. But there was more than bonding.

She came to make a major distinction between what she *could do* and what she *could not do*. She was able to realize that *her powers were limited*. Though that may seem like a practical reality, for her it had felt like a defeat. Now, in this highly focused atmosphere, it represented a pivotal reshaping of her mind. The combination of the group conversation and the *aura of the group continuity* was a heartening reminder, beyond resignation or defeat, of the palpable reality of a continuing existence. This opened the lens of her awareness to receive the hint of a world broader than her pain would allow; a world that included her son and her feelings. Together, the events of life join with the undercurrent of raw energy to build a richly textured reality; a humanistic extension reaching beyond simple pointedness into the experience of livability.

People depend upon this union between immediacy and its home, the vast range of meaningfulness. At a mundane level, what is common is that we cannot easily measure up to the surprises and pace of our experiences. Left to our own devices, we simply blur the attention these experiences deserve. Yes, one might say, I played the piano as a kid, and yes, I couldn't wait to go the library to get another book, and yes, I played games in the playground, and yes, I have had victory and defeat and companionability and spontaneity and more. All this deserves registration, even if it has been blurred by dominating events, such as the death of a parent or changing schools too often or feeling let down by promises not kept. Even the desirable experiences of confidence, endurance, laughter, and good grades are often diluted and our personal nourishment diminished. The variety of experiences registered within the therapy setting gives proportion to such special secular assets as wealth, physical prowess, intellectual accomplishment, and all the other components of the good life that frequently overshadow the basic rewards of being alive. The special circumstances of a created opportunity of psychotherapy explorations give people the setting and stimulation for catching up to themselves and restoring the elemental awareness that does not survive the complexities of everyday life.

Long ago, I became aware of what seemed like a strange phenomenon. Before each session started, people in my therapy groups gathered together companionably. They would talk to each other in quite animated and largely purposeless conversation. When the time came to start the session, I would say, "let's get started." I can think of little I could say that would so promptly stop all conversation, as though a paralytic wind had wafted into the milieu. Silence. Why would this happen? I thought of a couple of possible reasons. One was that an ongoing process had been interrupted, with nothing yet formed to replace it. But that was not enough of an explanation. What became apparent is that there was an amplified attention, as though a spotlight was turned on to everything being said. The promise of life examination placed people in an anticipatory mode, much as they might be at the start of a play or a novel, open to the flow of thoughts about intimate details of living. The people were on the cusp of new images of their own lives, the lives of others, and life itself. They were satisfying their reflex as storytelling animals, needing to give coherence and communicative excitement to their listeners.

This union of people offers a promise of group formations, guided by psychological principles and ignited by sharpened attention, a process I will flesh out later in this book. These groups are driven by an elaborated design that highlights basic themes of living. The life focus concept ushers in a concentrated attention to a large range of personal themes, examined in a communal climate. The importance of each person's story, along with the communal absorption in the stories, engenders a microcosmic implication—that is, while engaged in the immediacy of expression, the deep attention of a group affirms that local happenings are the stuff out of which life itself is made. If we stretch this small group experience into large communal groupings as we see them in religion and the arts, we enter a larger domain that reaches into the infinite, the moral, the beatific, the very depth of existence; into not only particular human experiences but experience itself.

The supremacy of content

It is important to note that the depth and significance of these group experiences must then integrate the power of simple concentration with the ever-present and self-defining happenings in anyone's life. While the storytelling is supported by a value-free concentration, its significance is fleshed out with events. The interface between neutral energy and the humanly insistent flow of happenings is remindful of the primacy given in Buddhist thinking to the raw energy commonly overshadowed in our lives by events and their values. The primacy of this content-free energy, while setting a standard for Gestalt therapy, differs from Gestalt therapy in its major lessons. While the content-free energy of the Buddhist perspective foreshadows the Gestalt concepts, there is a difference in emphasis. The Buddhist emphasis is to transcend our everyday concerns, replacing them with a value-free immersion in the flow of life as it unfolds and resulting in the absence of the sense of self. Therapy's intention is to *enhance* the self, freeing it from the admonitions of an invasive social value system. While recognizing the need to see things just as they are, the concentration factor is, itself, harmonious with Buddhist meditation. The Gestalt perspective, on the other hand, values most highly the awareness of personal experience and its integration into the whole person's being. It seeks to *experience* feelings, ambitions, fantasies, personal stories, and all the happenings of life that call out for attention. Thus, for the Gestalt therapist, content, despite its blurring of basic human energy flow, is a supremely important challenge for the integration of personhood.

I asked one of my patients what she was thinking, and she said, "nothing." I asked her to look again, and she said again that she was thinking about nothing. I jokingly remarked that she had accomplished what the greatest gurus, working 50 years, were still seeking. She laughed and began telling me stray thoughts that felt to her unimportant. Expressing these thoughts, however, led her to tell me about her feeling of unimportance, and through our conversation this feeling was replaced with an experience of the validity of what was in her mind. It was a step in the fruitful continuity of conversation that had no great significance in itself but was a significant contributor to her regained vitality.

While it is true that many can spontaneously keep up to date with the complexities of life on their own, for others some form of communal guidance is important. Religion is an obvious vehicle, of which psychotherapy is a modern variant. If the well-being of any particular person takes a back seat to the sense of cultural necessity, a promise for self-affirmation might seem too romantic. But the popularity of focusing on one's life throughout our society attests to the widespread need to keep tuned in to the lives we are living. The group experience both stimulates and assures this intra-personal attention for navigating the inner world. The hallowed quality of such opportunity is created not only by each person's need to get off the conveyor belt of modern life but also by the leader's commentary, other written material, music, films, poetry, and the collective excitement of self-examination. This expansion of simple concentration into the large arc of experience that forms the full landscape of living meets a universal need, represented not only by individual attention but also by the formation of communal systems of orientation and guidance. Among these, religion has been primary, and psychotherapy promises to be its heir, a part of the life focus revolution.

Fascination

While concentration is the major form of attention, by itself it lacks humanization. Fascination is a variant of attention that contributes value. It does not call for a moral or ethical bias, but rather it represents personal investment, as in being charmed, captivated, enthralled, awed—all words that carry a special sense of caring. Because of the risks of excessive involvement, fascination is a concept not much heard in therapeutic methodology, where dispassionate accuracy is more commonly sought. Yet the luxury of receiving continued and unwavering personal interest through weeks, months, and even years of dialogue is the grounding on which much therapeutic work is accomplished. To be able to give the patient such personal validation, the therapist is greatly aided if his mind is open to the inherent drama and urgency in what the patient is saying.

A misunderstanding about *fascination* is that only certain favored and compelling people are fascinating. Fascination is not so exclusive. It's not such a big deal to be fascinated when someone comes into your therapy office feeling that her life is on the line and open to revealing her most intimate experiences, many of which would make for intriguing drama. The surprise would be if you were not fascinated. Yet this failure to be fascinated occurs often, either because the therapist is not open to such feelings or, more likely, the patient is not up to feeling fascinating.

Many patients are masters at being uninteresting, a mastery carved out of a multitude of preparatory life experiences, all geared to take the vitality out of their existence. They exclude parts of themselves that are dulled by pain or too dangerous to be let out of the house. Yet nobody is so skilled at maintaining a colorless life that he doesn't leave openings through which the therapist may see. As I've previously written, "Patients may appear linguistically sterile, morally neuter, visually plain, or depleted in energy. However, these are all camouflage, intended to deflect from what is actually interesting." (Polster, 1987, p. 4) A professional challenge for the therapist, therefore, is to be fascinated through simple reactivity to patients, many of whom have made a life's work of deflecting from the most interesting aspects of their lives, either in general or in particular arenas. When the patient is superbly experienced in being uninteresting, the therapist pits her own openness to being interested against the unwillingness of her patient to be interesting.

One of my patients, Giaccomo, is thoroughly convinced of his uninterestingness. Giaccomo is obsessive, devoted to seeing himself and the world of people around him as uninteresting. I find him extremely interesting and am glad to see him every time he arrives. He is a complex man who always gives me a good argument. Among his many selves, he has a strong alienation between a superior self and a klutz self. The klutz is his rider and driver, crowding his mind with his difficulties in managing his world. He will not go into gatherings of people because he has nothing interesting to say. Nor is there anything interesting to hear, as his superior self readily reminds himself and me.

Most people are more likely to find him inaccessible than uninteresting. Inaccessibility would, of course, cause an eventual disinterest, though not as unreservedly as he portrays it. Although he thwarts my interest every step of the way, he can't succeed in getting rid of it because my fascinated eyes see beyond what he thinks he is showing. His perceptions about the world and the people he runs into are excellent, though grossly overgeneralized. I would agree with his values if he did not caricature them, as he does when he describes phony party behavior, people trying to make the grade in work, selling out on principles, and all the many other traits we humans exhibit.

Partly this is his cynicism speaking, but there is also the effect of his superiority. His opinions could be interesting to him, but he turns them into a nihilism that allows no contradiction to his set mind. I glory in his mountainous, chaotic, 300-pound physique; he sees himself as misshapen and blubbery. I once told this Gargantua of his Rabelaisian self. He was momentarily delighted to be seen altogether differently, but then quickly decided I was just playing therapist. But my greatest opportunity to allow my fascination full play is that, as a therapist, I don't have to make party conversation with him. I know, and I think he does also, that everything I say to him is as close to the truth as I can get it. I take his entry into my office as his invitation to be seen differently from the way he would be seen elsewhere. We speak vigorously all the time, something he would not permit socially. Although he thinks I'm very smart, he agrees with nothing I say. Is that his klutzy self speaking or his superior self? There is a loophole in every remark I make, and he goes for it like a moth to a flame.

At this point in our therapy, he has a lively time with me. Though he was originally severely depressed and in unrelieved misery, a function of his klutzy self, his pleasure comes from the exercise of his superior self as he duels with me—his version of a possibly admirable person. I have to be careful that he doesn't come simply to have a lively time rather than to actually experience himself anew and so change his self-configuration. To counteract any temporary pleasures and make sure his therapy represents growth, not merely entertainment, I explained that I do not want to be his drug of choice.

I see him changing outside of therapy only slowly. He has trouble seeing it at all because of his high requirements, but when I explain what I mean, he grudgingly accepts the increments that are beneath the notice of his superior self. He tells me of new experiences in his life when previously, practically nothing was worth mentioning: a new person he met and visited, the purchase of a car and all the details of his frustration and dissatisfaction, a weekend with his sister, a work assignment. All these are small in terms of giving him satisfaction, but they promise he may move out of his agoraphobic confines. I am quite convinced the restoration of his fascination with the world he faces and with himself, as well as my fascination with him, provide a significant chance for change, one small step at a time. If I were to let him imprison me in his own sense of dullness, we might as well not do therapy.

In supervising therapists, I have often seen them defeated by their own loss of interest. When they offer difficult cases for examination, they have already lost interest in the patient. They are discouraged about their failure to make progress, and also their patients make it hard to be interested in them. The patient's unyielding characteristics—repetitive complaints, unwillingness to register the therapist's observations, dangers of suicide or madness, the hopelessness they feel about therapy and their futures—all become unremittingly burdensome. When these therapists can bracket off questions of success and failure and concentrate on what is actually interesting, it's always there: a chance meeting with an old friend, a new pressure at work, a thought about travels. If we loosen the tight therapeutic format, these could all be fascinating even though they offer no immediate payoff. These topics may initially be no more interesting to the patient than to the therapist. Yet the elements of interest are there, and tapping into them successfully will increase the chances of relieving tension and returning to the fundamental fact that each person's integration of diverse qualities is a miracle.

Curiosity

Another variant of attention is curiosity, which is closely wedded to detail. This form of attention helps flesh out the abstractions people live by. People often live lives guided by generalities, as though providing titles to the stories of their lives. Titles are intended to attract curiosity, but they are empty commentary on the events and feelings that count. One always wants to know more than titles tell you, and it would be unthinkable to be satisfied by them. While titles are intended to make you want to know more, in psychotherapy people often feel they have told you the whole story. They are stuck with statements like "my father abused me" or "I'm lazy" or "I'm not comfortable in groups of people." Exercising curiosity, we explore the details of these experiences and the feelings that accompany them. Just what did your father do? When are you lazy? What groups are you thinking about? These questions would represent the barest hint of the exploratory process in the service of knowing more— not just a pathway to a better diagnosis or momentary empathy. That quest to know helps people feel optimal engagement. The therapist's question or statement must be more than a way to get the patient to realize what the therapist perceives. It should mean simply that you want to know the answer. You might strategically ask a person who it was that beat him when you know it was his father, but questions like that should be used sparingly.

In exploring the patient's experience, the therapist's curiosity opens a mutual process of discovery in which therapist and patient join. This is an important feeling for the patient to have. It beats the technically obvious guidance offered by suggestive questions. For example, a patient speaks circuitously about the absence of love from her mother. The therapist is not likely to know just what the patient means. So the therapist asks, for example, "What do you miss from your mother?" This gives the patient a chance to offer details about the relationship. The patient says that she was never sure about her mother's love because it was always intermingled with the admonition to become the best person she could. This never gave the patient the feeling of being loved. So it always seemed like she was delinquent, chafing inside about it. And she hasn't called her mother for a couple of weeks and knows her mother will be upset about that. When asked why her mother would be upset, she blurts out, "Because she loves me!" Suddenly she erupts into crying and realizes her grudge has blinded her. That feeling registers and evolves from the timing of the therapist's question, which the patient now can take seriously, a response to the therapist's enduring interest. She becomes ready to re-examine what her sense of love has been and what she allows herself to experience as love.

Communal implications

In the early 1950s, this enlargement of the teaching process was evident in the eye-opening integration of abstract principles with each person's life experience. While these training groups had a didactic intention, the learning experiences were an extension of a budding group therapy. This approach invited the classroom to become an experiential ground, one in which group members not only learned these new principles but also incorporated their personal experiences, transcending the familiarities of pedantry into directly describable conversational engagements. For example, if the theory emphasized the importance of fleshing out abstractions, the group members might tell each other about certain key abstractions they have about their own lives and then spell out concrete events that either support or contradict the abstractions. So, if a woman sees herself as a "scholarly person," she would describe what she does or feels that fits that abstraction. Perhaps she would tell about her reading habits or success in school. What might complicate the abstraction is her love for camping, which calls for an acceptance in the face of the original abstraction. During this process, the trainees would develop a pathway to a sharpened sense for the role of *abstraction* in therapeutic engagement. This process, multiplied by the entire range of theoretical principles, would indeed increase the personal involvement in the methodology and became the hallmark of the training process.

One of the surprising results of this approach was the *enchantment* felt about this new openness, a phenomenon I'll address further in the next chapter. A group of 15 psychological professionals met with Perls for a five-day workshop. Then the group continued meeting weekly on a leaderless basis for two more years. Each week's meeting was like a holiday, opening us to experience the enthrallment of pointed attention; a community converged to attend pointedly to personal experience. The hallowing of such deep concentration, nurtured in each group experience, was grounded in Perls' highlighting of concentration and awareness, each pointing compellingly forward in the continuing flow of life. This key expansion beyond the privacy of individual learning and beyond personal pathology was a natural offshoot of group therapy, a testament to its broad powers of illumination. This transcendence of the psychoanalytic search from the historical reason things happened to an emphasis, instead, on *what* happened and *how* it happened was a sharp awakening to direct personal experience. While this approach was serviceable for sharpening awareness, it also restored a natural biological surge toward the establishment and enhancement of attention, which proved to be an elixir for personal growth and a source of personal enchantment.

The developments I am describing nurtured a sense of assured belonging and inspired mutuality, creating a quasi-religious sense of a sacred place to explore one's personhood. This is paralleled in the arts, devoted as they are to the landscape of personal experience. Not only did the parallels of religion and the arts offer new stimulations and understandings, they also offered entertainment. The *pleasure* of activating the biological imperative of life focus has been overlooked, because pleasure seems shallow and popularity seems an undependable sign of validity.

The union of the personal and the general has been further developed in certain Gestalt therapy conferences. They have long incorporated "process groups" into the large format of a conference. These are small groups of perhaps six people who meet with each other at scheduled times to discuss their personal reactions to the academic presentations, to flesh out what might otherwise remain unsaid in the larger audience. This not only adds clarification and personalization of the material but is a considerable pleasure for many attendees. This personal opportunity draws time away from presenters, but it pays off in involvement and in fleshing out of personal questions for which the larger audience has no time or expectation. In my experience, these groups always *add* rather than subtract from conference purposes. Hallelujah!

Chapter 3

Concentration
Enchantment

Enchantment[1]

Building on the concept of concentration is the experience of enchantment, which represents a sharp amplification of attention. *Enchantment* is an extravagant word to include in the psychotherapist's repertoire, wary as we've been about the mysterious aspects of existence. We are instead commissioned to address immediate and serious problems that cause people suffering.

Let's look at what is meant by *enchantment* and why it might be an ally in the therapeutic process. Enchantment is, after all, a natural aspect of the human attention system. It must, therefore, as a mental reflex, be incorporated into a society that, incidentally, adores it. It's a phenomenon that arises untaught, simply making itself felt under fertile circumstances.

Enchantment happens when a person expands performance beyond ordinary reach, as in Olympic skating. The spotlight is on the dancer, and her balance, athleticism, grace, and daring entrance an international audience. It feels for the moment as though the dancer is all that exists. The audience is enthralled with the adventure they see unfolding right in front of them.

When we are enchanted, we may see into the transcendence of the laws of nature, as in magic shows or space travel. The magician cannot actually cut a woman in half and have her survive. Space travel also transcends what we thought were natural laws, a mere wishfulness, perhaps, or a songwriter's fantasy.

We have examples of enchantment in the beauty of nature—ethereal sunsets and glorious mountains. Or we feel it in deep sensations, like romantic love or visiting a childhood school.

How do we, therefore, see such extraordinary experience in the seemingly mundane, such as a conversation in the therapeutic process? Always lying beneath ordinary events, in fact, there could be fascinating exchanges, so personal as to measure up to more universal attractions. There is an insistent promise of novelty and a compelling unfolding of events that create real drama and often result in a heartfelt reach into new understandings; the prospect of people being witness and star players in their own lives; perhaps even life itself. While enchanting events happen sporadically, they are generative forces, lighting up experiences that affect life beyond the exhilarating moments. They engender an aura that is the source of enlightenment and entertainment. Such a populist attraction is a key force for psychotherapeutic entry into the workings of the public sensibility, reaching people with a pleasure that is more than light hearted. For therapy to become a populist experience, enchantment is a great attractor, offering people an orientation and guidance through the challenging landscape of living.

I will illustrate this awaking to life focus by remembering the spell cast upon me in my first experience of therapy, a step in my graduate student training, 70 years ago. I wasn't looking for a cure, as patients normally would, but, as a student, I wanted to experience the rudiments of psychoanalysis. As I walked into a large apartment, into what served as a waiting room, I didn't know what I was getting into; I felt only a sense of an indeterminate adventure to come. I knew it was going to be about me, but I had only the barest idea what form it might take. The room was dimly lit, with large hangings on the wall, a level of acculturation that added mystique to my naïveté. I knew that there was someone who had preceded me into the inner sanctuary who was already having a private experience that I judged to be more deeply pertinent to whatever life was about than anything I was familiar with. My turn would be next. Then I went in—to the strange privacy of the analyst, curtained off from everyday living. It felt like an initiation into self-realization. While I knew I was there to talk, there were no assignments. My analyst gently guided my next moments, with little pressure other than those that were my very own.

A few questions from my conjured monk-like image and I was on my way to a detailed account of my life, which I never dreamed would merit a devoted listener. My analyst listened to me, not only as any interested person might in everyday life, but for *session after session*, always with a sharpened sense of implication. What was amazing was how important everything seemed. With his guidance, I told him about many experiences; some recent, some placed on the shelf long ago, some about a dimly sensed expectation of my life ahead. The stories just flowed. Some of them had never crossed my ordinary attention. I told him about my first athletic experience, throwing rocks at the rats scurrying outside our apartment building when I was three. I told him about my awe at seeing a movie screen for the first time. I told him about my first sense of the ominous, which I felt as I heard a radio report of an auto accident. I told him about being lazy; about being quiet; about my Walter Mitty fantasies of being a ballplayer. I told him about a dream in which my hair was the color of flames. This man listened to it all. No matter what I said, he listened. No matter how many times I came back, he still listened. Never had anyone listened to me so enduringly, with such absorption. And I could tell by his sensitive responses that he knew what I was talking about, as though he was at home with my mind. This pointedness funneled me, first, into a new respect for what I had to say and, second, into a trajectory for saying things I would never otherwise have thought important or safe enough to say.

I am well aware that this is my story and hardly a universal story of psychotherapy. In fact, it's far out of date to the style of therapy prevalent nowadays, and I, myself, came to do therapy quite differently from this early experience. What has stayed with me most prominently—and what I have witnessed in the subsequent years of my work as a therapist—was the deep absorption that colors this mysteriously private setting. Even though we were just two people talking about the events of my life, I now realize more clearly than ever that this special environment, with its sharpened attention, was an invitation into a new world filled with "experience" and heightened sensibility. I had only the most innocent glimpse in those early days of what I see more clearly now: *the primary enchantment with the exploration of the life experience.* I doubt my medically oriented analyst saw this either. We looked past the enchantment of this engagement and packaged it in the wrappings of a professional healing. The *adventure* of my enhanced life focus was overshadowed by a targeted but dimly understood search for *personal improvement.* Instead of realizing clearly that I was in the grip of a biologically driven human need to explore the landscape of living, I saw it as a practical, though humanly rich, medical instrument; a vehicle intended to modify the consequences of my innermost psychological dynamics. That is to say, my mind was directed by the widely recognized medical purpose—the solution of acute problems and the accompanying medical intention to change people's lives.

Valid though this perspective was and still is, it may be overshadowed by the common interest in how our minds work. The excitement of this exploration is reflected in the devotion of the huge number of people who have flocked to therapy and the various forms of mindfulness. Driven originally by a sense of personal disability, many have discovered an attraction not unlike those that accompany other biological imperatives. What has become recognizable is that paying attention to our lives is just as natural as eating, sex, movement, talking, or any other of the biological basics. These are all so crucial to human existence that people are driven to exercise them, irrespective of their biological purpose. We eat because of our appetite, not to make us healthy; *yet eating makes us healthy.* We have sex because we feel its urge, not because it replenishes the species; *yet, it replenishes the species.* We move because muscular activity is a biological necessity, not only because we need to get somewhere; *yet moving gets us there.* And we engage in life focus because we are biologically geared to pay attention to what is happening, not because we seek the orientation and directedness it provides; yet we learn the nature of the world we live in and come to feel at home in it and are, indeed, guided in how to live our lives.

Of course, it's true that focusing on one's life can have undesirable effects. Just as we see deplorable sex, pathological eating, or poorly directed movement, there are examples of excesses and distortions in life focus. There has been considerable commentary on the "Me Generation," a literature that rightly gnashes its teeth about self-centered thinking, reflected in people becoming so enamored with the self-exploratory process that they lose track of the daily demands of personal purpose, accomplishment, and relationship. We must not, however, let potential excesses of paying attention to our lives overshadow its benefits. The need for a rightful proportion underlines the importance for *guidance* in the enhancement of life focus.

Furthermore, there is another compelling attraction to the role of enchantment and the life focus process—the experience of *microcosm*, which takes its place alongside other forms of enchantment as a universal and mysterious experience. Microcosm is the phenomenon of the immediate event represented a universe of events. This provides a sense of a box within a box synchronicity between individual existence and the world at large. That membership gives local experiences more importance than if they stood alone; often inducing a sense of enchantment with this convergence of worlds. This enlargement of the meaning of the single event heightens attention to it. We see such enlargement in role modeling, where a public figure, be it an athlete, politician, or actor, is experienced as a worldly exemplar. We see it in soldiers whose courage represents their country. We see it in songs that portray the character of a certain form of relationship. The therapy group and its offspring, the Life Focus Group, have a number of characteristics that foster the experience of microcosm.

Here are five of them:

1   These groups provide a special place, a special time, a special frame of mind where people explore not only their own lives but, also, indivisibly, life itself. This assurance of worldly significance provides a starting point for connecting whatever is happening here to whatever is happening in the larger realm, resulting in a sense of membership rather than isolation.
2   People feel a brightened sensibility when they join up with others. When individuals go to bars, theaters, lectures, ballgames, concerts, or conventions, they become part of a larger entity, amplifying what might otherwise be a less notable private experience. When people see a funny movie in a theater, they laugh more heartily because there is a world of other people laughing with them. A large attendance at a lecture punctuates the importance of the speaker or the ideas. For many people, prayer is felt more strongly in church than when expressed alone. Similarly, the aggregate of people in the Life Focus Groups stimulates them not only to live in the moment but to tell others about living; not only to live but to hallow and anticipate the living, stretching them beyond immediacy.

3   The convergence of minds into a simultaneous attention to a sharply stated theme combines individual and communal experience. While meditation is commonly seen as an elemental amplification of attention, the communal concentration is aimed at a broader content. Each person's stories contribute singularly to a *communal conversational vitality*, a stretch beyond the self. As in activities as broadly different as chanting and voting, there is enrichment in everyone paying attention to the same theme.
4   The content is broad, highlighting feelings, sensations, memories, fantasies, and perspectives that are important both universally and personally. The content will include worldly themes, relevant to all: jealousy, misunderstanding, hilarity, love, or ambition. The individuality of each storyline has its particular detail, but it is shown that it crosses over individual minds into a larger universe of comparable experiences.
5   The group may use music, poetry, lectures, film, and real-life stories to give *lyrical attraction* to a range of human experience. These vehicles reflect, animate, telescope, and color the substantive themes of life, which are not only intensely personal but also vital to the world outside the self.

These guidelines tap the microcosmic stimulation to integrate one's immediate experience with experiences that are common to the society at large. Such recognition of the universality underlying human individuality takes on subtle proportion when we address an actual set of themes commonly associated with life itself. Among such themes are non-pathological mourning, comparison of self with others, timeliness of sex and aggression, having pre-fixed opinions, and facing the risks of the future. Of further importance would be such developmental concerns as birth, puberty, marriage, personal loss, divorce, geographical displacement, and death. Other more relational themes might be forgiveness, conflict, competition, destructive impulses, and happiness. All of these are about the small world of the self as well as the large world of everyone. It is timely to expand communal invitations to this cornucopia of experiences, guiding people to a sense of both themselves and the host world, in which they can discover their own idiomatic reality.

This promise of cosmic embeddedness beckons large numbers of people to religion, philosophy, transpersonal psychology, spiritual practices, and psychotherapy itself. The Western religions in particular are well-known for providing ambitious answers to mysteries of a supernatural host universe pointing to the certainty of God, afterlife scenarios, and a sacred range of moral values. A comparable enchantment is available in the Life Focus Group guided by psychological understandings, attending to common life themes, communal conversations about life experiences, the role of mind-shaping conflicts, and the accentuation of purposes that drive behavior and feeling; all leading to a sense of where we belong in this incomprehensible universe. This humanized context honors the question we hear over and over: What is this life all about?

The Life Focus Group experience provides a revelatory sense of the ordinary experience into an ethereal embeddedness; a euphoric appreciation of the extreme beauty of each person's perceptual possibilities. This is a very ambitious expectation.

Lightness and depth

Here is a therapy session that illustrates the union of lightness and depth. It shows the way ordinary experience can evolve into a stream of exceptional events. This session was held with a conference audience of more than 1,000 people and reveals the important effects of the witnessing experience:

> The opening interactions included ordinary banter and lightheartedness, a lubricant for warmth and trust. I asked this person her name, and she said, "Michelle," to which I said, "That's a big name nowadays," an allusion to Michelle Obama. In quick rejoinder she said, "It was big in 1969 also" (the year of her birth), to which I replied, "Let me count." She laughingly saved me the trouble by saying she was forty. I replied that I was more than twice her age, and she said, "And still fabulous," at which the audience applauded in approval. I said, "Thank you very much. That takes care of my therapy, now let's see to yours." The audience roared. This humor was no competition for the professional comic, but it was timely and engaging and it set a tone that, I believe, paid off in deeper emotionality. What was introduced by this audience engagement was the expansion of vitality through their witnessing and cheering support. Whatever followed would become greater than itself, enlarged or even enchanted through a community of friendly participants.

Getting down to business, Michele told me that she had been very troubled that she was unable to love. I asked whether she felt unable to love some particular person or whether this was a general feeling. She said it was general, that she had no love in her life; then she demurred, thinking of her kids, whom she can love very well. Clearly she was treating that love as irrelevant to her supposed life-without-love. Actually, it was most relevant, even though it did not represent the romantic love she may have had in mind. This was an opening— re-experiencing a personal truth, rising above a mistaken conclusion about her life.

She went on to tell me more of her story. She had been married for 13 years; then two years ago she came out as a lesbian. She joked that had not helped the marriage or relieved her of guilt. Because her basic orientation in life was to take care of people, she felt guilty satisfying her own needs at the expense of others, especially her husband. Then, she shared that she was learning to enjoy being what she called selfish. I asked whether we might celebrate this new pleasure. The idea of celebrating lit her up, making her laugh whole-heartedly, as though she were mischievously getting away with something. Her laughter was so surprisingly free that it was contagious for both the audience and me. I asked her to tell us what her laughter was like for her, and she was surprised to notice something that she would normally overlook: that she was feeling her laughter more deeply inside her body than she would have expected.

Encouraged by this light heartedness, she asked whether I would like to do a little dance—a rumba or something. I said, "Okay, but I'm not sure I can do it." By then, she and the audience were laughing about her turn-around from the presumably guarded person who said she was unable to love and who was now behaving so warmly and openly. I said laughter had turned her into a new person, that she had previously looked as though she were in danger and now she looked as though the world was hers. We never danced because she went on to other things that were on her mind.

Primary among these was her difficulty in distinguishing between wanting sex and wanting love. Though coming out two years earlier, she had, surprisingly, not had any sexual relationship. She said she couldn't separate her need for sex from a pressure to take care of people. Because she is conflicted about taking care of people, to have sex would be troublesome. She was joking about all this and then said her laughter was a cover-up. I said that her laughter looked to me like a real pleasure—not merely a cover-up. I asked her to notice whether this pleasure committed her to some accommodation to me or anyone else.

She felt no such commitment. Then, just as real as the pleasure, she thought about her husband and tears came. She was surprised at the depth of these feelings. She told me how good a person her husband is and how badly she hurt him, and yet, how well they do together with the children. He loved her so much.

Here we have a significant change from her original concern: that she is unable to have love in her life. I asked her how many people can say they are loved as you are loved, to know the love, as you do, even in the face of its unhappy aspects. I asked her to try to absorb this feeling of being loved. She paid close attention and said that a familiar tightness in her chest had loosened. Then I asked her to talk to me about something she loves. She started by telling me about her 11-year-old son, who still climbs up on her lap and she is going to let him do it as long as he wants to.

Then she told me about loving "minimum" days at school, where she is a counselor. And she went on to tell about her love of exercise. Then another turning point! She said she would love to make connections with people at the conference. She had been afraid she would be rejected, and her eyes became moist at the realization that people might actually accept her. There was a long pause while she pondered this possibility, and I asked whether she would like to put it to a test by just standing and saying, "Here I am standing in front of you." When she did it, the audience applauded wildly. She gasped, "Oh, my," and giggled, saying, "There are a lot of you out there." I asked her to let her feelings of embarrassment soak in and to think whether she has a right to be loved. At this point, she began to sob deeply for about 30 seconds. When she came back into engagement, she talked about her feeling small and vulnerable and how hard she has strived to be strong. I told her she doesn't have to *try* to be strong; that she *is* strong, with great character. When we ended the session, with pleasure and love in the foreground, she left without any sense of the irredeemable obligations so familiar to her.

In examining the role of lightheartedness in this session, we see that laughter became a fundamental part of our engagement. Many might think such humor would be a distraction from a person's "serious" needs. Or even if it serves a seductive purpose, drawing the person into a soft and misleading friendliness, a distraction from engagement rather than a substantive engagement. The difference is important, but it's not an on/off phenomenon. We need to understand that this person and this therapist have had serious purpose built into the encounter and that this purpose, not easily taken off track, can be lubricated by humor. Heartfelt humorous interplay must be differentiated from avoidance, and it's a judgment call. The validity of each emotion must be understood within the continuity of what happens; in this case, whether the humor helped her face what needed to be faced or distracted her from it.

The entire session had an enchanting quality, but the climactic attention, almost unreal in the wide-eyed absorption of the audience and herself, came when she stood before all those people and *received* the sweeping affirmation. That flooded her mind, erupting in a wrenching cry so deep as to endear her even further to so many people. This moment was not only crucial as authentication of her enhanced hospitality to love, but it was also a testament to the power of a large group of witnesses to induce enchanting experience, mind-opening in its own right and also arousing a communal empathy.

The early parts of this conversation were simply an ordinary bantering introduction to our relationship, a way station to a deeper experience. To set such a deeper experience too far removed from the ordinary would make the deeper experiences such as enchantment feel like a foreign body, irrelevant to life except for a momentary pleasure. Recognizing the indivisibility of the ordinary and the extraordinary allows us to integrate the complexity. To fail in this integration romanticizes the power of enchantment in our lives, limiting it to moments of special pleasure and absorption. However, enchantment has a larger role. It also serves to light up the ordinary life that follows it. We are not only absorbed by the enchanting event itself, which is a giant source of both insights and entertainment, but the enchantment may also light up the ordinary, offering a new measure of recognition and significance to the ordinary experience. The ever-present affirmation of enchantment lights up our lives and honors us in a stream of worthy moments. To converse with a neighbor, to write a letter to a friend, to laugh at an apt turn of phrase, to drink a glass of water when thirsty, these are the stuff out of which a life is experienced. While these experiences are not usually seen or felt as enchanting in their ordinary form, it's a short step toward a lesson learned motivating people to give their attention to whatever the mind is dedicated. Concentration is so independently interesting that it rises above the ordinary standards for what is interesting and important.

It is often difficult for people to differentiate enchantment from such familiar pleasures as a surprise meeting with a friend in a city in which neither lives. Many would also find pleasure, but not enchantment, in a musical performance or a beautiful horse just before the race, or a joke told by a TV comedian, or the sight and sound of your panting dog. These are the stuff from which a life is formed, and paying attention is an approach to enchantment that can further illuminate our feelings and direction.

Psychotherapy conversations have a large range on the emotional scale, some aspects reflecting misery, others telling of banal happenings, and others reflecting large emotions and revelations. While the exceptional experience is what we see in enchantment, it is important to recognize that the exceptional must take its place in partnership with the ordinary. That can be easily accommodated, as the ordinary is the ground from which the exceptional is formed. A patient may, for example, speak dispassionately about visiting his family over Christmas, telling of his excitement about the exchange of gifts while sitting around the tree. A very ordinary account, until he comes to realize how much he misses his grandfather, who was a great storyteller. The ordinary vanishes, and he cries as he tells a special story he remembers. Enter enchantment, the palpable affirmation of dearness.

Such experiences happen under circumstances relatively untainted by life's endless pressures. To set complexities aside and witness life with sharply pointed attention helps us recognize the relationship between the immediate experience and its broader dimensions. To feel this harmony is no small revelation, and it's hardly the moment-to-moment experience in most therapy sessions. However, when it happens, it is cherished, as it accentuates a life beyond the ordinary. It is the consummation that makes life feel that it's all of a piece, a confirmation of the best we can do. We enter into a world where we ourselves are basic and yet indivisible from the bountiful world in which we live. Perhaps this is too romantic a perspective on psychotherapy. Psychotherapy is however, designed to make us feel whole; to bring together the mundane details of existence against a backdrop of human prospect. This movement is, therefore, embedded in a convergence of diverse experience: in song, in poetry, and in the sense of relief from the obscuring complexity of everyday living.

To say it another way, the root of therapeutic enchantment lies not only in the ineffable, but in life's rudiments as well. We are the beneficiaries of awareness and responsiveness and the integrators of a complex stream of personal experiences. We feel, we think, we want, we go, and we function in countless ways operating from the beginnings as in a simple sperm/ovum interaction, each stage of which is a miracle of convergence and mutuality. Only in certain moments does enchantment happen, when existence is seen through an eye-opening magnification. But this exceptionality is based on an ever-present system of stimulation, which can erupt under many circumstances and always deserves recognition.

Through their skills at lighting up experience, artists are an example of the human microscope, pointing people beyond the dimmed understandings that dominate our lives. We read their books, look at their paintings, watch their plays, listen to their music, and reside in their designed environments. Artists transport us into a cryptic reality, inviting us to witness novel versions of a world of events and feelings, filling in missing pieces in the landscape of living. They convey us into softened boundaries, where fact and fantasy may be indistinguishable, where anger and kindness may interweave, where tragedy and blessedness can alternate in a flick of an eye, where the comforts of the familiar can be joined with an open-ended freshness.

These contributions to the cultural climate and to individual people often provide profound insights, but for many consumers of the arts, such depth is not what is sought. For them, the arts are just good entertainment. After walking through a museum, or reading a novel, or hearing a concert, many people come out happy, having been *entertained* by seeing a world compellingly portrayed. They are more drawn by the drama or the beauty than by the subtle influences on their own lives.

Many artists would blanch at such a description of their work. Entertainment by itself is less deep than what artists intend. They underestimate the importance of entertainment, I believe. The raw truth is that most people do read novels, look at paintings, hear music, and go to the movies primarily because they like to. But so-called entertainment is not necessarily lighthearted. It's not a casual experience to hear a Bartók concerto, read a novel portraying the struggle between India and Pakistan, or feel revulsion in seeing Picasso's *Guernica*. Has anyone seen a Charlie Chaplin movie without being touched with empathy for the honest underdog? Clearly, artistic experience is a pleasure that is not just incidental. It is part of the reward built into the innate function of life focus, the artist's fundamental instrument.

That is true of psychotherapy, too. People commonly experience anticipatory excitement, even though the prospect of a session may also be ringed with anxiety. Trouble notwithstanding; there is a great attraction for many people in being safely guided to address their personal motives, tell intimate stories, explore dreams and fantasies, and expand their versatility of behavior and clarity of feeling: to know life in a range, beyond the ordinarily reachable. You don't need to be "cured" to derive these pleasures. I'm reminded of a woman I worked with who had made important strides in her therapy, but she continued coming to more sessions. I sensed that she was now making up problems because she liked therapy so much she wanted to stay in it. We talked about the fact that if she wanted to come, that was okay as long as she felt it was best for herself. But she did not need a problem as a ticket for entry. Furthermore, it was important that she accept the reality of her pleasure, so she could more clearly accept the pleasures also available to her in everyday life.

She found the conversation a great relief, taking her outside the realm of pathology. It was plain to her that her pleasures in therapy were not flimsy pleasures. These were the pleasures of honest communication, of appreciating her life, of putting troublesome feelings into context, of experiencing freedom from the judgmental. Moreover, these pleasures, entertaining though they were, were the seeds of a major life change. Entertainment notwithstanding, therapy is serious business.

The future ahead

I am, therefore, proposing that a paradigm shift is developing in the healing profession; one that takes us beyond the remediation of psychological disturbance to a larger and more public focus. The original medical purposes still serve well as psychological troubleshooters. This medical invention and its huge consequences have a paradoxical benefit. The medical frame of mind has benefited from governmental support and the inclusion of limited psychotherapy into insurance policies. Accordingly, much therapy nowadays is done on a short-term basis limited to specific problem-solving. While this is a boost to the accessibility of therapy to the population at large, it has also been accompanied by a huge social movement, varied in procedures and perspectives, but all devoted to the lives people live rather than to narrowly focusing on specific personal problems.

What is potentiated is a public enchantment. This cultural development is an advance beyond the resolution of specific problems and inspires a spirited communal ethos. To use the word *enchantment* may seem an extravagance of both language and experience, because the surface of therapy is often just two people talking to each other. That being said, it has always been apparent in common conversation how vital the therapy sessions have been. These people refer to their therapists as saying this or that, as though they were the messengers of life itself. A large part of this illumination is the explicit intention to enter deeply into the mystery of a person's lifetime of experience. Riding above these mysteries is a series of awarenesses of the ordinary arriving at new perspectives or highlighting familiar, cherished ones.

Such accentuation is familiar in our everyday lives. Weddings, for one example, are felt to be enchanting. They are celebratory and solemn and hallow the entry into a new arc of experience. A lot is riding on the promises for the future, and the celebration is a lubricant for both the couple getting married and the witnesses, affirming a deeply important move.

Religious experience also banks on enchantment, setting the stage for everyday living. While there is disagreement about the principles of particular religions, both psychotherapy and religion are devoted to clarifying the nature of life and offering guidance. On and on we might go, but it is enough here to point out that the attractions of enchantment are key agents of public orientation.

Note

1 A version of this chapter, "Enchantment: The Secret Ally of Psychotherapy," appeared in *Gestalt Review* 24.1 (pages 1–13).

Chapter 4

Figure/ground relationship
Basic process

Introducing the concept of figure/ground relationship was a milestone in advancing the understanding of how the mind works. It replaced the psychoanalytic emphasis on the unconscious, a compartmentalized player in the workings of the mind, overshadowing and alienated from a conscious reality. While the description of the figure/ground concept incorporates a huge universe of personal experience, it does not have the linguistic charisma of the *unconscious*. The unconscious has the aura of a mysterious driver, riding on one's shoulders, directing each person to incomprehensible behaviors. Still, while one cannot hum the figure/ground relationship as a tune, it engenders a compelling vitality, and it's illuminating to spell out the life experiences it fertilizes.

The figure/ground concept starts with an obvious observation: people live in a world of happenings, and only some of these happenings come to the clear attention of any of us. These are figural, and they are housed by the ground, which is everything that happens in a person's world: learning to read, laughing, fighting with siblings. There's an insistent reality that nothing exists by itself. These figural happenings are always contained within a background of total life experience, and they derive meaningfulness through the reverberations between them and the context of a total existence. Whether we are open to personal risk, for example, depends on whether the risk is welcome to the totality of our lives. Of course, some happenings are more important than others, and we don't fully understand the effects of the background on any particular person's life. Still, the challenge is to unify this figure/ground relationship so that not only can we be sharply engaged in what is happening but our experience will be relevant and acceptable to the sweep of our lives, and perhaps to life itself. Enter the psychotherapist, who is commissioned to explore this relationship between the world of experience and the happenings that are front and center.

What is important to Gestalt therapists is the fluidity of anyone's experience in a perpetually operative figure/ground relationship. You have only to glance out your window to experience how freely the flow of your attention can dart from one part of the panorama to another. You see a tree starting to bud, and you give it your attention. Suddenly a bird launches from a branch, and you follow its flight. A cloud of intriguing shape distracts you from the bird's flight and sets off a train of thoughts about the sky once experienced in distant Boulder, Colorado. This is how experience develops. This fluidity reminds us that at any moment that which is figural may recede into the ground as something else moves to the foreground.

Innocent flow is only part of the story. Studies show that the perceiver not only structures what she perceives into economical units of experience, she also edits and censors what she sees and hears selectively. She harmonizes her figural perceptions with her background of inner needs. For example, a hungry individual will more likely perceive an ambiguously presented stimulus as food. Our inner experience colors and determines our current experience, just as a hungry person perceives food even when it's not there.

Extrapolating from such basic perceptual activities, we see that human concerns reflect integrative requirements that are holistic in nature. Our whole life is the material from which we select what to bring to the foreground of each present moment. As we do this, many of the specific events in the background disappear like a single bubble in boiling water. Current events must be coordinated with their background, including the person's characteristics, such as kindness, knowledge, ability, and ambition. Under ideal circumstances, these will be consonant with current behavior. The background of personal qualities sets the stage and influences the experiences that emerge.

All of this sounds pretty elemental. It is, however, a simple statement about a most complex chain of experiences. For example, for the person who cannot abide his own homosexual possibilities, any behaviors that tap into these fears will either be neutralized, confusing, or anxiety-inducing. A sense of well-being might be diminished by the seeming incompatibility between his actual behavior and feelings, on the one hand, and the background of his tainted beliefs, which would otherwise provide support and new meaningfulness. Fear of homosexual implications might, for example, create a taboo against sensitivity in a male world of toughness. Accordingly, a person may have a harder time permitting sexual thoughts or feelings to emerge when they are threatening, whether a mild discomfort or full-on panic. The job of psychotherapy is to increase the individual's sense of harmony with his background, largely by highlighting new experience. Restoring vitality to the immediate experience with the therapist is crucial because otherwise, prior beliefs dim the aliveness of immediate experience. This restoration in the therapy process of a fluid immediacy provides an inspiration, one that energizes and clarifies the resulting happenings.

When such new experiences pop up from deep in the background where they previously were receiving little or no recognition, the whoosh of excitement is great. This may be exhilarating or it might create anxiety and shock for those who live with a fixed forbiddenness. The new experience influences the ground. Such figure/ground resonance is at the root of fluidity. Ideally, every experience, under the right circumstances, could be figural. One would come in touch with the gamut of emotions, from the most painful agony to the joys of personal enlightenment. One could know one's kindness while also knowing one's cruelty. One can reach into the reservoir of the ground for experiences of gullibility, vindictiveness, competitiveness, nausea, caginess, passivity, stubbornness, and all the other characteristics that reverberate between figure and ground. The clarity and the effervescence of one's life are profoundly affected by *the mutuality of figure and ground.*

When a person has swum, traveled, run a lap, planted flowers, ridden a motorcycle, made wine, painted a picture, parachuted, he has increased the fund from which he may draw for new figural developments. In other words, as the background of he experience becomes more diversified, it also becomes potentially more harmonious with the whole range of happenings. The resulting diversity is more likely to assure relevant background for anything that might be happening. This is a rule of thumb implicitly subscribed to by parents whose children have dancing lessons, music lessons, travel experiences, museum visits, and outings in nature. The wisdom of expanding the range of one's background lies in the greater resonance between whatever is happening now and the full array of a person's life.

Helen, for example, who had been reared by a perfectionistic mother who emphasized abstract precepts to the exclusion of human considerations, was distressed trying to resolve her own uncertainty about how to be a good mother. She wanted to be free and non-judgmental with her children, but she felt she had to maintain unrealistically high standards for herself, about how her home should look and how much work she should be doing during the day. This left her frazzled and irritable with her children and guilty about her shortcomings. The rub between allowing herself and her family to live freely and keeping her home tidy was chronic and abrasive. She was having difficulty deciding which to give her focused attention, how to decide which to prioritize. One day in a therapy session, I suggested to Helen that she might try putting people values above property values. Her face lit up, and she recognized that when the struggle was framed in these terms, she had no problem loosening her mother's standards and following her own evolving standards, which she sensed were right for her. In this context, Helen's own warmth and loving could emerge, effortlessly.

The flow of mind

For most of us, a single-minded purity is hard to achieve, because experiences have variable force and variable primacy. Some thoughts, wishes, and images are like blips on the radar, and to give them premature emphasis is aborting the process. Minds are not so tightly organized that each occurrence is equal. Each person is governed by a unique sense of which events come into lively expression and which are only mild appearances of a figural flow, not ready for vital birth, let alone prime time. People must grow into a confidence in their figural flow, including varieties of human experiences, thoughts and wishes, and disappointments and challenges. Things either become stray wisps in one's effervescent system or move into the center of a reality that calls for recognition. It is evident that in postulating figure/ground formation as the basic dynamic of awareness, we are addressing how accessible our experiences are to us and what composes the context for events in our lives. If there is any psychological principle that many theorists share, it's that there are dynamically powerful forces within each individual that are not accessible to his awareness, but which nevertheless influence his behavior. The most prominent of these psychological principles, of course, is the psychoanalytic view of the unconscious, to which figure/ground formation is the Gestalt counterpart.

The concept of the unconscious contributed much to the twentieth-century person's knowledge of our own nature by dramatizing the power of that which was not available to our awareness. It is not surprising, therefore, to find that in spite of its eminent position as an orienting principle, certain drawbacks have become apparent. First, this view of human beings creates a conscious/unconscious split, dichotomizing the person, overriding a holistic view of his nature. The free flow between the accessible and the inaccessible, although paid some slight notice in the concept of the pre-conscious, went largely unrecognized and unused. The unconscious became the core concern in determining a psychotherapeutic methodology. The search for unconscious meaning created such great leaps from one's ever-moving psychic reservoir to a mental gymnastics that it overshadowed trust in consciousness. Once removed from overt experience, people became deflected from immediacy, in order to discover what was "really" going on.

The figure/ground concept, on the other hand, supports the individual's surface experience as a source of therapeutic leverage. When you are willing to stay with what is present, speak clearly, move from one moment of actual experience to the next, discovering something new in each, life becomes as plain as the nose on your face. As this process moves forward, a theme develops, and the result is an illumination of what was inaccessible in the beginning. Thus the sequence of actualities, rather than a clever diagnostician, tells the tale. Interpretations and symbolic equations are bold attempts at divining exciting drama for those in the flow of life. This is a special game ingeniously played, offering challenge and confirmation for excellence and psychological marksmanship. For the person observed, it may offer illumination and sharp surprise. When the interpretation reaches its mark, it will tie together one's consciousness with new data and a new reality. Interpreting the nature of a person's unconscious neutralizes that person's own developmental process, however. This process is more firmly established when it is based instead on the person's own awareness from moment to moment, each new awareness riding on the momentum of the previous experience.

Here is an example of how the sequence of figural formations may unfold in a therapeutic session, without interpretation of the unconscious process. Cleo was a 35-year-old woman, long divorced, classically unsatisfied in spite of successes in her work. She chronically maintained her aloofness, fixing into the background, those feelings without which she was left in a vague state of longing and incompleteness. One day, Cleo became aware of her fear that if she got close to people, she might fall in love.

This would be unbearable if she were not loved in return, and Cleo feared being in need of the other person. The experience of her fear was a new figure for her, one she had not previously allowed. As she spoke, I asked her to describe how she felt. She said there was a twinge of sensation that she could not describe, but she also felt afraid. The fear was palpable and specific; another new figure. As she focused on this sensation, at my suggestion, Cleo began to feel that if she yielded to it, the feeling would get so strong that she would have to do something that she was not used to allowing. Another new figure. I asked her to close her eyes and allow a fantasy to come to her.

She fantasized a scene in my office, another figural step. When I asked her to visualize what she would like to do there, she saw herself coming into my arms. Then she saw herself crying. The color rushed to her face, and although she didn't actually carry out her fantasy, she felt great warmth inside herself and none of the fear she had imagined. She said it felt whole and surprisingly independent, not at all vulnerable. A new configuration had been formed. She could talk seriously and warmly with me, presumably from the support of her inner sensation. From this point her relationships outside of therapy began to take on greater warmth, as her security with people was dramatically increased.

This story shows how the non-interpretive movement from figure to figure can happen. The patient is going her own route, making her own choices at each stage of the game. Her experience in therapy became pivotal in the resolving of her unfinished business about allowing deep sensations. The process of moving from one moment to the next reflects the existential view that whatever exists, exists only now. Flux is basic to experience, so if one can allow each experience the reality it seeks, it will fade into the background in its turn, to be replaced by whatever is next. Only hanging on can maintain a semblance of sameness in life. Once Cleo was able to experience warmth and closeness, the flow of her awareness was restored.

Each figural moment contributes its share into the whole experiential process, much as a single frame contributes to the continuity of a film. If the projector is stopped, even though there is still a figure sharply focused, the quality of aliveness disappears, and we are left with a stagnant version of what might have been a vital process. The restoration of movement throughout time is a pervasive theme of therapy. Where movement has gaps or is interrupted, life becomes awkward, disconnected, or meaningless, because it has lost the support of the constantly rejuvenating cycle of development that is native to the ongoing life process.

The Gestalt perspective puts a premium on novelty and change—not a pushy premium, but a faith-filled expectation that the existence and recognition of novelty are inevitable if we stay with our own experiences as they form. Beisser (1970) has described this as a paradoxical theory of change, because change rests on the full recognition of what already is happening. Such paradoxical games require a profoundly artful discrimination in accepting the status quo, while anticipating change.

If the letting go process is forced, we abort the natural continuity each movement stimulates. It's important to learn the difference between staying with an experience until it is completed and hanging on, trying to squeeze out something more, from a situation that is either finished or barren.

The basic clue is whether attention to the issue is a loose, unfixed, mobile attentiveness or whether it feels glued to the object. Those with a bug-eyed stare, a clinging grasp, insistent preoccupations, a sense of desperation, ready-made sermons, an unwillingness to leave when conversations are finished, all are hanging on. He is hanging on if he is 20 years on the job with no rewards or if he is 10 years in a marriage with someone he doesn't even like to be with, maintaining a desired self-image in the face of all kinds of contrary indications.

An example in which the immediate situation is consistently out of harmony with the individual's needs is that of Ken. Ken, who had been beguiled by the status and security he felt in his academic life, was miserable with the actuality of his role as a professor. He felt oppressed by the need to publish and the endless committee meetings and fantasized about the countless other ways he would have preferred to spend his life. Ken was an excellent businessman and dreamed of running a resort community. He even had some innovative ideas about how he might do this while maintaining some professional connections through lecturing and consulting. But he hung on doggedly to his college appointment, ignoring his needs and clinging to his image as a secure academic whom everyone looked up to and respected. When disharmony persists and no efforts are made to change the circumstances, someone is hanging on.

Open attentiveness to alternatives and maintaining a sense of choice among possibilities are hallmarks of staying with it. Staying with a pleasant experience is an easy choice to make. Staying with a choice that involves considerable unhappiness can still retain the flavor of a decision made through choice. A student who hates graduate school but knows that he wants the training to support his future work is staying with it, if he experiences the decision as valid in the context of his life needs. A man who is married to an invalid wife and who chooses to stay with her and remains fresh and loving in the process is staying with it even though the pain may be extensive.

Though these examples have aspects in common, in each instance the individual's personal judgment and the deep absorption with which he continues his engagement are crucial. There are no hard-and-fast rules to govern the distinction between hanging on and staying with it. It is the unique responsiveness to the flow of life. One person might say in retrospect about living in St. Louis, "I should have left long ago," while another may say, "I'm so glad I worked through the troubles and came out blessed by my patience or creativity or luck." Clearly, what for one person is hanging on, for another is staying with it. The task is to stay in touch, meeting each moment with a sense of opportunity and an inspirational vitality.

The accessibly hidden

Because Gestalt therapy has made immediacy of experience a centerpiece of its theory, to understand the *breadth* of this theory is pivotal to perceive some of the richness of the content we all live with. One expansion of the limits of immediacy is the concept of the "accessibly hidden" regions of the mind. With this term I include the wide landscape of experience in every person's life, much of it available for immediate arousal, although only a limited part of this landscape is relevant to what is immediate. Some thoughts and feelings are on the edge of expression but are outside the relevance of what is actually going on. If, for example, I am speaking about my dislike of hot summer weather, it wouldn't be relevant to tell about a fire I put out in my kitchen. The need for the "accessibly hidden" to fit rightly into the existing experience is vital for a sense of depth and detail in one's life. If something accessibly hidden doesn't fit, it may create unnecessary complication or derail the flow of experience. On the other hand, there is great benefit from stimulating the lively present; this arouses thoughts and feelings that are, indeed, ready for prime time. Invoking available content is a continuing process that is more friendly to people's current mindset than the mysterious challenge of the unconscious. Its simplicity is user-friendly, and its fruitfulness is immediately apparent in the resulting fluid conversation. Because these thoughts and feelings are not hidden, they satisfy our immediate will. When the time is ripe, the effervescent sense of continuity of experience will arouse thoughts and feelings that otherwise would remain dormant, outside our immediate attention even though they're well worth arousal.

Let's look at an everyday life scenario to illustrate how accessibly hidden content sits in the background, waiting for the signal to call it onto center stage. My wife and I, because of my hearing loss, went to a technology store to buy a wireless headset so that I could more easily hear certain

TV programs. The manager spoke to us, then sent someone named Mike over to help us. This was a tiny diversion from our continuity but nothing much, just part of a routine sales sequence. Mike was an interesting phenomenon in his own right, the source of a lifetime of potential storyline. But it was not relevant to our purpose. Then I silently noticed a scar on his jawbone. What is that about? I thought about that for a second, not long enough to draw him out. There was the promise of an interesting story, but Mike was not there to become revealed nor I to explore. That's O.K., but that part of Mike remained hidden, though probably accessible. Under the right conditions, even in the store, it could have been the source for a personally interesting story.

Then he begin to tell us about his grandfather's hearing loss and how a certain wireless headset had worked effectively for him. Again, this is a promise of the appearance of the accessibly hidden that was left out of the conversation. We know nothing else about his grandfather, although he may have been the mayor of Peoria. Nor did we care.

At each step of this matter-of-fact engagement there was much more that could have been said but was not. Naturally so. The tiny surprises, the sidestepping of elaboration, the guiding influence of purpose: this is the normal stuff of everyday life. We override the untimely possibility, or we could not live our daily lives. Even this routine exchange, however, had a throb from the accessibly hidden, hints of potential information by-passed in favor of headset education and purchase. The pleasure of dwelling at the edge of this unknown background was intriguing, because with Mike's intonations and facial expressions, there was always the sense of a mysterious underground, even in the information that had a place in this business sequence. Likewise, in many normal life situations, we're likely to be affected by mysterious potential; even when we don't follow through, its unacknowledged influence pulses through the continuing business at hand. This potential for novelty affects our absorption, affording a measure of drama to otherwise routine experiences.

Now let us look at a non-business scenario, where there is a greater latitude in conversational choices. When I meet you for lunch, the vista from which the silently imminent may appear is broader. As you speak, I feel an anticipatory attention either because of my history with you or because of how you are speaking to me now. Whatever you're saying, I feel there is more to come; an anticipation that amplifies my interest. From the accessibly hidden region of your mind, you may have a story about your wife, who might have banged her head this morning, wouldn't go to the doctor, and you're now wondering whether she has a concussion. Or you may have just signed a new contract to sell an exotic coffee from Brazil. Or you may wonder why I did not respond to your last e-mail. On and on, the approaching unknown spurs our conversation and, while much of it may be accessible, its appearance is unassured, to be determined by the way our conversation plays out. This level of suspense ranges from barely noticeable to highly charged.

Many people are excellent at creating an expectation of impending novelty and need little help in revealing it. They characteristically convey an unspoken promise of the more that is to come, perhaps with a breathless tone of voice, perhaps with intriguing ideas, perhaps with observations about politics or movies or a chance meeting with a mutual friend, perhaps with their pleasure in the conversation. Perhaps, perhaps, perhaps.

The therapeutic experience is especially powerful in inviting the accessibly hidden into the light. By its hospitality to personal storyline, it creates a conversational suspense and induces sharp attention. The resulting expectation will arouse personal expression, telling thoughts that have depth but are not retrieved from a buried mental reservoir, as represented by the unconscious. What emerges is, rather, a synchronized response to whatever is happening.

Here is the story of one person in a 12-person Life Focus Group where there was room for conversation. The group had been meeting for about 20 years. Oliver was artful, kind, effective in his work, and living a satisfying life. Still, he was bothered that he wasn't using his full potential. He felt that he was too careful in the way he spoke, in the goals he set for himself, and in using his imagination. There was one major exception in his life. He loved to improvise on the piano, and when he did, he was quite free, playing fully in the spirit of the moment. In his reckoning, however, this freedom didn't count because it was private, not something he would ever do in front of other people.

As the conversation warmed up, I thought he might be ready to play the piano, improvising in front of us. We were meeting in the house of one of the members, and, happily, there was a piano in the room and, more happily, Oliver consented to play.

The music he played went beyond any of my expectations, exquisitely melodic and free-flowing with no sign of uncertainty. The others listening to him were spellbound too. For Oliver, there was a shy thrill, and more importantly, a new insight. He had *lost himself in the music, as though he would dissolve.* The pleasure he felt was a surprise to him. He had always dreaded this feeling, which he deemed a weakness; softness in scary contrast to the secure stiffness he usually feels. It took a few conversational exchanges before he could see that his softening, as he put it, was not a muscular softening but a heart softening, opening himself to the resonance of the music.

Then, in thinking back to his everyday life, he remembered that the thought of "dissolving" had been on his mind recently. He realized, "everything I am doing these days that I most value is slowing down, softening—the way I am with my clients, my poetry, my relationship with my wife." I asked whether this softening made him feel weaker, and he said, "No, I feel larger, warmer, more alive, and more capable and competent. It's actually delicious."

I have witnessed surprises like this over and over in the years of my therapeutic work. People bring up a problem as though they'd never thought about it, when actually they have, already, by themselves, started to solve it. Glimmerings of improvement, even unacknowledged, have made them bolder in bringing it up and taking a next step toward dependable improvement. Oliver's sudden willingness to play the piano in front of us was not so much a novelty as a continuity, a punctuation for what he had already begun.

This was an important experience for him. And for the group, the experience tapped into their lives too, and we discussed what it meant to them. One person spoke of her own love for singing and how she could only let her voice soar when she had a friendly environment. Moved by Oliver's experience, she could see how she might focus on her own actions rather than be preoccupied about what others were thinking. Another spoke about his lectures and how he has learned that when someone leaves the room, they might be going to the bathroom. Another spoke of her role in giving psychological testimony in court and how she got over being intimidated and achieved a victory over a bullying lawyer by sticking to what she knew.

The discussion highlighted two things. First came the *enhanced realization* that Oliver's experience applied to their lives too. And second, it sparked an increased pleasure in a renewed connection they now each felt with others in the group. The experience not only helped them name and spell out their own struggles; it lubricated their kinship with one other.

In addition to the obvious arousal powers of group communication and the power of setting themes, there was a general excitement in the ordinary conversation that may be tapped by the accessibly hidden; particularly if there is space for conversations to go in unspecified directions.

Implicit within this recognition is the function of past and future, the creation of storyline, and meaningfulness through increased understanding, belonging, and guidance in the Life Focus Groups. It is crucial to invite storylines that paint living pictures of people's experiences, and to find a support for a dependably lively sense of belonging and communal engagement.

While it's true that the concept of figure/ground lacks the linguistic pizazz and mystery of the idea of the unconscious, it fosters some crucial aspect of life and of the therapeutic endeavor to portray and enrich life by arousing interest. The concept of the accessibly hidden elevates the suspense inherent in human engagement and a continuing sense of life unfolding as we move through its process. It incorporates the past with the immediacy of now and opens us to freshening the old with the new.

Chapter 5

Figure/ground
Here and now/there and then

Because holism is crucial to Gestalt therapy's figure/ground concept, we must re-examine the theory's love affair with the experience of here and now. Theories always need freshening up, or their concepts, exaggerating one point, blur the larger intentions of the theory. In this spirit, let us examine the inherent contradiction between the figure/ground concept and the identification of Gestalt therapy as a messenger of the here and now. Even though the here and now always includes the present acts of remembering and planning as here-and-now events, in the world of psychotherapy, many have taken the here and now to be in the exclusive arena of consequential living. It is therefore worth looking for a pathway to the escape from the present.

For the psychotherapist, it seems only natural that the full dimensions of time and space be taken into account, because things obviously happen in a specific time and place. It is therefore curious that the more narrow emphasis on here and now should have gained almost cult-like ascendancy over the past 60 years. Shortly after World War II, many people began to believe, with ramifications still present, that the here and now was the center of psychological living. Although the reasons are not altogether evident, I offer some obvious speculations. For one thing, there was an increasing call for immediate gratification in reaction to the oppressively familiar delays for almost everything people wanted and did. For another, there was a growing impatience with the psychoanalytic emphasis on the past and the lengthy extent of treatment.

This cultural frustration was joined by important technological advantages. We discovered that the mind's extraordinary resiliency increased when it was freed to concentrate on the immediate experience and the natural movement into nextness. Søren Kierkegaard (2011) long ago recommended that purity of heart was to will one thing, and his credo—originally intended to invoke total attention to God—was then applied to more mundane events. It became clear that if you cut out distractions, internal and external, the resulting concentration would release additional personal awareness and maximize fertility. We see this in the achievement of excellence in the arts, sciences, sports, and animated conversation—all focused pointedly without loss of context. At the same time, there is a risk of narrowness. Holding both poles of a paradox simultaneously is a prerequisite for the attainment of excellence and the feeling of satisfaction.

Thus the here-and-now emphasis serves as a bridge to absorption by underscoring simplicity in a world gone haywire in complexity. This narrowing of attention—at times compartmentalization, even dissociation—helps close off many debilitating habits of mind that normally fence people in and make therapy slow going. Focusing on the here and now was an exciting turn of the psychological kaleidoscope. Any single point of keen concentration could trip off a chain of internal events, even a simple sensation like an itch. With concentration, we amplify one thing, then move to another area of the body, then back to the original place. In continued concentration, each awareness might ignite the next until the whole body would be warmed. Sensations rise instead of falling, collecting waves of feeling, which release pent-up energy, invigorating the person who originally only had an ignorable itch. Sharpness of attention and fertility become joined in continuous attention.

These were impressive commentary on the effectiveness of the sharply pointed here-and-now concept. It was much easier to say *now* than *how*; and this emphasis on the present did indeed reduce the complexity of attention, fostering improved concentration. Unfortunately, the instruction to stay in the present caught on more rapidly than the integration of a lifetime of experiences, and it was not long before large numbers of people endorsed the idea of living in the present. Presumably they came to realize how much they had lost by allowing their lives to be delayed and deflected. For them to put life on the back burner until some future time when they would graduate, get married, or retire was understandably no longer acceptable. Nor was a brighter twenty-first century consoling to the underclass of the society. Many people came to believe that the present was all they had in life, the only reality. Perls, among others, was unusually skilled in publicly demonstrating the power residing in simplified experience. His followers were often amazed at the depth of the experiences he speedily induced.

Because the present is simply a point on a time continuum, it is actually neither experience, nor awareness, nor reality, just a point. An experience is an *occurrence* in time, not time itself, just as a jewel in a box is not the box. A person has the choice to describe his sadness about his mother's death without caring about time; caring instead only about sensations, thoughts, intentions, and hopes that may enter his consciousness. On the other hand, he could relate his sadness to time by saying that he is *still* sad about his mother's death two years afterward, or that he's sad because she's going to die *soon*. All details of experience exist within time and space, and everyone is free to take these dimensions into account as he sees fit. Minds will not stay put, and their freedom to roam is self-evident.

Many of my fellow Gestalt therapists would cry foul at my sticking Perls with his own slogans, and they have a point. Despite its simplistic overtones, the here-and-now approach of Gestalt therapy was from the beginning more comprehensive than its reputation for focusing on immediacy. Remembering, imagining, and planning are validly taken as *present* functions. This qualifier does look beyond the present and restores dimension. However, it suffered the fate qualifiers often do; it took a back seat and was widely disregarded by practitioners and laypeople who were superficially knowledgeable. The consequences of this misunderstanding are one element in the cultural configuration that has popularized the notion "the future is now."

Too tight a focus on the "here and now" forecloses much that matters: continuity of commitment, implications of one's actions, preparation for complexities, responsiveness to demands, and so on. When these requirements of living are chronically set aside, alienation from large parts of society is one consequence; living life as a cliché is another.

One example of a person infected by the stereotypes about present experience will help show its *narrowing* effects. Abigail, a 25-year-old woman, was alienated from her parents who, for religious reasons, objected to her living with a man if they were not married. Though greatly distressed about her distance from them, Abigail stood firm on living with this man, whom she loved. While her current life was predicated on emphasizing the here-and-now aspects of life, she nevertheless wanted urgently to reconcile with her parents. I asked her to talk aloud to her parents, imagining them sitting in my office. She had them ask whether she was going to get married, and she told them she didn't want to talk about it. Normally, in actual contact, she would melt at this point dripping tears or go into catatonic-like paralysis. I encouraged her to be as generously verbal as she could, cashing in on her knowledge by saying what she knew to be true. Then, taking both sides, she played out the following dialogue between herself and her parents:

Abigail: The reason we haven't gotten married is because we enjoy living together and I don't want to do something just because I'm supposed to... I have to feel like it's important inside.

Parents: (Caustically): Well, isn't the church a good enough reason for you?

Abigail: The church is very important to me. To me what is important is the spiritual part of it, to experience God. To me it's not just following the rules. According to our church, marriage is a sacrament. And I don't know why... I don't understand it at all. (Cries, looks confused again, resigned.)

A crucial point was reached. For a moment, Abigail did well stating her position clearly. Then, characteristically, she got confused. She couldn't allow the support of her own breadth and perspective, which went beyond her parents' narrow views. She was caught between her parents' righteousness and the unconvincing shibboleths of her new here-and-now aura. Neither was quite right for her.

She told me, as she visualized her parents, that they were looking at her critically, neither understanding nor attempting to. She felt she was doing something wrong. In spite of her disagreement with her parents, she was still attached to them, beleaguered like a punched-out boxer looking for his corner. She needed them not only for the relationship itself, but also because she felt disconnected from her own independent past. This was like an amputation, which cut her away from her own perspective, leaving her with a cosmic whine. Feeling bereft about losing her parents was sad enough, but the malaise was multiplied when she invalidated her specific lifetime of experience, which was not owned by them.

She looked as if she wanted to stop talking to them, because she thought they wouldn't listen. I suggested she might be stopping too soon. Whether they would be listening or not, she needed to formulate the clarity that words can provide. When I asked whether she would be willing to go on with the conversation, she agreed. Again, she played both parts, this time in a softer tone. Her parents told her how deeply hurt they were by her leaving the fold; they said they were worried about her wasting her life, that she had no future.

> Abigail replied,
>
> I don't think that's the way it is. I have a darn good future. To me what's important is what I have right now, not 20, 30, 50 years from now. And it should be. I don't know what's going on that long. What I have right now has nothing to do with the future. This is the way I have chosen to live my life now—it may change, I don't know (*starting to get a marked whine in her voice again and sounding contrived*). What I know is that I am happy with today. (*Unconvincing*)

She seemed enmeshed in the liturgy about present experience, narrowing her perspective in a way that was parallel to the subservience to her parents against which she was struggling. I observed that she started out saying she had a darn good future, then abandoned this belief by discounting the future entirely. I explained that she probably does have expectations about the future, some subtle and some evident. I suggested that her parents thought she was wrong when she told them the future doesn't count, rather than, as she had started to say, that she merely had a different vision of her future.

While the aura of her current relationships was to honor the here and now, her life was filled with the ordinary immensity of experiences by which she could be oriented. After all, she did go to school knowing it would be important to graduate. So she needed to acknowledge the breadth of all she knew and find a way past the dictates of her parents, her current relationships, or the ideology of the here and now. Otherwise, she was caught in a cultural insistence that bypassed her own judgment. At this point, I suggested she speak to her parents again, saying what was actually true for her.

Abigail:

> When you say I have no future, that has no merit, that if I'm not married it could end too easily and if I were married it couldn't and wouldn't. Nobody could just drop out of it... I don't think this is true... I believe we have a very strong commitment to each other... Whatever problems come up between us, we think in terms of long-term, not in terms of it's good for now only and we'll not be married because it's easier to pick up and leave.

Her voice lost all trace of whining. She was clear in her gaze. Ordinarily, she would have had a questioning look on her face. Now she seemed unconcerned with whether her parents accepted what she was saying. She believed what she said, and when I asked her how it felt to say it, she simply replied, "Clear." She now looked like she was well grounded and later remarked about her lifetime of accumulated understandings, "It's a process of changing what I was taught and taking everything else I've learned and putting it all together."

What was apparent in Abigail's mindset was the ascendant place of the present. This focus permitted her to have a relationship that her family background would not allow. Because she could not manage the contradiction, she had to cut out her parents' influence but not her own acquired perspective bringing in large regions of understanding. Everyone's past is much larger than their parents' attitudes. Everyone's life experiences are a hospitable background to their current life. This interwoven mosaic of her past, present, and future can become hopelessly confused, much like the state of a brainwashed person. Putting it all together was not as daunting as she assumed, once she recognized the truth in her own argument. Once she believed in her actual future instead of relying on jargon, her right to have a relationship with the man she loved would fit the continuity of her life.

Storytelling

A major avenue for escaping from the present is the human impulse to tell stories. Each moment, in a person's life, the mind is host to an infinite number of events, and as these events occur, the raw material for stories is formed. Those that live in memory and in story remain understandably dear; they are carriers of a personal sense of enduring reality, prime vehicles for linking together the selected survivors of personal experience. Without this linkage, only the most dim sense of reality would remain—isolated, unmarked pulses. Although the role of stories in marking a lifetime seems evident, there are some notable questions worth further examination to see where storytelling fits into personal affirmation.

Jean-Paul Sartre's 1938 novel *Nausea* (Sartre, 1964) paints a gloomy picture of life. He bemoans a cosmic contradiction between actual living experience and the telling about the experience. Through his depressed character Roquentin, he says, "Nothing happens while you live. The scenery changes, people come in and out, that's all.... Days are tacked onto days without rhyme or reason, an interminable, monotonous addition." For him the solution to this nihilistic state is to tell about these happenings, and he even thinks, "For the most banal event to become an adventure, you must (and this is enough) begin to recount it." He goes on, though, to moderate this seemingly hopeless contradiction by saying, "But you have to choose: Live or tell." The implication is that if you only "live," there is nothing really there; the fleeting experience is nonsense, hardly worth the attention it commands. On the other hand, if you tell about it, it can, through the telling, be a vibrant, adventurous experience. But once you start telling, the living is over.

Roquentin's gloom represents the hopelessness of having to choose between "living" and "telling." Though the dilemma is not as hopeless as he sees it, it is one we must take into account.

Setting aside these nihilistic implications, it is important to recognize that paradox is no stranger to human existence. This paradox is neither more nor less vexing or challenging than others. In fact, it is illuminating because through Sartre's confrontation of the paradox between raw living—untold—and confirmed living—that which is told—he gives unaccustomed centrality to storytelling. It is difficult to relive an old experience lacking the power of immediacy. We must make it alive in the retelling.

This integrative function is a reflexive reaction to complexity, requiring dexterity in a paradoxical world. Such dexterity is evident in a broad range of functions. It may be as fundamental as the coordination of the disparate functions of the brain hemispheres to the frivolous trick of patting the head while rubbing the belly. Such deftness is necessary for coordinating events with telling about them. Vital telling is a feat which, in spite of Sartre's Roquentin, many people accomplish every day. Some people do it better than others. Some are fooled by mistaking the tale for the event itself, repeating their stories over and over as though that will restore the living experience itself. What is most important is that the telling, itself, be a vibrant example of living, as well as just telling *about* living. The psychotherapist can help bring the vitality of storytelling into the process.

This split between the vitality of original events and the second-hand reporting of them was further highlighted by Perls, who warned against the excesses of what he called "aboutism." He didn't want life to be about something other than what was going on and was wary about the substitution of stories for current events. He cautioned about looking outside the experience of the moment to recount earlier and no longer vibrant experience. While this put a damper on some storytelling, it was actually a unifying statement: the past is to be incorporated into the present rather than be an isolated reality. History resides in the vitality of being revived, rather than only in the original events themselves. A story, told freshly, is not just about an external experience but is living itself.

People vary in the liveliness, clarity, and meaningfulness of the stories they tell, varying in the connectedness between the living and the telling. For some, telling a story enhances the living to which it refers; for others, it distorts. For some, stories are marvelous elaborations on what is only a simple experience; for others, the most complex event is worth only a grunt, the punctuation mark in a story to be fleshed out. Some people are wary about telling things that will make them look bad. And on and on.

Much of what happens in life floats on the periphery of awareness. Jane may ask, for example, whether I thought Agnes was unfriendly to her; she is having a hard time knowing. John seems to talk more about his ex-wife than he used to. Agatha vaguely senses that there is more music in her life these days. These are all dim awarenesses, suggestive but undependable. In spelling them out by telling stories, details can be added yielding broader perspective and greater clarity. Hints become realizations; bare facts, when recounted, expand like yeast; unvisioned feelings and associations become revealed. When the poet is moved by seeing a tree, the tree is just a hint of what she wants to say. The tree may be beckoning her to climb it, or she may be remembering a summer in the Adirondacks, or she may be noticing that the branches form an umbrella. She may become clear about fertility or gnarledness or grace. When most of us see trees, they are only trees. For poets who write about them, they become much more.

In psychotherapy, we give special attention to the elusiveness of experience, especially to experiences that are troublesome. We are beleaguered by abstractions that color our lives. On the contrary, stories that might flesh out the abstractions are either missing or distorting the reality of the original experiences. We want to change our lives, but often can't put our finger on just what it would take. Ingrid, a woman in our group, spoke about having a general sense of shame, fear, and self-criticism, unrelated to anything that would account for her feelings. All she could think was that she "should have it more together, be more confident, more successful, more loving and more accepting." Her "shoulds" didn't stand still long enough to hang a hat on, and she was stuck with "shame" as the title of her story. Then, when pressed further to spell out what she was ashamed of, it took a while before she said that when she disagreed with people, she got mad, gritting her teeth and becoming silently unyielding. That, she said, is what she was ashamed of—the dishonesty of her silence. This was a trigger for storyline, and suddenly her shame seemed a little less elusive. Next she added detail: her mother preached honesty at all costs; although when Ingrid practiced it, her mother couldn't handle it. With lying immoral and truth unpalatable, Ingrid was in a bind. She wound up silent and forgot why.

Now we needed more. In an attempt to flesh out the story, I took Ingrid's concern with her mother's two-sided attitude toward honesty to suggest that rather than stay stuck with the contradictions about truth, which only paralyzed her, she try an experiment in lying, assuring her it need be only for the moment. She got excited, transforming a worried look into one that was loose, even a little wild. Tongue in cheek, she told about the really tough week she had, working so hard around the house that her fingers split open and her nails crumbled. She "cleaned at the office, watered plants, did lots and lots of work and lots and lots of reports, lots of letters." At this point, she was still caught in the phoniness of the lie. But she was getting warmer. There were giggles about all she had done for the people in her house, when suddenly she realized she was saying something true, truths she wouldn't normally tell. Then she licked her chops and went further to tell a true story about how she recently entertained Norwegian relatives. Clearly her experience by now is no longer elusive. Here is how it goes:

> I cooked for these people, I entertained them, I listened to all their problems, their frustrations, I poured them drinks, emptied their fucking ashtrays. I spoke Norwegian for them so they would like me and be entertained by me, and I gave them all hugs and kisses and I cleaned the whole fucking house Norwegian-style. I mean, I worked my fucking ass off. Then I set this beautiful table, with lace cloth and flowers and candles. I even asked my uncle to say a prayer before dinner, so they would feel at home, and comfortable. I did this three nights in a row for three sets of people. I did an incredible job.... There is a lot of excitement to that.

She could have gone on forever, but she stopped herself at this point in her prideful account. As it happened, in her family, men were allowed to go on and on about their experiences, tall stories included, but women were supposed to tone themselves down and to serve. This realization clarified her shame about not being *counted*. By now though, she *felt* counted and her shame simply evaporated.

To elicit stories, the therapist sometimes has a mind-bending job, trying to lay bare the stories that actually count. On an easy day, these stories may be readily apparent and one may gather them like picking stones up off the ground. At other times, they're deeply imbedded in the host psyche and only through sensitive, patient, and inventive efforts can the therapist recognize the signs of the existence of these stories and succeed in eliciting the right ones.

People often have difficulty telling their stories, even when the outlines are already apparent. One woman spent her childhood getting beaten up by her father but was reluctant to tell about it. For the listener, the violence would have been assimilable, but for her, the overstimulation of telling it might have drastic effects, like screaming or feeling as though her head might burst. She might also feel like a coward to have allowed the beatings, or a wanton mischief-maker, or a betrayer of her father, whom she also loved. Thus the actual story may remain veiled, but it's always there, waiting for the right sequences of conversational development to bring it out into the open. The noted scientist Loren Eiseley (Eiseley, 1975) wrote:

> Everything in the mind is in rat's country. It doesn't die. They are merely carried, these disparate memories, back and forth in the desert of a billion neurons, set down, picked up, and dropped again by mental pack rats. Nothing perishes, it is merely lost till a surgeon's electrode starts the music... nothing is lost, but it can never be again as it was. You will only find the bits and cry out because they were yourself.

The difficulties in finding the storyline are further exemplified in the writings of Proust (Proust, 1924) as well as a number of other twentieth-century writers, including Kafka, Joyce, and Faulkner. Proust is especially well-known for obscurity in storyline. He paradoxically tells about his own early enthrallment with the novel. He loved it because of the dramatic clarity with which it condensed a lifetime of gradualism. He saw the novel speeding up life's process, replacing life's gradualism with a "mental picture." Through ingenious acceleration of events, the novelist crams his pages with "more dramatic and sensational events than occur, often, in a lifetime."

In his writing, however, Proust frustrates the expectation that the novelist will rescue the reader from gradualism. Instead of providing an easy storyline, he disseminates detail so luxuriantly that the elements of storyline are veiled and only gradually revealed. The story is there, of course, but recognizing it may seem like finding faces hidden in a drawing. As a result, a legendary number of Proust's readers have been awed by his perceptual masterfulness while never finishing his novels. Though the ingredients Proust lays open are far more scintillating than the ordinary sensations that people regularly experience, his gradualness requires the reader to be continuously attentive with unusual perceptual acuity to ferret out the advances in plot.

The therapist, similarly, must also attend carefully to the emergence of storylines by highlighting the patient's "mental pictures," including small details, such as Ingrid's concern about lying that might otherwise remain shadowy or concealed. What usually stands out for the patient, emerging from almost undifferentiated gradualness, is a generalized theme that points to events long ago, but still anxiously throbbing for a return to awareness. This thematic structure, often no more than a hint, is a guiding factor in each person's orientation toward himself. It's like the title of a novel points to the novel itself. Whereas a title without a novel would be absurd, we often find it difficult to look beyond the titles assigned to the experiences in our lives.

One woman saw herself as having had a terrible sexual relationship with her ex-husband, but at first she could tell me nothing about it. All she knew was that she had a Terrible Sexual Relationship. She surely knew more than the title. It alone was too tight a summary. I pointed this out, saying she probably knew more than she thought she knew. As she spoke more, it became clear that she did, but oddly, hadn't realized that it mattered. As she went on, she remembered that every night her husband would watch Playboy TV, which implied that he was no longer interested in her. That, by itself, added substance to her feeling degraded and dismissed. Warming up to the details, she then found it worth telling me that he had herpes and was contagious two weeks out of four. Moreover, he wouldn't tell her when he was contagious, so she, herself, had to be on the lookout for it. Fortunately, she never caught it. In addition to these severe inhibitors to his availability, the pernicious effects on *his* self-esteem were great and he compensated by treating her with disdain. Her Terrible Sexual Relationship, more than a title, evolved into a fleshed-out tale of misery.

This may seem a special case of shame, preventing her from telling her story, but when she told it, she didn't seem prohibitively ashamed. Once started, she easily went into considerable detail with little probing. Limiting herself to the titles of her stories was simply a familiar style; she was merely unaccustomed to fleshing out the events that gave her life substance. This form of narrowing was more than one woman's neurosis; abstractions are a common shorthand system through which people assume too much about themselves and know too little. The titles to the stories of life are too often given so prominent a position as symbols or guides that they come to be accepted as substitutes for the real thing. For someone to say he is country folk, for example, will not be as uniquely identifying as the details of the Baptist revivalist meetings he grew up with, the games he and his friends played, getting lost in the woods, and the whippings he got.

Patients who come for therapy are commonly oriented to their own special abstractions, the content of which—marital troubles, homosexuality, school failures, or fear of elevators—crowds their minds. Only by expanding such titles into specific elaborations will the special qualities of each life event be restored. Once actual happenings can be re-experienced for their own sake, the titles may change and the patients' lives, too. Marital Discord may become Boiling in the Kitchen, or The Homosexual Life may become Better Than to be a Boxer. Yet, no matter how intriguing or even helpful the new titles may be, they can never be a substitute for the story. Though many people hope they can change their lives by changing the titles, in fact only the full stories highlight the reality of each lived life. Engaging this way includes much that is ordinary: support, curiosity, kindness, bold language, laughter, cynicism, assimilation of tragedy, rage, gentleness, and toughness. The principles of Gestalt therapy orient therapists to notice not only *how* people presently live, but also how they *have lived*, and *will live*, not only *here* but also *there*; not only *now* but also *then*.

Chapter 6

Figure/ground
Life focus groups

The importance of the figure-ground relationship is evident in the formation of Life Focus Groups. These groups are created to explore the range of human experience as it is reflected not only in the lives of individual group members but also in the Community at large, as there is a need for both individuals and the Community to have orientation and focus.

This expansion of private psychotherapy principles to a public exploration is a contemporary development. In the early days of psychotherapy, Freud was faced with the medical necessities of helping people to resolve pathological behaviors and feelings. However, the benefits of psychotherapy have always been joined with personal enlightenment. Freud, himself, was exasperated to see the enlightenment aspects of psychoanalysis overshadowed by its medical intentions. Yet he was a physician, and, though he had a flair for the exotic in life, he was quite occupied with practicalities of his curative method.

His method became pointed, therefore, to curative purposes. Understandably so, as the cultural need for solving psychological problems was inviting. Nevertheless, the method was always grounded in personalized attention to the way people lived, incorporating the larger realms of events and feelings.

The consequent shift from private therapy to large group meetings called for a departure from the familiarly unstructured format. In the private office the therapist, faced with the uniquely troubled individual, does not know in advance which personal themes will be crucial in dissolving this person's troubles. Because of the patient's singular life, the pathway to remediation gets lit only through the therapist and patient talking to each other.

Not so in the Life Focus Group, where the aim of resolving a specific presenting complaint is replaced by the purpose of addressing more general human concerns. These concerns represent a wide range of themes that reflect those challenges of living faced by most people in the group, albeit each in their own individualized ways. They face challenges created by their own experiences with friendship, humor, and loyalty. They are vulnerable to failure. They are faced with family interrelationships; with prospects and consequences of guilt about greed, neglect, and cheating;

with worry about ambitions they can't satisfy; with pressure about duties they feel they should perform.

These are only a few among the many themes that mark our lives. They are selected from the entire menu of human experiences and become the arousal for personal stories that flesh out people's lives. The design of the life focus meetings taps into these stories, which are responses to the vital human interests represented in their themes. The stories may be further stimulated, as I shall show, by instructional exercises, abetted by music, poetry, or film. In telling these stories to each other, people laugh about familiar idiosyncrasies, identify heroes and villains, cry when sad, reveal prideful and shameful experiences, give and receive praise: each person's stories providing both individuality and a sense of common humanity.

While there are many possible designs for these meetings, the example I will present here has a five-step sequence. I will illustrate this process by describing a session conducted at a psychotherapy conference where there were approximately 100 people in the group. The following account will show details of the group experience, augmented by my observations and by verbatim commentary by the group members.

Step one: introduction

The first step is to introduce a theme that matters to the people in the group. I chose the theme of "home." As part of the introduction, I read a passage about my own sense of "primal familiarity," described in chapter one of this book. These words were not exactly about "home," but my thoughts about familiarity were close enough in meaning. This looseness represented an idiomatic rather than routinized response to the idea of "home."

Then I invited four volunteers to serve as an opening panel, to show the plenary group a conversation about "home." The plenary group would then divide into subgroups of four where they would soon have a chance to hold their own conversations. Witnessing the demonstration would warm up their minds, giving them quicker entry into the stories they would tell each other.

Step two: subgroup demonstration

After forming the demonstration panel, I said, "So, that's what 'home' calls forth in my mind, and I'm sure it will be very different for each of you. I wonder what comes to your mind?" Then I listened to the demonstration group conversation and joined in occasionally with remarks that would help the flow of conversation.

Person A: began by telling the others about the smell of cooking and how his aunt, who was like a second mother to him, taught him how

	to cut an onion. He could experience himself at her feet in the kitchen. He told of sitting on her lap and remembering the warmth of the room. Then he spoke of his love for his aunt while aware of how much she loved cooking. This story was told wistfully and received attentively.
Person B:	told a very different story. He said that the concept of home was not pleasant for him. Then, after a few remarks about these unpleasant experiences, he went on to tell us where he did find home—in the smell of prairie grass in Illinois and remembrance of the land and sunset in summertime, when the dust in the air was all red and golden. He said he was much more at home there than with any people. His words were a testament to nature in the raw—not people. His tone was warmhearted and warmly received.
Person C:	then spoke, expressing little sentimentality but impressed with the creativity that he saw in making a home. He had an interesting twist, though, flipping the experience over from being the finder of a home to the idea that he was "discovered." While this may sound like a passive experience, even vague, it came across more as his way of yielding to a providential world that welcomed him and from which he received a bountiful harvest.
Person D:	said he had not had a church for many years and missed the sacred quality of that experience, and now he was feeling that quality—by being part of this community. He observed that everyone is looking for home and a connection with others and that such experiences are "sacred." He went on to say that speaking this way was scary for him but he felt it was going to be okay. Then he added that I reminded him of a *good* preacher, not narcissistic but accepting. Then, after a thoughtful moment, he said he wanted me to know how much he experienced me as a good father. After I jokingly asked whether he would write a letter of reference to my son, we ended this part of the meeting with laughter and a strong feeling of connection.

Observations

Introducing the session by reading my own words might raise alarm bells. Would not my own thoughts about "home" stack the deck against people speaking their own thoughts? The possibility of inappropriate influence has plagued psychotherapists always, beginning with Freud's insistence on the psychoanalyst as an ambiguous figure. But neutrality has its drawbacks. The fear of undue influence can have a depersonalizing effect if it forecloses influence itself. The therapist must, after all, accept responsibility for the timeliness and proportionality of his influence, exercising humility about the limits of his powers to know what's best.

The range of possible introductions is wide, certainly not limited to the musings of the leader. It might include some orienting thoughts of the leader or poetry or music or philosophical gems. What matters most is that the tone of the words and the delivery model a heightened sensibility about the role of "home" in our life experiences, both ordinary and extraordinary. The introduction needs to point toward the stimulation of a deeper-than-casual examination of the theme, going beyond abstraction into specific events. While starting the group with my own experience could have had a skewing effect, it did not seem to diminish the group's idiomatic sense of "home." Each spoke of experiences quite different from mine in both content and style. Perhaps the example did help them reach the deep feeling tone more quickly than one might expect of people telling their story for the first time in front of a large group of strangers. We don't know whether the emotional tone of the introduction influenced the quick emotional reactivity, but if it did, it would have served its purpose as stimulation rather than domination.

Though the individuality of each person in the demonstration panel became apparent, it's important to add that their communal convergence was also apparent. These four people, who did not previously know each other, seemed genuinely glad to be together and conveyed a strong sense of mutuality and acceptance. And they played off each other, developing an undercurrent sweep of mind in which each story elicited the next, creating an organically felt affirmation. While the sequence of stories did not follow any mandated direction, the details of each speaker's life swelled the group storyline like metaphorical yeast, creating a group statement. While the hallowing of the experience by one of the members at the end of the session may or may not have expressed the way everyone felt, it was a punctuation for a strongly felt conversation.

Step three: subgroups

The next step was to move from the plenary group to subgroups of three or four people each, so everyone could have a chance to speak. In introducing this phase of the meeting, I added a key stimulus: an evocative song to further accentuate the idea of "home."

Here is what I said:

> OK, I'd like you to divide into groups of three or four now. I'm going to play a song that's written by a woman who also sings it. Beautiful voice. She is the daughter of a missionary and grew up in Tanzania. The song is a story about her experience growing up there. What I'd like you to do is listen closely to the music, just letting it sink into you and as you drink it in, it will find some place in you. (Aside to reader: Alas, I cannot

replicate the beauty of this song and voice, but assuredly its beauty played a role in creating a poignant feeling about home and about the community in which this music was heard.)

"Then when the song is over I would like you to tell each other what the song evoked in you. We'll take some time for this. More time than we took for the demonstration. The idea is just to talk to each other. Not to do any therapy with each other but just to talk and to let each other know your experience of what the song evoked in you."

Participants listened to the song: (Johnson, Deborah Liv, 1995. "Tanzania." Across the White Plains. CD: Mojave Sun Records).

Step four: report to the plenary group

After the music played and the subgroups talked to each other about their sense of home for about 20 minutes, I asked people in the subgroups to report to the plenary group about the conversations they'd had. What seemed most noteworthy, even in these succinct reports, was the rapt attention to the theme, the openness of people in talking to each other, and the quick development of a communal spirit. The following verbatim remarks go a long way toward portraying the communal bond that this conversational bazaar created:

Person 1: "I had a warm feeling, of being *met*. Also to hear from others was touching. One spoke literally of home—the home he's going back to; another spoke of all the different feelings of family and places and people that it evoked for him. This notion of home—what he felt with the music. We also noticed that none of us had an ordinary home; that we all had a lot of longing."

Person 2: "My experience listening to the music—as soon as she hit the refrain of I want to go home to wherever she was going, I just started weeping—not much content (that came later) it's just grief, appreciation—not unhappy but sad."

Person 3: "I'm just aware of how fast my heart is beating right now. So, I know that I've been very touched by this experience and very appreciative to you and my small group and the large group as well. I don't know why I'm always so amazed by the power of group, but I don't ever want to become not amazed by that. In the beginning I was "current" when the song started to play, and I started thinking about how many bodies of water and ponds and oceans and rivers we all cross to get here. Then I started very quickly to think about my parents, not so much in a sad way but in a longing way. I won't have my mother's loving arms around me ever again because she's dead. I'm so thankful that I have had this and that I've created other ways to have that in my life. There is something wonderful about the fact that we are in the room together."

Person 4: "I had nine years of psychoanalysis—A waste of time! I had an experience sitting here that I've never had before. That song, this whole environment, gave me something to think about and feel that I've never experienced before in all my 86 years of life. Thank you very much."

Person 5: "I had two really significant associations. First was my mom. She's 90, and I was home just a couple of months ago to throw a 90th birthday party for her, so there were a lot of things about us. Have I done enough for my mom? With what little time that's left is there time to do what's left for her? So, it was a mixture of feeling good that I sort of celebrated her just a couple of months ago, but also some regret at the time that's left or whatever there might be there for the two of us, because we've had problems in our past and in the last 10 years or so have tried to repair some of the feelings and problems."

Observations

For the members of this group, the idea of "home" hit home. This theme mattered greatly to them, tapping into feelings of belonging, devotion, and gratitude, as well as longing and unfinished business. Their level of concentration was remindful of the meditation process, especially in the depth inspired by the evocative music. This created an amplification of experience that had a broader range of content and relationship than one usually gets in meditation. This sharp focus created strong feelings of comradeship and community. What was especially noteworthy for me was that people seemed altogether accepting of their own contributions, each with its own validity and with no pressure to do anything better than the way they were doing it.

Step five: consolidation of theme

The plenary discussion that followed the subgroup reports went beyond participants' current experience. Some people spoke about their interest in other theme possibilities for future meetings, such as courage, generosity, family, and gratitude. One man said, "I was thinking about courage because in that song there was something about going across the sea and leaving. There was such an echo in me that it spoke to me in a very personal way about courage."

Others observed that society's well-being depends on personal well-being and people caring about each other. Someone else added that courage applies to everyday challenges, not just to heroic scenarios. Still another person spoke of a dear friend who had died a month earlier and just wanting to bring his memory into the room. The last person to speak said,

> When I think of religious institutions, a lot of people go there to confess their sins or feel that they can acknowledge their weaknesses and that they are less than perfect, and I also think about the role that "shame" plays in our society. I'd like to see these groups address those topics because I think that what you are doing structurally is great. You are looking structurally to give people a place to go to connect with family and society and values that are no longer being given by the institutions that used to do this.

The group then came to a close.

This is one example of a large range of possible exercises; all holding significance for people at large. They elicit a sharpened attention to a designated theme, while at the same time, the whole of their lives is tapped, offering a broad landscape of personal experience. They tell each other about places they've lived; people they've cared about; and struggles, hopes, and beliefs that have filled their lives. Communal togetherness and enhanced awareness of key themes of living that rise beyond ordinary social norms create the high interest and self-acceptance so evident in the subgroup reports. This form of congregation optimizes the power of directed concentration to refresh and give luster to the stories of people's lives. The drama thus experienced points poignantly to a common human desire to tap into the *accessibly hidden* described earlier in chapter two.

Design options

I shall now describe five other possible design components:

1. Individual therapy in the presence of the group

Conducting an individual therapy session in front of a plenary group addresses both individual and communal needs. On the face of it, a personal session may seem too private to be conducted in front of a community of people. I have found, however, that the presence of an audience is more of a support for the person than a hindrance. The live attention and empathic presence of a friendly audience create both safety and stimulation. While one person's therapeutic work is the center of attention, the witnessing group is resonant with what they see, vicariously receiving an illumination of their own lives.

Every therapy session contains some common human threads within it, so the themes of one person come alive for many others. After witnessing the therapy session, the group members respond with their own stories, and these stories almost always reveal a group empathy for the observed person and a lesson for all. Discovering that we are all in the same boat while also distinctly different frees us from the isolation that differences might otherwise create.

2. Films

Another design component is showing a film that represents themes of living, such as sibling rivalry, recovery from trauma, acceptance of diverse styles of life, or the ups and downs of success. Films make human issues come alive by replicating situational and relational realities, which in their vividness serve as springboards for subgroup discussions.

Flying Without Wings, for example, is an absorbing and inspirational account of a life turned around by personal trauma. The film portrays the life of Arnold Beisser, a psychiatrist and Olympics-level tennis player who became a paraplegic polio victim. The film is a treasure of wisdom, courage, despair, heroism, and ordinary decency. Beisser was unlucky enough to be in the pathway of tragic fate but was enterprising and grounded enough to transform this uninvited fate into a transcendent experience. The storyline itself is poignant, and the film ignites viewers' interest in their own lives and how they might navigate through inevitable difficulties. The design for the group meeting would invite people to divide into subgroups to tell each other about the implications of Beisser's experience for their own lives (Estrup, Liv (2010). *Flying without wings: Life with Arnold Bessier.* Film Available through LivEstrup.com).

3. Practice

Two "cousins" of Life Focus Groups are prayer and meditation. They are part of the daily regimen of many people and an intermittent activity of many more. While prayer and meditation are different from one another, each induces high concentration and rapt personal involvement.

Prayer, in its role as a communication with God, warms people up, not only to their relationship with God, but by extrapolation into their relationships with people. Over and over again, by saying predetermined words created in religious liturgy, or individualized words spontaneously spoken, people come to feel their sacred words have been *heard.* For those who practice well, this reception by a supernatural otherness promises an eternal relationship, where deep feelings can be dependably expressed outside the stream of social complexity.

Meditation, on the other hand, usually includes little conversational content. It is directed toward transcendence of the everyday happenings of life and when successfully practiced impels the mind into a raw sense of life itself, a life beyond wants, conflicts, and thoughts; a life that joins each person with a universal energy. Meditation can thus provide a sense of internal unity that transcends the fragmenting experiences that often populate our lives. As products of antiquity, both prayer and meditation pass the test of time as instruments of life focus. The fullest dedication required for repeated practice of either prayer or meditation is a tough act to follow, and, of course, there is considerable variation in the success of its practitioners.

Our purpose in the design of Life Focus Groups is less ambitious than prayer and meditation in the sharpness of concentration required. It is more ambitious, however, in extending the practice into a socially interactive process that addresses the diversity of other people's personal experience. Practice programs might include activities as simple as addressing someone by name, but, mostly, they include more complex practices like expanding friendships, enriching time spent with children, or reading more extensively. The options are vast. As Miriam Polster and I have written,

> A few hours are hardly enough time for growth. A few weekend workshops a year, although certainly capable of powerful mobilization, are hardly enough for growth. Something has to reach beyond the guided therapeutic tour to assure a potent level of impactfulness.

How might the Life Focus Group enter into this process? Suppose, for example, that a group theme is the experience of kindness. The group orientation about kindness and the exercises evoking stories about kindness would be only a starting point for practicing kindness. The subgroups might explore what each person in the group could do in their everyday life to practice kindness. Perhaps this could include writing an old teacher who had been helpful. Perhaps it would involve bringing home a special gift for a spouse. Perhaps it would be making a donation to a cause one likes.

People would be free to choose their own particular forms of kindness. Some of these forms might feel sappy or too delayed or too contrived. No one would be urged to do anything that did not feel fitting for him or the recipient. For some, there would be a preference for kind acts; for others, kind words. Some people may feel kindness in being softly confronting; others would be altogether supportive. Each person could practice her own forms of kindness and report the effects back to the group for discussion. As members become more aware of the role of kindness in their lives, they might become more open to expressing it.

The process of conversation and practice could be applicable to a wide range of themes, such as expanding your social engagements or reporting comical experiences. Or, if the theme of "novelty" were to be addressed, for example, people might be asked to write down two or three experiences that they saw in a fresh light. Perhaps they noticed the color of their spouse's eyes more clearly than they normally do. Or perhaps they noticed a friend's smile more consciously than before, or heard a song more pleasurably, or read a newspaper article they may previously have passed up. The same would be true of negative experiences, like envy or anger. Each person might be asked to notice his envy or anger more freshly and write down whether this attention made any difference.

Practice is frequently associated with homework and has connotations of fulfilling authoritarian requirements, often with little obvious relevance to the person's life. Some of these examples may represent aspects of a person's life too small to care about, too difficult to accomplish, or too self-conscious to be graceful. But in the Life Focus Group, no practice will be required. Those who choose to practice will self-select and will have a hand in modifying the instructions or uniquely fleshing them out. Practice ideas can be offered to the group at large, expanding on themes presented at the meetings, or they can be based on conversations in the subgroups. For some, simple practice will significantly enhance their life focus. Others will have a chance to express their individuality by choosing not to do what others are doing.

4. Music

Many forms of music can serve life focus purposes—from the reverence of a Bach concerto to the ethereal sounds of John Adams to the heartening hopes of "We Are The World" or the warning that "The Times They Are A-changin'." The broad range of folk music, rediscovered in the 1950s, is remarkably rich in human spirit, highly entertaining, and largely disregarded nowadays. A renewal of the folk repertoire has a large range of evocative social and psychological relevance and calls out for personal response. Meditation music is another vehicle that enhances the look inward and registers a sense of calm and acceptance. Still other music might be selected or even composed directly for its value in framing specific themes.

All these musical options, the inspiration of the rhythms and melodies accompanied by content-rich lyrics, stir people to examine themes that mark our lives. Optimism, generosity, despair, dread, love, celebration, mystery, and other life focus subjects are widely examined in musical compositions. The range of music available to the Life Focus Group would depend on the leaders' and members' repertoire and stylistic preferences. We have already seen, above, how the musical rendition of the theme of "home" affected the tone of a meeting. While musical accessibility is understandably limited in private therapy, it would be easily available for Life Focus Groups. An obvious precedent is the historically vital music in religious services, creating both an arousing and a calming effect, inviting people into an increased awareness of the prayers they recite and a devotion to life itself. Such musical vehicles have been almost entirely absent in psychotherapy practice. Psychotherapists have commonly been wary of their inspirational effect because of its potential for dominating people. But it is also quite evident that dancing, singing, and chanting incorporate color, feeling, and a union of minds.

5. Perspective makers

Verbal presentations by leaders are a familiar form of guidance. To call these "lectures" gives them an academic accent I do not intend. To call them "sermons" would imply a greater level of moral insistence than I intend. However, the leader's perspective can offer careful orientation about the themes to be examined and can create two broad forms of illumination. First, it can provide an educational experience that widens the group's understanding of whatever life theme the group is addressing. Second, it offers the leader's experience, understanding, and inspirational skills to convey the importance of the theme. Among the many possible themes are competition, sacrifice, generosity, vacations, family activities, politics, optimism, tragedy, and standing up for oneself. The professional literature is vast, and popular lessons about life are everywhere, apparent in the cultural extravaganza of information and instruction. What is emotional intelligence? How should we treat those who cannot fend adequately for themselves? What do we emphasize in raising our children? When is divorce desirable, and what is the optimal way to handle it? How does adoption fit into our lives? All these questions are illuminated in the popular media and are good candidates for lecture themes.

It can be useful to augment the orientation format by having concrete illustrations to flesh out the theme. If, for example, spending time with your family were to be the theme, a specific family could be invited to talk about its experiences. This exploration of a particular family's life could have illustrative impact for the whole community. The discussion afterward, either in the plenary group or in subgroups, would show both the contrasts and the commonality between one person's concerns and those of the membership. As they come forward, people almost invariably discover great harmony with the audience, and emboldened by this, they enter deeply into their own psyches.

The above suggestions illustrate the range of possible design elements. Some exercises could take on a repetitive tenor, like liturgical content appearing over and over in our familiar religions. The content of these themes would evolve over years of experience. One group with whom I meet starts their meetings with drumbeats and ends with arms around each other, singing the song "Bye, Bye, Blackbird." The drumbeats remind participants they're about to enter a new region of relationship. Nobody knows how the singing ritual began, but it denotes an end to the meeting and invites people to return their attention to the everyday lives to which they'll soon return. Many groups will create rituals unexpectedly, with a sense of the dearness of the experience.

Underlying whatever design specifics are created, there are two fundamental constants that support the variety of possible designs. First is the goal of transforming important themes from abstractions into concrete complexes of events. An abstraction is a convenient summation of experience, a condensed view that invites an unfolding detail. It is empty, however, when the storyline underlying the title is either missing or diluted. We therefore seek to restore storyline. The second constant is the stimulation created by the communal ethos. There is special power in the simultaneous entry of a single theme into many minds. This converging attention amplifies the substance of what many people live with only dimly, providing testament to a vibrant reality residing just outside everyday familiarity.

Chapter 7

Figure/ground
Belonging

The "need to belong" is one more psychological phenomenon that helps to flesh out the figure/ground concept. Belong to what? To family, workplace, profession, book club, or other of a multitude of groups, which we can call hosts. Belonging offers key satisfactions of acceptance, dependability, inspiration, and meaning, all pertinent to knowing what life is all about. Although this need to belong is important for the geography of our minds and is a universal phenomenon, there is also a paradoxical need to feel one's individuality.

For nearly 1,000 years Western Civilization has favored individual empowerment, but conformity remains everywhere. We see it in the inculcation of values in political parties, race groups, economic classes, gangs, and professional affiliations, as well as in garden clubs, residents of the same street, and customers at Starbucks. In each of these groups, those who think differently from the well-defined positions of the host group are no longer secure in their sense of belonging. Conformity is a price that may have to be paid. Nevertheless, our society still treasures individuality, adopted in many circles almost as a mantra. The resulting dichotomy of motivations is so interwoven that people spend a lifetime seeking proportionality between them.

The societal aura

There are many reasons people band together. First, there is safety in numbers. Joining together protects us against danger, whether from predatory animals, earthquakes, or human competitors. Second, many tasks are best handled by cooperative endeavor, such as setting moral standards, building complex structures, and expanding knowledge.

Psychotherapy has always been an individuality-oriented process, although it recognizes the indivisibility of the individual from his environment. The iconic messenger of individuality Adam Smith posited that the aggregate of individual activity, exercised without regard for societal interest, best serves the needs of society. The individual, acting spontaneously in his own interests, would, in almost mystical purposiveness, be guided, as

Smith famously said, "by an invisible hand to promote an end which was no part of his intention. Nor is it always the worse for society that it was no part of it. By pursuing his own interest he frequently promotes that of the society more effectually than when he really intends to promote it" (Smith, 1965).

Surprisingly holistic in seeing each person's contribution to a societal destiny, Smith's theory of individual preeminence also suggests that nature has a built-in coalescence between individual need and the common good. In other words, even this quintessential protagonist of individuality recognized society as a vital collaborator, the host who benefits from the mysterious confluence of individuals. Without particularly intending to help the community, individuals will, like metal filings around a magnet, come together for the mutual benefit of all. Without directly taking the society into account, Smith believed that nature would see to it that the well-being of individuals was basically the best ensurance of the well-being of the society.

Of course, the practical question is this: though there is obvious merit to the idea of an innate impulse to merge individual interests, there is also, equally obvious, much interference built into the merger. The perverse truth is that it is just as natural for things to fly apart as for them to hold together or alternately to coalesce around a cult of personality. The premier of China, some years ago, said in an interview with Charlie Rose that he applauded Adam Smith's "invisible hand" and imported it into an otherwise communist scenario. He said it was important to have all hands functioning well for optimal results, pointing to China's efforts to accommodate the needs of the huge numbers of people who were otherwise not contributing to societal well-being. He concluded that the "invisible hand" must be coordinated with the "visible hand." The individual, the community, and their skills were to be interwoven in their purposes and results.

The American priority for individuality has long been identified with freedom, eloquently nourished in the writings of Emerson, Thoreau, and Whitman. Each of their testaments to individuality resonates powerfully with the American psyche. A more recent contrast to this perspective is that of Wallace Stegner, a literary witness of the American experience. He ruefully recognized the losses created by these freedoms, including the absence of belonging. He said,

> Not only is the American home a launching pad, as Margaret Mead said; the American community, especially in the West, is an overnight camp. American individualism, much celebrated and cherished, has developed without its essential corrective, which is *belonging*. Freedom, when found, can turn out to be airless and unsustaining. Especially in the West, what we have instead of place is space. Place is more than half memory, shared memory. Rarely do Westerners stay long enough at one stop to share much of anything.
>
> (Stegner, 1993)

Ironically, in a society where hero worship often fills the blank spaces of identity, this individuality has not always created the intended freedom. Stegner portrays the American West's homage to individuality as a mythic enlargement, evident in the common imitation of society's idols. He says, "Plenty of authentic ranch hands have read pulp Westerns in the shade of the bunkhouse and got up walking, talking, and thinking like Buck Duane or Hopalong Cassidy" (Stegner, 1993).

Alas, Stegner's view of the American West is no longer geographically bounded, and it is hard nowadays to go a day without reports of the diminishing sense of belonging and the reduced accessibility of such enduring hosts as families and neighborhoods. There have been many observers of the disconnections between our government and various classes of the population, but perhaps it is enough to note here that the well-being of constituent people often depends on the will of existing authority, the economic circumstances, the niggardliness of geographical happenstance, or the threats of geopolitical strife. Nowadays, and perhaps always, the agonies of isolated individuality and failure to belong fruitfully is insinuating itself into the lives of alarming numbers of people (Schlesinger, 1992).

Let us look, for example, at Robert Kennedy's statement of a governmental need, remarkable for an active political figure:

Even if we act to erase material poverty, there is another greater task. It is to confront the poverty of satisfaction...that afflicts us all. (Quoted by Sandel, 2010)

He goes on to say,

> Our Gross National Product now is over 800 billion dollars a year.... But that Gross National Product counts air pollution and cigarette advertising and ambulances to clear our highways of carnage. It counts special locks for our doors and the jails for the people who break them. It counts the destruction of the redwood and the loss of our natural wonder in chaotic sprawl. It counts napalm and counts nuclear warheads and armored cars for the police to fight the riots in our cities. It counts...the television programs that glorify violence in order to sell toys to our children.

> Yet the Gross National Product does not allow for the health of our children, the quality of their education or the joy of their play. It does not include the beauty of our poetry or the strength of our marriages, the intelligence of our public debate or the integrity of our public officials. It measures neither our wit nor our courage, neither our wisdom nor our learning, neither our compassion nor our devotion to our country. It measures everything, in short, except that which makes life worthwhile. And it can tell us everything about America except why we are proud to be Americans.

> (Sandel, 2010)

This concern with being proud to be an American may seem like political sentimentality. However, it resides within a fundamental human need for a hospitable context, one that offers a benevolent home base. While all of Kennedy's concerns are focused on the executive role of the government, his observations also point to the psychologist's practical concern not only with resolution of acute individual problems but also with response to the *public* need for dependable and continuing orientation and guidance.

Addressing such societal purposes, we recognize that Life Focus Groups are part of a mushrooming movement that reaches into many corners of modern life. Ignited by the invention of psychotherapy, this social dynamism has gone beyond the language of disturbance to look at the way people live their lives. Huge numbers are participating in a wide range of social applications. We see this popularity in the "mindfulness" programs that are sweeping the country, in widespread "spiritualistic" practices, in the large variety of self-help groups, and in the prodigious sale of self-help books. We see it in journalistic perspectives appearing in books and magazines. We see life-exploratory conversations in men's and women's groups. We see the life focus need addressed in book clubs, where people identify with the novel's characters, who provide enlarged recognition to obscured aspects of their own lives. Newspapers and magazines respond every day to a public thirst by reporting "human interest" stories.

The beat goes further, into the workaday world. We see the expansion of life focus practices in commercial organizations, where the formation of in-house groups is flourishing, bringing employees together to learn how their emotions and attitudes affect their work. While they may begin by exchanging ideas about solving bottom-line problems, they glide into telling about personal needs and characteristics. They recognize that the diverse personalities of their fellow employees must be coordinated for top-flight productivity. The procedures in these meetings, therefore, range from a sharp attention to decision-making itself to an examination of how the psychological priorities and habits of employees may be modulated to affect organizational effectiveness.

We also see a new level of person-to-person exploration in religious organizations, which have formed relational groups that augment the more familiar worship formats. In these groups, people are guided to talk to each other, telling each other about their concerns, reflected in stories about their lives. While God is commonly in the background of their orientation, they are, more than ever, directly engaged with one another, examining what they feel, think, hope, and want. They offer acceptance and expanded understanding of each other's feelings, and they are hospitable to whatever their members want to say.

On the cusp of the future, we see the exercise of life focus in the wildly growing phenomenon of networking. Facebook alone has over two billion users worldwide. The total numbers are monumental. The range of purposes includes planning, reporting, requesting, celebrating, and complaining—an expansion of opportunity for people to talk about things they might otherwise say to each other face-to-face, but don't. Internet correspondence offers an unprecedented opportunity for people to go beyond ordinary conversational exchange into personally vital engagements. This provides each person with an enlarged and hospitable arena to tell and hear about experiences that mark their lives. These conversations are often very personal: revealing people's values, their ambitions, their animosities, and their loves. They tell each other about what's happening in their daily lives and how it feels to be talking to one another. Clearly, we are witnessing a commanding openness to person-to-person conversation, a social eruption of communal accessibility.

With these baby steps of the social networking phenomenon, it is too early to know the full story of the benefits and dangers. We can already see that it can have many negative, as well as positive, consequences; venom intertwined with affirmation; the motions of engagement without empathy or consequentiality. Social networking calls for vigilance and creative design. What is unequivocally evident is the compelling need for people to join together to focus on how they are living their lives. While that need is being insistently expressed, the jury is still out on finding the safest and most effective means of engagement. Electronic communication has, however, opened the widest opportunity yet for the expansion of life focus into a communal force for relational connectedness.

In this variety of applications of life focus, we see a large range of purposes. At one extreme, people are searching for answers to ethereal unknowns, such as life after death, extrasensory communication, or foretelling the future. These are enticing fields for speculation, inspiring people to transcend familiar observational limits. At a more common level, there is clearer ground for direct observation. People explore experiences that directly matter to them: their surprises; their fears; their guiding beliefs; their experiences of pleasure, adventure, and dismay; their bodily sensations; the everyday happenings in people's lives; and the like. We see life focus also deepened in the poetry and novels that clarify elusive personal themes, such as love, contradiction, tragedy, and survival. We see life focus too in the religions that direct behavior and perspective. All of this is part of a human mission: to probe the nature of our existence.

Communal imperative

The community is a substructure of society and provides a more intimate option for people to join their lives together. Communities have many faces, ranging from the large entities, such as business associations, neighborhoods, libraries, families, schools, and churches, to the many other social units that invite people to belong. Communities also include such smaller units as friendships, favorite hangouts, choirs, book clubs, knitting groups, bird lovers, or any other interest groups. We increase *belonging* when we have pets. We belong when we are among nationality groups. We belong when we happily go to certain restaurants. Yes, belonging is all over the place, and we are free to join up and also to notice which groups matter to us.

This need to belong is primal: a fundamental attraction, often having absorbing, even addictive effects. Nonetheless, membership in one or another form of community is vital for personal belonging. At the same time membership brings up conflicting needs and demands. Further, some affiliations are inherently in conflict with others. Can one faithfully belong to a group of atheists while enjoying the spirit of religious services? The multiplicity of options makes belonging seem like a moving target.

A familiar example is intermarriage. A Caucasian person marries a Black person, and all hell breaks loose. The security of belonging is shattered. This is an old story, portrayed famously in *Romeo and Juliet* and many recent plays and novels that depict the struggle between such abrasive differences as in levels of wealth, heritage, intellect, education, social habits, place of birth, and other differences that turn someone into "not one of us." This is a clash between imbedded identities and the challenge of otherness—a struggle between familiarity and novelty.

In spite of the large difficulties, the human reflex toward unification is real, and each of its moves is a stepping stone to peaceful and vibrant belonging. We affect our belonging when we marry, by the work we do, where we live, whether we have children, and by what movies we see or novels we read or songs we listen to. We also sense that a choice to belong in one place can threaten that of another. Can a politically left person, for example, still feel belonging in a politically conservative family? Can a truck driver fit with a mate who loves art? Perhaps every move we make adds or subtracts from the compatibility of the realms of our belonging with the host universe of experience. We start with a reflex for unity as a huge genetic mission to put things together, to resolve dissonance. The reflex is not enough, though, and the integrative process must be husbanded, sharpened, and tailor-made to serve the individual person.

Of course, what I am addressing is a very large social challenge. The resolution of the split between simplicity and complexity enters into every region of our lives. Part of the resolution lies in the progressive orientation of a society—one that is consonant with new discoveries, new needs, and new social circumstances. All we can do is to face the problem and address it with our most impactful instruments. One is the Life Focus Group. To this end, I will examine the ideas of congregation and ethos, key factors in transposing the distance of strangers into a comradely connectedness.

Congregation

Congregation is a venerable word, used to identify religious assemblages. Through religion's historic role in tending lives, the concept of congregation offers lessons to the Life Focus Group. The first is that the congregation provides a primary place for people to come together to solemnize their lives and give them purpose and meaning. Second, the religious congregation is usually larger than the therapy group, which gives it a more distinctly communal flavor. Third, in contrast to the therapy group, the congregational continuity endures over a considerable period of time. This dependable continuity offers assurance of relationship and opportunities for exploration. It enables members to immerse themselves fully.

The term *congregation* is closely identified with religion. This is so different from psychotherapy that adopting this designation would be misleading. Nevertheless, religious congregations are an interesting precedent for therapy's group formations. It is especially relevant for a future dimension of the Life Focus Group and its numerous predecessors and successors in the mindfulness movement.

The designation of *group* is more familiar in the history of psychotherapy, but it, too, has implications that contrast with my portrayal of the Life Focus Group. The *group* designation is closely associated with the "therapy group" and has too much curative implication. If you are in a therapy group, you are likely to be there because you think something is wrong with you that you want to correct. This accentuates pathology, which overshadows the equally fundamental need for a look at what our lives are like.

The Life Focus Group emphasizes the importance of bringing people together to satisfy a mutually felt need for enlightenment, and it names life focus as the operative instrument. The Life Focus Group parallels both the congregation and the therapy group by creating a special atmosphere of heartfelt, open-eyed interest in examining the landscape of living. It is a place to find release from the pressures of the everyday world, while at the same time receiving guidance toward understanding and participating in that world. It provides a combination of respite and stimulation, a communally based time-out for marking pivotal life experiences. People can, for example, examine the role of listening in their lives, or their uncertainties about love, or the way they celebrate their pleasures. They can even be more detailed in telling each other what it's like to have a new baby, or sharing their frustration about surprise visitors when they are dead-tired, or expressing the sadness of nursing a sick mother. In a climate of mutuality, people are enabled both to satisfy the need to be individualistically heard while, at the same time, feeling that they *belong among each other*.

One of the major challenges for the group is to coordinate individual needs with group productivity. That is a normal human requirement. Though it can be difficult, it is supported by a natural configurational skill that serves the normal potential for wholeness. Union between the individual and the group does not seem out of reach. In my 11-year-old granddaughter's dance groups, the children really enjoy not only their own individual dance talents but also the coordination of their movements with all the others in the ensemble. Some children do better than others, but all are intent on coordinating, and it is exciting for them to do so. Examining evolution, Richard Dawkins sees a comparable predisposition in the communal behavior of birds. He tells us about a flock of starlings that demonstrate a miraculous communal synchronicity. These flocks may be composed of thousands of individual birds flying at great speeds, and yet they never collide. "Often the whole flock seems to behave as a single individual," he says, "wheeling and turning as one.... What is remarkable about the starlings' behavior is that, despite all appearances, there is no choreographer and, as far as we know, no leader. Each individual bird is just following local rules" (Dawkins, 2006).

While human beings in their choice-making complexity face a more challenging group mutuality, the inclination to join up is, nonetheless, a compelling phenomenon. We see it at the tiniest cellular level, where the organizational imperative silently commands the creation of a whole organ or a whole organism out of a diversity of minute cellular beginnings. At a higher level of this organizational reflex, we see that humans are gregarious beings, joining together because of innate pleasure as well as for strategy. Neurological studies more and more recognize the phenomenon of mutuality. High among their discoveries is the recognition of mirror neurons, which fire up when people have vicarious reactions to other people's experiences. While this research is in its early stages, there seems to be a neuronal web that spurs common understanding and inter-relational mutuality. On a behavioral level, this empathic resonance reminds me of the two-year-old child whose reflex upon seeing another toddler crying because her mother was absent was to take her hand and lead her to her own mother.

Ethos

Closely interwoven with the enabling activities of the congregation is the mandate for a benign ethos. This has not always been a standard for religious congregations, though, which have varied greatly in their level of benevolence toward dissident members. For the therapist, it has been fundamental to assure safety, even in the face of troublesome eruptions. The safety assured in private therapy must be transposed into the enlarged membership of the Life Focus Group. Among these people, some may dislike others, some may compete for centrality, some may take up too much time, and some may become too easily defensive. While members of the Life Focus Group vary in both readiness and skill for maintaining safety, this is, nevertheless, an important condition, because only in safe situations will people at large speak openly to each other. Hence the benign ethos must survive differences in perspective, one-upmanship, and other adversarial challenges.

An illustration of this union between individual expression and a communal grounding is the report of Daniel, a member of a longstanding Life Focus Group. When he was asked to tell about his experience of his own individuality within the group's experience of communal connectedness, he said,

> When I am here, I can dig a hole and pull things out and I'm saying "Oh my god look at this" and you are all just sitting there looking and saying "oh my god, look at that" (Laughter)... you are with me. And so over time I have come to feel at home here amidst you. And that feeling of being at home here and having you look at something that I have brought out about myself that I didn't even know if I could look at. It's like there's a ground to put that into and it takes hold and it's real, and so when I leave here I carry a sense of substance of those ideas, that they've planted themselves, they've taken root.
>
> I then feel the substance of that way of being; outside here. I have this big buffer around me of my experience here. The storms would still blow in about my imagined "judgment-by-other-people" but I am buffered here. This is so profoundly important to me. And it has something to do with us and how we have known each other for a long time. Let's just go deeper; it's really the way we treat one another.

While there is no sure formula for such resonance between individual and communal behavior, what's clear in Daniel's account is that he was able to say what he individualistically needed to say and he found his group to be a place where these stories belonged. The search for self-actualization, a familiar goal of individuality, is not just a cold enterprise. It flourishes in the relational hospitality of the surround, one hand washing the other. This is no casual phenomenon. It is the foundation for belonging and the accompanying pleasure of feeling at one with the world.

A common contrast sees the adversarial component as an important *spur* for growth. I am reminded of some people in our Gestalt therapy training programs who, wary of conformity, felt there was not enough anger in the groups. For them, the absence of anger was a sign of inauthenticity, a surrender to the communal ethos. Yet however valid our vigilance against conformity may be, it is just as important to recognize when a benign atmosphere is authentic. In an environment where each person's concerns are honored, there is less reason to be angry with each other than in a competitive or pressured atmosphere. While my experiences are only anecdotal, in the Life Focus Groups I have either led or witnessed, the participants have been decidedly respectful of one another's reactions, while honoring their own well-being. Further, they have been quite open to expressing strong feelings, clear self-interest, and novelty of storyline, all of which color their lives.

Contagion is a key factor in the development of a group ethos. That may seem an unfitting word, as *contagion* usually refers to pathology, as in catching the measles. It can also refer to the toxic spread of psychological conditions. As Yapko (2009) noted regarding the social contagion factor in depression, "Drugs may address some of the depression's symptoms, but they cannot change the social factors that cause and perpetuate it."

A more full view of contagion, however, would recognize its *healthful* role in creating a collective frame of mind, where people gravitate toward each other's ideas and feelings. In training groups I conducted, I would tell participants at the start that we were forming a learning community in which the rightness or wrongness of behavior was not predefined and that, within limits, they should be faithful to their own ideas and behaviors. Yet, despite this invitation to freedom, some people, later in the process, would say they didn't cry or express warmth or make critical observations because that's not how the group did things. Apart from their being mistaken in that conclusion, we also see that, for these people, the modeling of actual behavior was more influential than the abstract rules of the game.

While the reasons groups behave as they do are complex, the role of contagion itself must be taken into account. In some groups, laughter is prominent, while in others people are more sober. In some groups, looking to the leader for direction is the norm, while in others, members are inclined to go their own way. In some groups, agreement, benevolence, or happiness are suspect, while in others, the ethos welcomes the positive—freely accepting mutuality, patience, and helpfulness. With such contagion operative, the leadership must be alert to the specifics of what any group imbibes, distinguishing between abstract conclusions and the current reality.

While norms can represent mindless conformity, they may also be part of a spontaneously formed personal style, a dialect, resulting not from inculcation, but as a social familiarity. That is, whatever people authentically say to each other may well become recognized as a group characteristic, one that fittingly represents the group's mode of function. To call this a dialect has different implications than to call it conformity. This is more than tricky semantics. *Dialect* reflects a group norm that does not sacrifice individuality.

For example, we all speak in a dialect, its tone growing out of New York City, the hills of Appalachia, or a country other than one's own. But none of these dialects interferes with people saying what they mean to say. Having a Scottish dialect or a dialect of the American South does not identify one as conformist. When a group has developed its own dialect, it still leaves room for considerable individuality. Just as individuals differ in magnanimity, surprise, or rebelliousness, groups will also differ in the ways they address ideas that come up. Some groups will work best when music is a part of the design; others will prefer perspective-setting lectures. Some will be interested in social issues, others in family relationships. Some will want to spend a lot of time on one exercise; others will want the exercises to be short.

These illustrations of some of the conditions for a benign ethos in the Life Focus Group draw from a foundational belief that a benign ethos depends on benign engagement. It develops responsively within the group because of the shadowy goodwill that forms a large part of human priority.

We are thus commissioned to reexamine the lesson we learned—too compellingly—long ago, that conventionality is disabling. This notion causes many, especially creative people, to become excessively vigilant about losing their freedom. Some recent cultural samples of this vigilance are the responses received by psychologist Dr. Caroline Paltin when she was forming a Life Focus Group (2014 Personal Communication). Though there were many heartily welcoming responses to her announcement, there were a few who believed it to be a threat to individuality.

> One person said, "I don't like the idea of a group, and especially an ongoing group, because my experience in church or organizations is that the organization takes control and the individuals are lost. Dissent is a crime. It becomes all about group think."
> Another said, "I like my individuality. I've never really enjoyed watered down group activity. I always leave feeling glad to be able to think my own thoughts."
> A third said, "I don't like the feeling of losing myself in a crowd of other people's ideas. I like to think my own thoughts."

In contradistinction, when the group of 50 people actually met, the tone of the meeting was represented in such words as these:

> It achieved what I am hoping for: moments of sadness and laughter, thoughtfulness and a deeper connection with a community of people who are also searching for connection, as well as a moment to… just be alive and be reflective in a different way from any other way… I'm so motivated to feel a part of a positive community, both to meet my own needs for connection and support, and also just as a reminder that there are so many good, and caring, people and authentic people in this world and I am not alone in that.

Of course, neither of these spokespeople has been elected as representative, and I am not quoting them as scientific evidence. Rather they are illustrative of the dangers of stereotyping and remind us to examine individuality and community in more than an either/or way. The Life Focus Group is a cheering section for individuality, and this attitude rarely threatens its communal function. There is no incompatibility, for example, between everybody in the group simultaneously examining their ambitions and the unique role ambition plays in each person's life. Those who are too vigilant about their individuality look past the many communal influences that provide support for individual enterprise. There is surely a societal support for individuality. Contrastingly, there are, of course, also many examples of social pressures to conform about sexual preference, religious beliefs, and occupational priorities. The line between societal affirmation of belonging and the pressures for conformity can be murky, but the assumption of its negative bias must be balanced by the recognition that a communal receptacle can be the container for individuality. Whatever failures the community creates are failures of integration, not incompatibility. Every community must balance its existence as a communal entity with its service as a support for individual constituents.

Chapter 8

Awareness
Fundamentals

The role of awareness

Gestalt therapy's use of sharpened and expanded awareness helped transform a Freudian overemphasis on insight. But the increased attention given to awareness and its accompanying immediacy would be empty if not joined with the reciprocal phenomena of relationship, imagination, skill development, and meaning. Indeed, if anything were to be "everything" in Gestalt therapy, it would be the integration of all the person's functions, a fundamental condition for depth of experience. The value of surface experience is not in ignoring depth but in inspiring attention to everyday experience, the ground upon which depth depends. Someone may, for example, say it was hard to leave home this morning, a simple awareness. This may lead to telling about sickness of a child and, as the story proceeds, to a sense of the relative values of family and work. Indeed, the stimulation that comes with a sweep of awareness creates vitality and purpose, opening the person to safe engagement.

This overt and describable surface of awareness replaced the view of the unconscious as a silent partner, mysteriously masterminding a person's life directions. To show how fertile and surprising the attended surface may be, here is a report of a student in a psychology class who was instructed to attend to his inner experiences. We can resonate with the excitement of his focalized awareness, as he concentrates on his bodily sensations:

> Normally—that is, before I let my "attention wander through my body"—I was aware of my body sensation merely as a general hum, a kind of poorly defined sense of general vitality and warmth. However, the attempt to subdivide this into component sensations was a source of genuine amazement. I became aware of a series of tensions in various parts of my body; knees and lower thighs as I sit on the chair; the region of the diaphragm; the eyes, shoulders, and dorsal neck region. This discovery was quite astonishing to me. It was almost as if my feeling had entered a foreign body with tensions, rigidities, and pressures entirely different from

mine. Almost immediately upon discovery, I was able to relax these tensions. This, in turn, caused me to be aware of a sense of looseness and even elation; a very sudden freedom, pleasure, and readiness for anything to come.

(Perls, Hefferline, & Goodman, 1951)

Though this report says little about an actual therapy session and the complexities of using the awareness process in an ongoing life, it shows how powerful a pointed awareness can be in amplifying the person's energy and engagement. Such expansion of import, experienced in simple personal concentration, moved the student into a generalized bodily aliveness. What was important to Gestalt therapy was the simple and vital radiance that guides all human activity, whether sexual, conversational, or intellectual or whether it involved planning, laughing, crying, reading, screaming, or anything else.

In addition to the recognition of a baseline bodily vitality, another advantage of the concept of awareness over the concept of insight is the importance of the entire range of worldly happenings.

In my own work, awareness led me to become more interested in how people talked, how they sat, how they chose their favorite topics, how they related to their spouses or coworkers, and how they imagined their futures. We start with simple sensation and expand like yeast to feelings, of purposes of values, of relationships, and all the experiences of which lives are formed. Serendipitously, insight is an indispensable constituent of awareness. At the insight level, interconnection among events is revealed. Focal events are placed into perspective, and observing this can produce enormous enlightenment. But the awareness of both therapist and patient is not just occasional, as is insight; it is always present.

Awareness and meaning

Meaning can be achieved in two ways: horizontally and vertically. The horizontal dimension of meaning is reached through a continuum of awarenesses, as they unfold into a realization of the connections between what has preceded and what follows any particular awareness. Meaning evolves through a step-by-step process of experiences, never by isolated experience. Each step leads, gradually, to a new understanding of the context of our experience.

The vertical dimension of meaning is plumbed by interpretation and insight. When, for example, we realize that our complaints about our boss are an outgrowth of always feeling shortchanged by our parents, suddenly the contemporary world can become more accommodating, and this experience opens us to being more creative in getting our needs satisfied. Vertical meaning, often dramatically realized, pierces through to the obscured meanings by relatively sudden illuminations, often shortcutting an otherwise gradual process. There is considerable overlap between vertical and horizontal meaning; meanings do not come altogether suddenly or altogether gradually. However, since the awareness concept also encompasses insight, it offers the therapist greater choice than the earlier concept of insight alone. I believe therapists of all persuasions should be open to both. Insight by itself excludes too much of the patient's ongoing awareness and requires impeccable timing. Step-by-step awareness, on the other hand, can become interminable without some revelations contributed by either therapist or patient.

Given such a union between awareness and insight, Gestalt therapy has had to attend to the gap between underlying energy, steeped in a flowing immediacy, and the contradictory but unabandonable depth of human existence. Might such an exclusively phenomenological experience as represented in the above student's report provide a misleading sense of wholeness? It necessarily and temporarily disregards his complex of wishes, thoughts, and plans. Should we not be hospitable to the client's childhood experience in the dark bedroom closet, where he was sent to ponder the fist fight he had gotten into?

The concern with the superficiality/depth dimension is a key requirement in the search for experience that matters. Whatever is going on always takes place in a larger, unmanifested, depth-inviting context, including both the unconscious and all our other experiences, which Gestalt therapists call the ground. Immediate experience is always positioned in this experiential housing. Still, depth is commonly understood to exist when experiences are highly significant or strongly felt or very clever or very obscure—experiences that include being deeply in love or deeply concerned about certain governmental policies or deeply immersed in reading a novel. The depth to which I am pointing, however, is the depth one achieves by relating any awareness to whatever context is accessible for that awareness. In this sense, depth is the undoing of the isolation of any single event from others that matter.

The cryptic unconscious celebrated in psychoanalysis as the geography of depth is only occasionally unscrambled. Very few of my patients have had memories in therapy that they had never had before. Usually, what happens that comes close to the fabled return of unconscious material is that people start to pay closer attention to what has been sliding off the side of their minds. Or they suddenly see old things in a new light. The sudden emergence of the repressed is an old romanticism; it has kept many therapists frustrated and distracted from the more immediately available depth as they seek in the unconscious what is percolating right in front of their eyes.

Much of what is recovered from the "repressed" has been simply set aside, readily knowable but not associated with current experience. Connecting what one is doing now to early experiences provides depth, because it's no longer an isolated experience. To know, for example, that the fights a person is getting into nowadays are connected to childhood experiences of being beaten provides depth to current experience, even though that person has always known about being beaten in childhood. We may experience the depth of a current success in college by connecting it to years of practicing the piano. We may experience our current tenderness for people in trouble by connecting it with the loss of a cherished dog. But these distant connections, important for restoring context, are not all that is required for the experience of depth. Valuable though these connections may be and as habituated as therapists may be to believing they are signs of depth, there are also other, perhaps more accessible, ways to the experience of depth.

An example of depth at the surface is the experience of a patient at a party. She soon remembered times when she had been captivating, and these memories reassured her about herself. But they didn't create a feeling of depth. The feelings of depth came when I asked her to close her eyes and tell me what she felt inside. At first she found it difficult to close her eyes, accustomed as she was to shallow awareness and feeling frightened about what she might find. For some people (those heavily defended against internal experience, and especially borderline patients), to focus internally might be too much to ask; it could set off terror. But she was not over her head and was able to do it.

During this sharp internal focus, she told me about a number of her sensations, including the key awareness that she had a tight band of tension around her abdomen. After a further short period of focusing, she told me that her breathing had become very quiet. Then, when she continued to concentrate on her internal feelings, the tightness just disappeared and I could see that her breathing became amplified.

This new opening to her breathing had led her to a direct realization and description of inner liveliness. No more guesswork about whether she was or was not captivating. She said this feeling was better than feeling captivating and that she was surprised at how peaceful she had become. In a sense she felt the wellsprings of being captivating without really caring about it any more, transforming her self-evaluation from superficial to deep.

Composite and ingredient awareness

Expanding the range of awareness from which depth can be recognized, all awareness is composed of composite and ingredient awarenesses, interwoven. This combination incorporates readily accessible experiences with those that flesh out the original awareness and provide color and implication. Let me explain.

Composite awarenesses are those that are in the center of attention, the ones people notice without detailed examination: a phrase spoken in conversation, a feeling of sadness, a recollection of a visit to a childhood neighborhood, an angry reaction to bad advice, a disappointment about a canceled trip. These statements, actions, memories, feelings, and reports are valid just as they are, taken at face value. But they all also invite details that can provide fuller delineation of the experience.

Suppose you are biting into an apple. This is your composite awareness. To be aware of biting into the apple may be all that matters. But the ingredients of the experience, if brought into awareness, will influence the depth. Whether the apple is sweet or sour, whether you have bitten off too much, how good it would be to join this apple with a bite of cheese, whether it reminds you of the apple tree you swing from in your backyard, whether you are an apple grower—these ingredients offer dimension to the experience of biting into the apple.

For another example, suppose a patient says, "I drove here today so peacefully." This composite awareness has many ingredients, some of which may be brought into awareness. The tone of voice, for example, may be soft or quick or reminiscing or inviting or challenging. For the patient to become aware of the qualities that are subsumed within his awareness of a peaceful drive gives the words a greater depth than for the sentence to stand by itself, unsupported by the ingredients of which it is composed. Whether these words are spoken with a shrug of the shoulders or with conviction gives dimension. If the words are spoken with bitterness or irony, that would be quite a different dimension than if spoken by someone who felt, at last, a moment of peace.

This process of interweaving awarenesses and the reverberations of fluctuating attention results in a throb of perpetual excitement, which makes experience fresh and vibrant. This interweaving process is the soul of knowledge, the appreciation of the continuing ramifications that one thing offers another. From these perceptual dynamisms come the roots of personal fascination, the transcendence of ordinariness that makes experience continuously inviting. Through restoration of the simple vibrancies of awareness, fleshing out the composite awareness, the release of the pertinent lifetime of experience will be facilitated and options for self-identification increased.

Though this process may include what therapists often think of as tapping into the unconscious, it is more inclusive than that. Ingredients may or may not be within the range of immediate awareness, and they do not have the causative implications that are imputed to the unconscious. They are simply elements embedded in a complex composition.

Tight therapeutic sequences

A further aspect of the relationship of surface to depth is the phenomenon of tight therapeutic sequences. The fluidity of our moment-to-moment experience is easily overlooked, because it's going on all the time, even when it feels choppy. What stands out most clearly, even more than the continuity, are the *events* that populate our sequences. These events may not seem connected or purposefully directional, but in the stream of them, housed within the passage of time, they are inseparable. Their fluidity is irrepressible and constant, without prejudice about the past, present, or future. The passage just goes on.

The content of experience, in fact, can throw a monkey wrench into the works, thwarting otherwise recognizable directionality. We get so caught up with goals, the organization of our thoughts, and their acceptability, that the smooth flow of time becomes lost to us. We are impelled, however, by our need for wholeness, to extract this veiled continuity from its unruly content, the details of which intuitively seem more crucial to our existence.

Enlarging on his emphasis on the primal role of awareness, Frederick Perls introduced the idea of an *awareness continuum*. He proposed that people who were continuingly faithful to their own *stream of awareness, step by step*, would be impelled into an organically determined pathway to their own goals. He saw each moment as having its own influence on the next. This continuingly free process differs from the concept of destiny, which has a fixed consequence. But without pre-set goals, Perls' process offered a holistic confidence that our best chance to reach our best personal destination was to stay faithfully *up to date* with ourselves and the world around us. With full-flowered concentration on each moment, choices always remained open. Multiple possible directions would always be available in each moment, and the ones actually taken would meet each person's ongoing needs. This organic process could be tainted by fixed attitudes, fears of whatever is suitably next, contradictory purposes, and so forth. Such conditions are barriers to the fluidity of living and often result in pre-set determinants about what to be aware of and what needs to be next. Therapy can help keep the continuity free of pre-fixed determinants. To accept each awareness on its own merits requires an appreciation of the promise of continuity, as I will show later in this chapter.

Building on Perls' insights, I will describe the role of *tightened therapeutic sequences*, which broadens the concept of the awareness continuum to include action and contact. Tightened therapeutic sequences look beyond the here and now into "nextness," accentuating the fluidity of experience. This highlights a faith in our need to attend to each moment of awareness, and a faith in the personal validity of a nextness, unimpeded by distorting life influences.

In ordinary living, we usually ignore the direct connectedness of moment-to-moment. It's too pressured a way to live. Instead, we play loosely between one thing we say or do and the next. In such desultory sequencing, we might say we spent the day running errands. Someone may respond that she did too. Soon we are talking about a possible trip to New York and then about a friend's recent accident or a political campaign. That is the way people actually talk to each other, and it can be very interesting. There is neither the wish nor a need for tight sequences.

In therapy, this looseness gives people room to develop their thoughts. However, pointed attention has its advantages. Selectively tightening the chain of events heightens attention and forestalls wanderings, irrelevance, repetition, and other interferences with graceful and fruitful continuity. In directing the therapy process, each moment's expression throws off *arrows*, pointing momentarily, sometimes contradictorily, toward nextness and an indistinct future. The therapist enters into the moment-to-moment impetus by riding these arrows; suggesting, reminding, and encouraging the person to move into an organically right nextness, as I shall soon show. In paying careful attention to where these arrows point, we are enabled to heighten the impetus of each expression, increasing a trust in the ongoing process.

In the service of helping people develop this continuity, it is tempting to look far ahead to potential lofty accomplishments, but the less glamorous tightening of sequences is the simplest, safest, and often most rewarding approach. Paying close attention to the moment-by-moment process, we lean forward each step of the way, concentrating always on the transition point between now and next. In its early stages, the ultimate destination is largely mysterious and thus becomes exciting. The heightened attention is stimulating. An important consequence of simple sequencing is that people may come to feel a *sequential inevitability*, a "yes" mentality that is a hypnotic-like confidence in nextness and its animated flow of experience. For example, if I count 1-2-3-4-5 in clear sequence, the listener will immediately expect 6 next. It is this sense of natural flow that a step-by-step process will induce.

Mihaly Csikszentmihalyi has done much to clarify and popularize this "flow" of experience. He describes the role of flow in great detail and from many perspectives, including good work, bodily experience, the creation of happiness, and the discovery of meaning. A key observation he makes is

> Although the flow of experience appears to be effortless, it is far from being so. It often requires strenuous physical exertion, or highly disciplined mental activity ... Any lapse in concentration will erase it. And yet while it lasts, consciousness works smoothly, action follows action seamlessly ... in flow there is no need to reflect, because the action carries us forward as if by magic.
>
> (Csikszentmihalyi, 1990, p. 54)

Daniel J. Siegel has also addressed the continuity imperative from a neurological perspective, describing a form of spatio-temporal integration. He refers to the brain as an "anticipation machine" enabling the person to "represent the future." The mind must always deal with a changing complexity of experience. To keep up with this challenge, its anticipatory reflex allows it to integrate the multiformed world of everyday experience and to prepare itself for consequences.

He says,

> The value of such a representational process is that it allows the individual to anticipate the next moment in time and in this way to act in a more adaptive manner, enhancing the chance for survival. Spatio-temporal integration may therefore be a fundamental feature of how the human mind has evolved.
>
> (Siegel, 1999, p. 305)

We are swept along by a string of sequences into a biologically determined connectedness that, through time, is our fundamental mission. The pathway is met by unpredictable dangers ahead, sometimes threatening our very survival, and this anticipation of danger commonly leads us to gird ourselves *against* the flow of experience, leading to a strained relationship with the future.

When people distrust simple, moment-to-moment directionality, they say things that are irrelevant, they change the subject, they ask questions instead of making statements, they lose the point of what they are saying, they delay, and they neutralize, all of which shakes up the linkage between an experience and its successor. To restore a free-flowing process, we try to move gracefully through time, gathering momentum toward a sense of closure. We know it won't happen smoothly or easily, but there are directional hints that can help.

Illustration of tight sequences

To illustrate the role of these arrows showing how moments build on each other, here is a therapy session I had with Anita, in front of a conference audience. Anita wanted intimacy in her life and hadn't been able to get it. She had been married for five years, and at the time of our session, divorced for two. Feeling that intimate relationships were impossible, she was now on the edge of trying to get close to people again, but she was always stopping herself. In her opening remarks, many arrows pointed the way: a need for intimacy, a five-year marriage, two years since the divorce, her sense of the impossibility of intimate relationships, her own attempts at intimacy, her resigned tone of voice, her feeling that she was the one stopping herself, and so forth.

Sequence 1: We can't follow all these arrows at once, so I had to choose one, and I chose Anita's belief that she was the one stopping herself from getting close to people. I asked her to tell me *how* she stopped herself. The reason I chose that arrow was that the self-recrimination in her tone of voice suggested that this was heaviest on her mind. Asking "how" invited her to get concrete, an antidote to her *abstractions* about getting close to people, since abstractions often cut off the impact of felt details. Her answer fleshed out some details, but she did not exactly answer my question. Instead of telling me how she stopped *herself*, she spoke of stopping *other people* from getting close to her—by criticizing them or feeling criticized herself. Her switch was okay with me, as I expect some slippage between question and answer. In fact, such slippages can serve as creative contributions, because the therapist's intuition is an approximation at best. She added that she might either argue with these people or withdraw.

Sequence 2: Her varieties of devices for stopping people were now recognizable, and I could choose one. She mentioned withdrawal, and I thought this was her most manifest style, so I chose it as the next arrow. I asked Anita *when* she had withdrawn, again tapping into her *concrete* experience and accenting her continuity. Why did I ask about withdrawal when there were at least three other specified options, to say nothing of the many unspecified? Perhaps it was her suppressed tone of voice. Perhaps her carefulness. Perhaps because of the absence of intimacy. Perhaps because it was the last option she mentioned. Perhaps because any of the options could be equally promising. I did, later, go back to one of the options left behind, her tendency to argue, as you shall see.

Sequence 3: Now, without the emotional cover of generalizing her withdrawal, my asking *"when"* scared her. She was afraid she might say too much. She didn't want to tell everything. Of course, she didn't have to, yet the underlying impulse to do so was there. She also said she was afraid that her reticence would make her *fail in her responsibility* to the audience and to me. She was in trouble whether she told everything or not. She was frightened about the continuity, intuiting the threat that the next step would open the door to who-knows-what.

Sequence 4: Nevertheless, Anita had now provided new arrows, and I chose "responsibility" as the smoothest transition into nextness. I warmly explained to her that she had no "responsibility" to the audience to say anything and assured her that failure was unlikely since I was not requiring anything of her that she wasn't doing. I spelled out my reassurance by telling her also that what counted most was that she and I were *simply talking together* and that it was a good bet that would *continue*. This sense of *continuity with me* moved her into a feeling of relationship, allowing both security and momentum, I believe, toward the closeness that she said she was seeking with others but could not develop.

Sequence 5: Our continuity enhanced, I went back and picked up on an arrow we'd left behind—reflecting another side of her, something she was aware of but that was not evident in her conversation with me. I reminded her that she'd said earlier that she would either withdraw in time of difficulty or *argue*. I could see signs of withdrawal, I told her, but no signs of argument. She took this to the next step by acknowledging this aggressive energy, telling me that her argumentativeness could not be seen because it was internal. By acknowledging this aggressiveness, she was inviting it into our conversation, restoring a sense of connectedness between two parts of herself—her hidden aggression and her surface composure. Then she took another step into a fluid continuity. Surprisingly, she said she did not really *feel* responsible for others; she had only accommodatingly *said* she did. She revealed that she actually knows what she wants very strongly. What a new confidence in relationship!

Sequence 6: Riding the arrow of disguised strength, I observed that she *looked* like people could get away with anything with her, but that she also had a *soul of steel*. This strong metaphor was a risky observation considering her previous reserve, but now she was up to it, and the word "steel" led her to speak of two sides of herself: the steely person and the gentle one. Then she went on to tell me a story about her steely mother and grandmother, telling me how harshly they cut people down. She intoned their harshness with a new level of energy and absorption. I think the flow of our conversation, going from one moment to each naturally next moment, swept her into the freedom to say things she would usually avoid and to say them with vitality. She now seemed much more connected with me, steeped now in the things we were saying to each other.

Sequence 7: Suddenly, Anita became afraid that her speaking so sharply would turn me away. I explained that for me it was more of an electrification than a turn-away and asked if she would be willing to experiment further with this way of speaking. She agreed and then intentionally spoke sharply; she did indeed feel strong but then again became bothered, this time because she thought that her domination would *exclude* me from the interchange. I was glad it mattered to her.

Sequence 8: The specter of excluding others was a new arrow, and I pointed out that she seemed *more* rather than less connected to me. This highlighted her feeling of connection, which, out of habit, she might not otherwise have noticed or might have disregarded. It made her heart beat faster, another arrow and the strongest sign so far of close relationship.

Sequence 9: I asked her what her beating heart would say, and she said she felt sad and her eyes began to tear. The sadness was about my actually *wanting* to listen to her, a feeling she does not usually let in and one that was very dear to her. Sometimes sadness, rather than pleasure, comes at the point of achievement, when the achievement highlights previous deprivation. Having felt the experience of connection with me strongly and the satisfaction of it, we ended the session with her experiencing a firsthand, undismissible example of herself affecting me and feeling affected, feeling more rather than less included through her strong words.

What I want most to point out about these sequences is the way in which each step was built on the previous one and how as long as the arrows I followed resonated with her, it became easy for her to say and experience things that would normally seem prohibitive. Furthermore, what seems apparent is that the process of connecting moments to each other has a striking similarity to hypnosis. The establishment of simple continuity provides guidance and a sense of *sequential inevitability*. This creates an inner permission to take what feels like the naturally next step, as hypnotic induction does, releasing a hidden fluidity. When one thing naturally follows another, the often surprising consequence is that one develops an "of course" frame of mind, which reduces uncertainty and fear. In this case, each step of Anita's moment-to-moment process called for the connecting link to the next, each successively moving her toward the restoration of her prospects for intimacy. Furthermore, the general sweep of her personality, including her strengths and fears, her life history, and her new openings to potential intimacy, were all evolved out of the larger undercurrent of her life. Out of this background, the moment-to-moment accumulation of experiences added up to a meaningful and representative vignette.

Loose therapeutic sequences

Riding the pathway of irrepressible nextness can have a valuable healing effect and offers grace, confidence, directionality, and realizability of one's existence. Still, tight seqentiality is hardly the whole story. The casual quality of everyday living is more the norm, and it is only now and then that we face consequentiality head-on. Mostly this or that nextness calls for little attention. We do what we do and are not much tuned in to what may or may not follow. Where we have loose sequences, we go on and on more or less haphazardly, minimally concerned with the direction we take. Sometimes our linear inclinations make us impatient when they remain long unrequited. Perhaps, however, the aimless quality will be interesting in its own colorful immediacy, in irreverent humor, in stories that don't seem to go anywhere, in parenthetical wanderings, in the pleasures of facial expression or tone of voice, or in purposeless exploration of ideas without intent to accomplish anything. When I tell a friend about a casual conversation I had with a worker bringing my drinking water system up to date, there is little purposiveness apparent. What interests my friend is just to hear me talking about my day and to have a chance to be heard also. We have no commanding interest in the continuing sequentiality of our remarks.

The psychotherapist is familiar with such looseness, listening while her patient is verbally warming up. Though tightening up this sequentiality is *ultimately* important, one should not programmatically force the pace of directionality. Patients will say significantly directional things only when they've developed a freedom of mind. I think of one patient, a deeply disturbed and introspective woman, who never looked at me during our first three meetings. She was obviously anxious about facing me, a barrier with others in her everyday life as well. By visually excluding me, she diminished the nourishment she might receive from seeing me. I felt, though, that she was putting all of her energy into just speaking to me, and I listened almost reverently to this fearfully brave person, who felt to me like a poem of confined expression. I think she sensed my absorption with her words, her grace, and her quietude. Because it was a huge expansion of her boundaries to speak to me at all, I surely did not want to rush her into looking at me while she spoke. Later, when she was sufficiently familiar with my presence in the room with her, she opened her lens to include me visually and was able to encompass my contributions and to smile and feel the freedom of simple relationship.

The ethos of Life Focus Groups supports this simple relational appreciation for another person's pace and style. This need to tune in continuingly without goal requirements is accentuated, and the satisfaction of it is repeatedly sought through illustration, discussion, and exercises. Every effort is made in this communal enterprise to enhance awareness of whatever level of manifest continuity exists as a preamble for timely movement. It is important, therefore, to realize that sequentiality is neither mechanical nor smooth. It resides in the intuition and perception of the person initiating the trip and the person joining and perhaps guiding. Still, a dependable linear directionality offers grounding for non-linear personal riffs that are surprises on the path to dependable sequentiality.

Another, more complex, loosening of sequentiality comes with the chaotic dynamic of our minds. Chaos violates our sense of familiarity and logic. Both syntax and context are missing. To many of us, the very viability of our minds is threatened by the absence of orderliness in our words or actions. Chaos mocks continuity and may offer its own brand of freedom, showing that continuity by itself may be a pale version of the way the world works. Neither surrealism, nor mosaic, nor disorganized patterns, nor surprise permit an easy sense of continuity. They show us a part of living that is just as natural as orderliness, offering depth, adventure, and fertility of mind. It is necessary, therefore, to take into account the strange fellowship between the unifying properties of continuity and the artfully mysterious arrangements of life's unruly events. As Virginia Woolf (1927) tells us in *To the Lighthouse*, in describing the Ramsays' oddly manifested love for each other,

> And, what was even more exciting, she felt, too, as she saw Mr. Ramsay bearing down and retreating, and Mrs. Ramsay sitting with James in the window and the cloud moving and the tree bending, how life, from being made up of little separate incidents, which one lived one by one, became curled and whole like a wave which bore one up with it and threw one down with it, there, with a dash on the beach.

In what sense, therefore, can we incorporate the seemingly chaotic within the need for the connectedness that continuity offers? One part of the paradoxical joke that nature plays is that continuity exists even in the face of chaos, surprise, and surrealism, calling for a special patience as we plumb the intricacies of living. Our whole-making imperative directs us to light up the obscure relationships of one moment to the next. It leads us to the discovery of hidden unity and prompts us to value the uncertainty preceding it, which provides both spice and anxiety to people's lives. In exercising the supreme organizational powers with which we have been endowed, we come to see that in the face of all the barriers to recognizable continuity, there lies underneath this disorderliness the consoling reality that one thing does indeed follow another. It is always there, even though that one thing may not be what one would expect it to be. Chaos is surely a part of the great mystery of the universe, but to live in it without respite is a painful violation, to be sure, of the humanly generic and palliative need for connectedness.

Chapter 9

Contact boundary
Fundamentals

The contact boundary is a pivotal concept in Gestalt therapy theory and is a foundation for relationship. This boundary is the point at which each person meets "otherness"—a phenomenon so basic that a world without it would be unimaginable. Contacting otherness is going on all the time, like blood flowing in our veins and neurons pulsating, and it is as easily overlooked as the air around us. It is composed of basic connections with the world around us, such elemental functions as seeing, hearing, talking, touching, and smelling. Important additional contact functions are imagination, remembering, and planning. These functions keep us connected with the world outside ourselves, a connection that is ever-present and largely taken for granted. Contacting otherness drives us to talk to a friend, get into a fight, eat, look at the stars, make love, thread a needle, gauge how far to throw a ball, read a book, or breathe the air.

By itself, the contact function is value-free. It's just there, a connecting process. To see you, for example, says nothing about where this fits into my life. But seeing you is interwoven with feelings, relationships, and meanings, all laden with personal values. While one or another of these functions is always happening, there is a wide range in the quality of the contact. When I tell you I drove a motorcycle to work, I may tell it routinely or with a sense of the adventure. If I listen to you talk about your visit to your children in Nebraska, I may hear it with great absorption or fade out into stray thoughts. To have a good conversation, it's necessary to speak clearly, point toward the appropriate topic, and have a sensibility for mutuality.

We can assess any contact as being of good quality or not. But contact is never free of other human functions, such as awareness of surroundings, implications, and especially relationship. In fact, it can be difficult to distinguish between contact and relationship; they're often seen as a package. If I speak too softly to be received, for example, that will affect the relationship. When contact is of a poor quality, the connections between us are diminished. Therapeutic procedures, therefore, call for attention to the quality of talking, listening, seeing, laughing, crying, and imagining, moving forward toward a meaningful meeting point between self and other.

Here is an example of a therapy session that accentuated the importance of good quality contact. Ann began the session, held at a therapy conference, by saying,

> What I'm dealing with is my developing as a professional and feeling guilty, depressed sometimes, angry a lot. It deals more with how our profession focuses on individuals. The more I look at the individuals, I start to think about what's happening around us and what's happening in the world and about how I am benefiting from the exploitation of people around the world. That contributes to my feeling guilty, and then I start feeling frustrated and confused.

I recognized her introduction as wildly ambitious. Ann was clearly aroused to affect large arcs of human experience. However, her message was abstract, and her aspiration beyond her immediate reach. Her contact with the world she wanted to affect was diffuse; glancing at distant horizons. Of course, contact is not an all-or-nothing proposition, and it's also true that her enthusiasm touched me strongly. That was good contact, and I was immediately in the grip of her concerns. While I felt the validity of her ambition, I also saw that her contact with this world called for a greater sense of proportionality and accessibility. Her present approach both to the problem and with me, as her therapist, was lacking in pointedness. She showed little or no humility or realism about how to accomplish her wishes, even though she told a touching story about her empathy and ambitions. So my task was to help her to improve the quality of contact. This required her to combine the enabling vitality of her purposes with the blurring abstraction, opening her to what was reachable. So I said to her, paralleling her enthusiasm and her purposes,

> Yes, yes. You've got a big job there. I understand the importance of attending to all those things, and yet there's so much in the world you're having trouble coordinating. Maybe you need a little more practice, as a circus acrobat might doing big flips. Maybe we can do a few of those flips here on the ground.

She responded by saying,

> Okay, okay—Let me see if I can even tie it into the conference. I'm angry at the profession for not including the issues of diversity, for not including issues dealing with women and underclass, for not dealing with issues. That's what I'm angry about. What I want is to make you and everybody else incorporate those issues so that I can learn and know that we as a profession are doing something.

Ann got it. She sharpened her message by pointing to the conference itself, giving a specific example of social inequality, an accessible challenge, and an invitation for others to join her. There was enthusiastic applause from the audience but no reaction from Ann, who just went on, unresponsive to the clear approval. She remained functionally alone, though on the verge of relationship. So, guiding her to incorporate the contact with the audience, I accentuated their response by asking,

"Did you hear the applause when you were speaking?" She replied, minimizing the reaction, "Yeah, I heard a couple of people."

She couldn't help hearing the enthusiasm of the audience, but she dimmed their quite palpable connection with her. I then asked her how she felt about it. This was to check out her sense of dismissal and revive her awareness of what was actually happening, pointing her to a more affirming contact. She acknowledged the audience by saying, "It felt affirming to know that other people are also struggling with that. And I'm wondering if other people are struggling with that, how come they still haven't addressed that here, now?"

I accentuated this concern by inviting her to explore her question, asking her to imagine a conversation with the audience. She then felt closer to the audience and went on to say, "As the demographics of the United States change, you're not only going to be serving white men; you're going to be serving a diverse population..."

She was speaking as though under great pressure and, again, impersonally to the audience. I said:

"Now wait a minute. Wait a minute. See what you're doing? You're not talking to them; you're making a speech."

She got the distinction between that and actually talking to real, listening people. Later in the session, she became more relational and proportional. Then I asked how it would feel if she were to have a greater sense of joining with them instead of feeling unconnected? She said that would feel affirming.

At this point I felt it important to introduce some form of action. Of course, too much specific direction can rob a person of initiative, but I felt in this situation, it would further accentuate the need for action and specificity. So, I said, "Yes. What if you were to get some kind of a notepad and get the names of the people who would like more people of color presenting, more women presenting?"

I asked whether that seemed too minor. I wanted to contrast the doable with her ambitions and check out whether she accepted this new level of enterprise.

The session soon ended, with her saying she was going to pass around a notepad, so that whoever wanted to sign it could.

Through all of this guidance, what was not said was that I was entranced with this woman, and I'm quite sure her enthusiasm invited me to this absorption with her. That phenomenon of unspoken absorption is an encouragement that goes beyond the explicit. It's part of a natural contact among folks, which is hard to spell out. It incorporates the presence of the other so naturally that one is more likely to notice the content than the personal inspiration.

Amplification of contact

In this session, we see an amplification of overlooked aspects of the conversation that might normally be disregarded. The pointed attention to her excess of ambition, dismissal of group support, and absence of direct action all heightened reality. It magnified what would otherwise be taken for granted, increasing the importance of stereotyped words, otherwise impassively residing inside her head. Such attention is an affirmative statement, and it mobilizes people for the exploratory process.

Transference

This attention to the immediate happenings is basic to Gestalt therapy, and it replaced the vaunted Freudian concept of *transference*—the idea that the immediate therapeutic engagement with the therapist was a left-over from one's childhood relationships. That is, if the patient was angry with the therapist, that anger might be interpreted as a replica of relationship with a parent. This notion diminished the immediate reality of the person's actual relationship with the therapist and was a distraction from the current experience.

The deflection of immediate experience to the past was unacceptable to Gestalt therapy and some other theories. The idea of transference did, however, have an unintended consequence. It highlighted the relationship with the therapist beyond that of other forms of professional consultations. It placed therapists inside the life history of the patient. Therapist and patient became *intertwined*, since the transference principle insinuates the therapist into the most intimate fabric of the person's life.

Through this microcosmic overlay, the therapist is no longer just another person; she has elements of the people who have mattered to the client. While this feeling offers expanded importance to the world at large, this importance does not diminish the actual experiences, which are important in their own right. Such consequentiality as the feeling of microcosm is extremely absorbing, occasionally reaching hypnotic proportions. This absorption and the accompanying trust, though, can be paradoxically frightening. The intense involvement leads to lessened deliberation by the patient, who has become opened to the risks of novelty. Yet the amplification factor is also inspirational, driving home the importance of the therapeutic dialogue.

I-Thou

The expansion of microcosmic depth and meaningfulness offered by the transference phenomenon was later joined by the poetic style of another great contributor to the psychology of engagement, Martin Buber. Introducing the idea of I-thou relationship, Buber (1955) used luxurious language in describing it, recognizing the intensity of engagement with words like destiny, covenant, soul, immortal moment—all to portray the profound connectedness of person to person in their fully experienced meeting. This deep personhood of the I-thou relationship was contrasted with an I-it relationship. The "it" was represented in the categorical, the practical, the taken-for-granted experiences of every day. These are important to ongoing existence, but they do not require the absorption of the I-thou experience or its implications for a union of self and other. While the I-it is the most frequent experience of the world outside, it does not carry the heartfelt implications of I-thou. From the standpoint of the therapeutic relationship, the therapist with an I-it perspective categorizes the patient as "patient," while the one with an I-thou perspective would see the unique person as part of a dual absorption, the union of both minds.

Many say Buber went too far in romanticizing contact. Does it not seem exaggerated to equate the connections with our patients with the hallowed relationship of religious people with God? Or even the microcosmically real emotional investment we have with people who are the most dear to us—our parents, children, spouses, friends? While recognizing these enlargements as pictures of life itself, may we especially experience therapeutic connections as a small version of a lifetime of experiences—much as a microscope magnifies—enabling people to experience connections in therapy that might otherwise pass by them? One cannot live every day in magnification of experience, but perhaps one must welcome those moments of high focus that will light the path, reveal a veiled connectedness, and make it supportable. All these relationships represent a promise of union. They are prototypes of connection with the world outside oneself. This absorption is a magnet for union, one that satisfies the compelling experience of "we."

There may be a biologically based example of union represented in the research of Andrew Newberg and Mark Waldman (2009), who took brain scans of meditators. Their brain scan studies showed that their subjects, at the height of meditation, did indeed literally lose a sense of boundaries. They report a decreased activity in the parietal lobe of these subjects and the subjects' sense of self beginning to dissolve, allowing the person to feel "*unified with the object of contemplation.*" While the research on specialized brain functions is still in its early stages, these observations suggest a familiar yet uncanny paradox: that while we live with a simple perception of separateness, we may, under the right circumstances, lose this distinctness. The therapy experience, differentiated as it is from everyday relationship, offers special opportunities for deep absorption, a magnet for unifying relationship.

The fetus is a precedent for such hospitality to the union of minds. We can imagine that the fetus does not make the differentiation between self and other. The infant continues what the fetus began, experiencing itself and the mother as indivisible. This changes during the maturational process, where the differentiation becomes more and more marked. Still, residuals of this infant sense of union are said to survive even into adulthood. We are all embedded in this history of seeming indivisibility, even as our more individuated personhood evolves. We acknowledge this continuing indivisibility even in such hackneyed sayings as, "You can take the boy out of the country, but you can't take the country out of the boy" and in the Jesuit claim, "Give me the child for his first 7 years, and I'll give you the man."

To reconcile this sense of union with its counterpoint, individuality, we must not fall in love with either. We start with the fact that people are far removed from *merging* with another. Even those who are captured or dominated or incorporated are always captured or dominated or incorporated by *someone else* and, except in the case of delusional perceptions, are never actually merged. I may belong devotedly to a certain group of people—family, country, or organization. I may even designate certain symbols such as flags, logos, and slogans as signs of that indivisibility. I may feel my interests seriously affected by what happens within that group. Still, I can always know that as long as I'm a member of that group, that's what I am, not the group itself. My personal identity will never disappear, except in cases of severe psychological disturbance. While the psyche's insistence on inclusion is strong, it always reverberates with an ever-present individuality. This coordination of individuality and inclusion is commonly accomplished but becomes a thorny issue when the contradictions become strongly felt. The Life Focus Group, therefore, must address the dual requirement of union and individual need.

Here is a story told by a member of a Life Focus Group as the group addressed the concept of "home." She says,

> I hope I can do this without crying but I don't know if I can. It was really meaningful to me, because I came across the ocean 14 years ago full of excitement to stay here for 1 year and go back home. It didn't work out that way. I met a man who persuaded me to stay, but I made him promise me two things: That there would always be money in the bank for me to go home and for me to be buried at home. I was panicked at the idea of dying in this country, which says nothing about America or the life I made, but it is a strong longing for me to return home.
>
> And there came a time in my life that it didn't matter so much to me where I was buried, and I thought it was crazy to think of it that way, but now I'm 68 and I do want to be buried at home. I don't know if it is a longing that is overwhelming. Maybe it's as simple as: there people meet in the cemetery and remember you and they water your flowers

and they talk about you. But it's again a strong, strong longing about going home. So that's what I was feeling and thinking about.

This story was ignited by several activities the group had just participated in. First, there was the theme of "home," then a poetry reading, followed by music that deepened memory, and by a storytelling momentum that provided communal safety. The member's thoughts had not been a deep, dark secret. But they had resided silently in a corner of her mind, ready to appear only under the right stimulation. The funneling of attention sparked her story, moving it into the stream of conversation. Not only did this provide her with immediate relational pleasure, achieving direct personal acceptance and understanding, but I would speculate that she was nourished by the integration of her hidden sense of longing and the manifest experience of her present life.

As for the therapy relationship itself, there is a fundamental excitement about entering into this mysterious setting. It does not take long for the patient to discover—most know it before they come—that therapy combines both the dread and attraction of engulfment into an unknown world. It is an invitation to join interests with the therapist in a symbolically rich union. Important personal consequences follow even the simplest of exchanges, giving high focus to the experiences out of which our lives are made. The prospects for amplification of experience become gratified in surprisingly simple ways. In this life-defining experience, an appreciative yes to a question, or an accurate observation about some remark, or a suggestion to feel how they are breathing when they speak of their mother, or laughter at a funny remark: such simple contacts provide relational assurance. Because of the high focus, everything counts more than in casual engagement. Just walking into the therapist's office feels to many as though they are putting their very selfhood on the line, entering a domain where the prospects for inclusion are awakened while the dangers of missed connections remain anxiously alive.

May Sarton (1966) is one of those artists who is deft in describing what professional therapists may be wary to say. She hallows experiences she had with her own therapist, brightening our knowledge of her contact with him in her poem "The Death of a Psychiatrist (for Volta Hall)," where the haunting refrain is, "Now the long lucid listening is done" (Appendix 2). She wrote:

> It was not listening alone, but hearing,
> For he remembered every crucial word
> And gave one back one's self to be heard.

Sarton recognizes not only his listening and her being heard, but also the overtones of silence, his face, which has been through the mill that grinds the coarser human experiences down. She knows he has lived a life among people like her and retained a mind of common concern; that he confirms the merits of her poem and lights it up at its birth. He provides a measure of dignity, giving proportion to her mourning, to her rage and her shame and her anguish, each of which may merit naming as a Self and be met with respect, and it becomes necessary to verbalize a fundamental split in the therapeutic method between technique and a simple personhood of the therapist who is permitted to do what is common to people in everyday life—free to sensitively offer help, to tell stories, to speak about friendships, to wonder about the things his patients love about their spouses or their work, the foibles that interfere with full concentration, the experience of a particular evening at the theater.

While May Sarton exhibits extraordinary literary sensibility, my interactions with an oppositional and less sophisticated person will illustrate a union of minds that had no implications for loss of individuality. This client had fallen into a life of isolation. He repeatedly discounted what he said, almost like a verbal hiccup. Nothing he said was important enough, because he "knew" his statements would not help. I told him I thought that these thoughts and observations and memories might serve as springboards for eventual resolutions. They did not have to help right away. He had no patience for remote prospects. I explained that his impatience was one manifestation of good energy, a quick reactivity and self-evaluation, which ultimately could be valuable to him. I proposed that he continue to be impatient as long as he wanted to, because even though he was impatient, I would be patient *for both of us*. No matter how impatient he would become, I promised him I would do my best to remain patient. He could depend on it. He was amused at this strange bargain and quite relieved that he could continue to be impatient and that I would make up for the deficiency. My assurance was that we had a mutual stake in his growth and that I was willing to provide something he couldn't do for himself. The understanding did not set an unbending boundary between his function and mine, and it did not exclude everything else we might do in our continuing conversation. Rather, with no diminution of the quality of our engagement, he accepted my mind as an auxiliary to his, a specified dependence. Perhaps he might become too dependent on me, in which case the merger would have a harmful effect. But he was in little immediate danger of that. Quite the contrary, he was excessively isolated and would have to come a long way in the direction of merger for this to become a new issue. The time to deal with merger as a problem is when it becomes a problem.

Common contact

Each time the patient experiences the ordinary qualities of the therapist, there is what may be called "common contact." This experience becomes a bridge to "technical contact," which is composed of professionalized procedures, invented by psychotherapists. These are tailor-made for an incisive clarification of personal needs and potential solutions. In the therapy office, the technical methods may seem too strange unless joined with the ordinary forms of contact, to which the patient is oriented by years of familiarity. Because the ordinary forms of contact are more familiar, it would be welcoming for therapy to include some easily recognizable contact. This would include such experiences as kindness, curiosity, colorful and clear language, palpable attention, endurance, gentle strong-mindedness, and many other interpersonal qualities that people seek in their everyday lives: moments of sharing common values, references to local or national news events, exchange of jokes, digressions about concerts or movies, opinions about office decor, and the like. Recently I had a special experience of common contact. It was serendipitous, but it serves to represent the power of the common. Even though it was surely no part of therapeutic technique, this strange happenstance had a clear therapeutic impact.

I had made a special appointment for a couple who could not come at their usual time. I arranged to see them early on a morning when I did not normally see patients. My office was in my home, and the office entrance was to the rear of the house. When the day came, I had forgotten about the appointment, so when the front door bell rang, I answered in my robe. I was as shocked to see my patients there as they were to see me in my robe. After a brief delay while I changed into street clothes, we proceeded with the session. At their next session, they both arrived in their robes, worn over clothes, and we had a hilarious laugh. This was a couple who normally had a heavy relationship with each other. The woman was just emerging from severe depression, and the man had strong blocks in his sexuality. The robe caper was a marker of a new lightness, and they were developing a signpost for continuing to enjoy their fun sides, too long in the background. In recognizing the deeper therapeutic factors so important and well known to therapists, it's also true that these fortuitous simple moments of contact happen even in so serious an experience as therapy. They should be given their merited endorsement.

Of course, therapy does create incisive focus well beyond ordinary engagement, and it is indeed serious business. It's not just small talk, a vehicle for being lightly together. It's important that it go beyond the casual; for the therapist, it's a judgment call as to the fertility of any specific simple talk. Nevertheless, the ordinary conversation is often an important introduction to the main event, perhaps even a major player. Here's the simple beginning of a session with Claudia, held as demonstration at a psychotherapy conference. She greeted me by telling me she was recovering from a cold and then went on to tell me about her experiences at a Colorado ski resort. She was chattering with me much as though she were talking to a girlfriend on the phone. I joked with her, wondering whether the cold made her nostalgic for her original home in Switzerland. None of this seemed like normal therapeutic style or content. My casual remarks implied I welcomed her to talk about whatever she wanted to. My casual reference to Switzerland showed up later in a significant storyline.

At this early point in the session, however, none of the coming story was evident. Claudia just went on talking about her skiing trip and the beauty of the mountain and the pleasure of the physical exercise, often with little guidance from me. Then she became aware of a sense of gratitude about her pleasure. She began to tell me about a lifetime of neutralizing her experiences. Then her next words showed her to be transcending her guilt about pleasure and success, and drinking them in. She said,

> It was just breathtaking. We were sitting on this chair lift in our group of learning-to-ski people. There was a young Dutch boy, and three of us were on this little lift and we were going up and I was going, "Oh, oh, oh." And we were all like, "Ooh. Oh." And we were looking around us, we were, you know, just in awe. And I said, "Isn't this incredible?" I felt almost, I don't know if I said guilty or like, do I deserve to feel this good? And she said, "This is how I want to be all the time."

I said lightly, "If that's up for election, I would vote for it."

> "That's right," Claudia continued, "This is how it should be all the time though."

Through this simple conversational exchange, Claudia's own exploratory process was facilitated. She built her story step by step, each step driving her forward. She went on to tell about her struggle with her mother, who had always blocked her pleasures. Especially, Claudia had made a momentous choice when she left a miserable marriage to marry a man in America, leaving her children behind. Now she has a happy marriage, and the children are doing well. Still, her mother dug into her with disapproval. After telling me about various ways her mother had blocked her pleasures, Claudia remembered a time when she returned to Switzerland on one of her frequent visits. She had arranged to pick up her daughter from school, but the plane was late and she called her mother to tell her there was a good chance she would not get there in time. After accusing Claudia of typical inconsideration, her mother begrudgingly agreed to pick up the child. Claudia did arrive on time, and her daughter greeted her gloriously, climbing all over her and very proudly giving her a pin she had made in school. Claudia said to me,

> Well, my mother had a heart attack, thinking "She gets a pin and she's not even here." It's like my mother just went mad. I mean completely mad because she remained in a bad marriage for me and my brother and my sister, and we don't give a shit about how she thinks and look what I've done and my kids are all over me. So she just, uh, I mean I didn't say anything. I just put my arm around my daughter. What can you say?

My acceptance of Claudia's light conversation was supported by my confidence in her basic purposiveness. She was not there to kill time. I simply was absorbed by each of her remarks and built on them through my interest in what her next thoughts would be. Sometimes I expressed this interest lightheartedly, sometimes seriously, but I was always hospitable to her storytelling. I offered personalized affirmation and minimal technical arousal for the flow of her mind. I believe that each part of the contact between us had a lubricating effect on the development of Claudia's storyline and on her realization of her freedom even in the face of her mother's disapproval.

In a continuing therapy one might also wonder, however, about the gender differences in leaving the family in the face of the children's interests, Claudia's means of staying in communication with her children, her overall relationship with her mother, and the quality of her life away from the family. Such guidance by the therapist is informed by ordinary human responses, by the professional's lifetime of experiences, her confidence in personal engagement, and a precedent of many trips through the landscape of living. Further, when the therapist is reflexively and continuingly interested, this interest will serve as an evocative reward to both parties in the engagement. Of course, one cannot take this fundamental pleasure totally at face value, for it is easy to distort, neglect, or overplay anything that in its right timing and proportion would otherwise be valid. This inner drive for connectedness is most dramatically experienced in times of great excitement, such as one might feel during a sonorous symphony or a deeply absorbing chant or cheering at a political rally. However, such experiences are also available in the sweep of ordinary living. The closer they come to the feeling of connectedness, the greater the defining sense of "we." Such unity sparks life, much as one log burning in the fireplace feeds off the others, which, isolated, would burn out.

Chapter 10

Contact boundary
Morality

We've now looked at the role of the contact boundary in the development of relationship. Next let us explore how contact and relationship are wedded to morality. The well-being of society is served by our understanding and influencing how people best live with each other. Morality is a guide, delineating the values that influence the way individual behavior can benefit the well-being of the community.

A key concern in the psychotherapy ethos is the clash between individual and communal interests. The concept of morality addresses the communal side of this controversy. Among many therapists, however, "morality" has a reputation for being excessively authoritarian, mistakenly insisting on certain behavior and imposing excessive punishment for disobedience. In the name of morality we often pigeon-hole people as cowards or careless or selfish, create guilt about sexuality, shame those with unpopular political positions, and demonize atheists. Excessive pressures like these have marked our human history. A fundamental responsibility of society, as well as of the Life Focus Groups, would be to recognize that these are complex issues. This recognition must be accompanied by education and the examples of parents and leaders, as well as a responsiveness to new understandings of human relationships. Easier said than done.

Mindful of the excesses and confusions about morality, most therapists have steered clear of telling people how they "should" behave. That being said, they have nevertheless created an ethos of distinct preferences. They foster empathy, listening with a welcoming mind, reciprocating good deeds, giving people the benefit of the doubt, telling stories honestly, and accepting responsibility. In spite of psychotherapy's wariness about the inculcation of behavior, the quiet truth is that many of psychotherapy's implicit moral preferences are quite evident.

Reflecting this insinuation of the psychotherapy ethos into society's moral positions, James Davison Hunter (2000) tells us about the paradoxically large impact of psychology, even within religious circles. He speaks of a "psychological regime," saying, "The vocabulary of the psychologist frames virtually all public discussion." While psychotherapy-influenced changes in morality are far from universally accepted, they are well known: loosened sexual prohibitions, lowered self-recrimination, heightened accessibility among races and classes, increased attention to personal self-determination, and freer interplay with established authority. These variations on the existing moral code have created a backlash in religious and political circles, where the loosening of familiar moral standards alarms many people.

Differences in content notwithstanding, it is clear that both psychotherapy and religious moral principles are charged with guiding relationships. If, for example, therapy leads a person to forgive a parent, this may not only be a resolution of this heretofore-alienated relationship, it can also raise the moral standing of forgiveness. If a patient stops badgering a spouse to go to church, that not only reduces friction in the household, it is a moral statement about freedom of choice.

Let us imagine the story of Alice and her husband, Franklin, who came to therapy because Alice caught him looking at computer porn. She became furious, feeling personally betrayed. From a problem-solving perspective, there may be many explorations of the context for each of their behaviors. Possibly, the porn was an isolated experience and does not have to interfere with their normal relationship. Possibly Franklin is addicted, watches porn at work, and is in danger of losing his job. Possibly Alice was unknowingly turning him away sexually. Possibly Franklin was expressing hostility indirectly. Possibly he likes to take the easy way to satisfaction. Possibly this, possibly that. Together, the therapist and the clients head toward an improvement in this troublesome relationship.

As the exploration evolves, Alice tells her therapist what she had never said before—that Franklin presses so hard against her when they are having sex that she feels invaded. Then she stiffens and becomes unresponsive. That is her practical response to feeling invaded. It is surely a relational mistake; she needs to discover a response that can lead to their finding a way to integrate their bodies, even in the face of his failure to do it well. What is relevant here is that she not only took the wrong relational step from a therapeutic standpoint, she also took the wrong moral step, rejecting rather than connecting. At the same time, from Franklin's position, he just finally gave up on her, let her stew in her own juice, and took the porn route. For him, turning to his computer instead of turning to Alice was not only a relational failure but also a moral one, from the point of view of a morality that frowns upon a passive and hurtful rejection of his most intimate relationship.

From a therapeutic perspective, morality is not the point and may even be a distraction from the problem-solving mission. It may shift attention from each of their own sharply felt personal interests to a broader, socially preferable standard. Suppose Franklin needs to rescue his individuality from the demands of marriage. That complicates his therapeutic agenda because he will have to integrate his need for freedom with his need for a better relationship with his wife.

Of course, morality may not always be so benign. Witness moral positions such as, "Don't get angry; get even," or "Keep a stiff upper lip," or "Never say die." All of these attitudes are crucial in the relational concerns of therapy, and they are also challenges for communal morality. That is, these behaviors not only carry implications for Alice and Franklin and their personal well-being but are important planks in a social system that strives for people at large to live well with each other—the realm of morality.

It is, of course, true that the therapeutic attention to each person's needs has been an effective therapeutic guideline. It has been practically useful as a vehicle for personal problem-solving, and this may justify selectively sidestepping the broader concerns of cultural standards. Private therapy is, after all, contractually arranged for the well-being of the individual client, especially when there have already been substantially harmful effects of strict moral codes. Therefore, even though the moral implications for the society are indivisible from the psychotherapeutic domain, therapists have understandably focused their energy on the practical mission of improving the lives of specific people.

If the experience of Alice and Franklin were to be presented to a Life Focus Group, the group explorations would tackle this story as a stimulus for each person to be free to develop their own reactions about the moral issues. A natural step, then, is to increase the resonance between what psychotherapy has learned about relationships and its relevance for the moral development of the society. This expansion of purpose must counter a historical wariness about the guilt created by violating moral generalizations. It may well be a sad reminder that a one-size-fits-all pathway to socially acceptable behavior is inherently booby-trapped, life being too untidy for social fixities.

These relational failures call for problem-solving, and they each also have moral overtones. From a therapeutic standpoint, however, morality is not the point and may even be a distraction. Therapeutic purposes notwithstanding, there are moral implications in failing to tell the truth, letting each other stew in their own juices, and distancing themselves from each other. When these individuated relational requirements are transformed into communal priorities about how people may best live with each other, we enter the realm of morality. When we consider optimal living in the communal world, we see other therapeutic issues in this illustration, which also are suggestive of morality: forgiveness of those who have erred, moderation of criticism of vulnerable people, filling in generously to make up for the weaknesses of family and friends, willingness to change one's characteristic behavior in the service of others, kindness to those in trouble, or considering one's effect on family unity. Clearly there are many avenues of convergence between Alice and Franklin's therapeutic problem solving and the possible morality of our culture.

Should we have "shoulds"?

The communal need for morality raises the question of whether we should have "should." The idea of telling people what they "should" do has a bad name in psychological circles. We know that many people will mindlessly obey authority and others will use authority as a base to control people's behavior. However, even though the establishment of a system of "shoulds" has had poor consequences for many people, "should" is an altogether natural phenomenon. It is an homage both to immediate and distant future, guiding much of what people do. Obviously, with some notable exceptions, most people "should" study in college if they want to be physicists; they "should" exercise if they want to increase their muscularity; they "should" respect other people's point of view if they want them to listen to theirs.

We also know that none of these "shoulds" is a *must*. To satisfy the standards for "should" is not the insistent requirement represented in the idea of *must*. It leaves an open space for perceptiveness, wisdom, experience, and humility. Thus, the need for good sense is unavoidable in the development of any but a robotic morality, which will inevitably bump up hard against the complexity of choice making. The "shoulds" of morality must provide a communal light for the unfolding demands of everyday living. Indeed, there will be loopholes and potholes in any system. Strict expectations are not impervious to contradictions between what one should do and what people can fit into their complex lives. For example, for a person to be strictly loyal to a family business would be troublesome to a person faced with a most exciting new job.

Let's look at a few examples of "shoulds" that would deserve recognition in a psychotherapy-driven morality. We as a society do not know everything we need to know about what people "should" do, but we do know a lot. And so do individual people. In the Life Focus Groups, issues of fairness, justice, compassion, dependability, dedication, sacrifice, and a whole range of potential "shoulds" are samples of the concerns that people face. In addressing such themes, the conversational exchanges provide personal storylines that reflect existing and potential forms of human morality, feeding experiences and perspectives into a *forming and viable morality*.

Here is a small sample of moral issues that would be addressed by such groups.

1. Looking anew at an old morality

Steve, a group member, is gay and grew up seeing this as a moral perversion. For him, the self-image of "disgusting sissy" was deeply implanted as a moral delinquency. In telling the group about it, Steve replays these feelings and breaks up his abstractions about his weakness and ineffectiveness with his own life details. He then affirms himself as a unique person, rising above this distorted self-image. He is sophisticated enough to know his self-image was distorted by an anti-gay morality. It's an old story for him; he knows he is not a freak. The knowledge becomes more real, though, as he tells his story and gives the rest of us details about his life. Not just once, but each time it comes up, he needs to remind himself that these stale abstractions are no longer the navigational coordinates of his existence.

While Steve is affirmed as a viable, desirable person and the group is moved to hear this happy ending after a tortured beginning, an enlivened morality also registers in them. Although his story is only a tiny contribution, like one person's vote in a national election, it registers as part of a cumulative understanding that forms society's morality. While this process starts with Steve's personal acceptability, it enters its perspectives into a growing social ethos about being homosexual. Such small steps create an evolution of morality, rebalancing existing perspectives on how people "should" behave.

2. Expressing and receiving gratitude

To feel gratitude is a greater part of the mutuality that colors our moral perspective than most people realize. We say "thank you" many times a day; most of the time honestly felt but so casual that it often goes unregistered. When, for example, I say, "thank you" to the waiter who just brought me a refill of my drink, I hardly think about it. Adding up the thousands of honestly felt "thank you's," however, reflects a mutuality that deserves recognition.

Other, more vital experiences call for stronger expressions of gratitude, but even these often receive inadequate attention. Some are lifelong contributions by parents, friends, employers, teachers, and physicians. They do things over and over that become part of everyday living. People are grateful when a friend smiles at them, for an insight from a teacher, or a helping hand from a doctor. Many people have no idea how important they've been to others. Only under special circumstances may some people reveal the key benefits they have received. These experiences become so much a part of the natural flow of events they're taken for granted, silently appreciated.

While it's true that there is plenty of room for improvement in expressing gratitude, to express gratitude may interfere with just living with it; letting it soak in and reciprocating with never a mention. Too much acknowledgment may upstage the naturalness of the act. For some people, to tell a friend years later about the importance of the walks they had together after a divorce may be better than to have been self-conscious about acknowledging the experience, explicitly, right then. Clearly, there is no formula for the best timing or frequency of expressing gratitude. Therefore, the institutionalization of opportunity serves a stimulating purpose, filling the gaps in everyday living. In Life Focus Groups, the design of meetings may invite recognition of both the everyday "thank you" and the highly significant experiences, memorializing them with communal affirmations, sometimes in the subgroup conversations, sometimes in song, sometimes in the recitation of a poem, and sometimes in the stories people tell when they have special reasons for gratitude. What is important is the reverberation between individual experiences of gratitude and communal recognition celebrated by the attention of the entire community. To savor each experience of gratitude every day, to be continually and consciously grateful, would upstage the spontaneous happenings for which we are, indeed, grateful.

3. Accepting moral dilemmas

Everyone faces the call for difficult moral judgments. For example, Arthur is about to go off to college when he is confronted with the sudden death of his father. Should he go on to college anyway and leave his mother and siblings to take care of themselves? Should he transfer to a local college? Should he get a job and delay going to college? Should he get married as he had intended to? Can he become self-educated while working to support the family? It's quite clear there is no systematic morality that can take full account of the practical and moral clashes that complicate Arthur's management of a vexing situation. Where no ironclad norms apply, the moral system should have room for a special empathy for the rightfully conflicted person.

4. The moral effect of key people

Our lives are dotted with people whose morality has influenced our own. Sometimes their morality is not spelled out, but just lived. A teacher who treats her students with respect is, without ever saying so, demonstrating her own brand of morality. A person who works when sick because his family needs the income; someone who smiles at you after you've made a mistake; an employee who stands up to a boss who is bullying a colleague: all are just living lives of a high-quality morality, not verbalized but reflected in their behaviors.

To acknowledge these nonverbal representations of morality by talking about them in the Life Focus Group accentuates nonverbal morality. This gives people a chance to frame moral guidelines and find a place for them within the group's sense of how we live with others. It offers the security of mutuality, and the free conversation also makes room for a diversity of perspectives.

Suppose, however, that one person's common way of behaving seems insulting to others. For him, this is just living honestly, and, in fact, many people accept his honesty knowing he is being more than insulting. Others would find this a flawed morality. Groups can assimilate such dissonance, within limits. If someone insults people frequently, a crisis of compatibility with the group may arise and require resolution. The group's morality may be able to live with the differences, or it may not. This struggle may be the engine for what becomes the new understanding, where exceptions to the common perspective are usually, but not always, assimilated.

5. *Righting a wrong*

Suppose I spoke to a friend about someone we both knew who was driven to suicide by his parents' cruelty. It was just a conversational recognition of something that happened years ago, but I failed to take into account that my friend's son had just committed suicide. I cringe to think of what I said. It was not immoral, rather quite accidental. Nevertheless, the potential harm was done, and I did it. What moral issue am I facing? Do I apologize and explain that there was no connection implied? Do I just ignore it and let the coincidence slide by in a continuing relationship? Do I ignore it but make sure my friend knows of my high regard for him; perhaps a special invitation to some event, perhaps a gift with the motives for the gift not apparent, or perhaps more frequent phone calls? Perhaps. Perhaps. What is clear in full moral flavor is that I owe some form of restitution for the wound I may have created. A scenario like this will evoke many stories from people in the Life Focus Groups, giving them a chance to air out some of their own relational gaffes.

6. *Biting the hand that feeds you*

Another option for group demonstrations is to set up a panel of participants to give their perspectives on a particular interpersonal issue. The panelists could be those dealing with the issue, or they could role-play characters with a delineated problem. An example would be the plight of a very religious person. Dave, in a state of futility, is psychologically and economically rescued by a lesbian woman, Arlene. When they met, Dave felt like the world was closing in on him. He was a bright man and a good worker, who helped Arlene take care of the grounds around her house. Arlene felt him to be a good person and was touched by his sorrow. She provided him and his wife a living space in her adjacent house and, later, advanced him some money to put down on the purchase of his own home. Then Dave's marriage broke up. His wife left, and Arlene continued to be supportive. After a mutually warm and considerate relationship, for an extended period, Dave began to shun her. She sensed this and, after a while she no longer would let the issue be set aside. She rightly assumed it was because he could no longer look away from her being a lesbian. He had known this from the beginning, but as long as it never came up, they had gotten along fine.

When Arlene confronted Dave with this change in behavior, he denied it, but as the conversation went on, he told her that he thought she was a sinner, and that we were all sinners, after all. She was wounded not only by his judgmentalism but also by his treating her as "a category" rather than the individual she had always been with him. Dave was dumbstruck. Her indignation immobilized him, and he lamely tried to explain that his view of *all of us* as sinners exonerates him from having been offensive. But she felt violated. She tried to get him to understand why she would feel that way, but the relationship ended when he could not change his own sloganistic notion of sinner.

What Dave failed to understand was the difference between the generic human sinner he felt himself and everyone to be and his designation of her as a lesbian sinner. One can argue the question of sinner-ness, but in his case it only camouflages the inaccessibility his fixed moral position puts him in. This conversation with Arlene was not an anthropological discussion about the nature of humankind, sinner or not. He just could not understand the fact that he was making a personal moral judgment of disapproval or the feelings he had aroused and instead fell back on religious slogans.

One could ask why Arlene cannot understand Dave's fixed position. But in a panel discussion, there is no way to know where the discussion will go. Wherever it goes, it will help clarify the way we make judgments and the way we camouflage them, a good starting point for developing a new openness to the experiences of others.

The leaders would play a guiding role in the panel's dialogue, with conclusions being drawn that would be relevant to the lives of many people in the group as a whole. One example of a moral conclusion, hardly the only one, is that if there is a common rule, such as "We are all sinners," such a rule can disregard the needs of individuals with different mindsets. To loosen up categories such as "sinner" may reflect "moral relativity," and it is a part of morality to take a stand on relativity. Unfortunately, moral relativity is often equated with a loose morality bordering on no morality. But it is valid to see moral relativity as grounded on *commonly held basics*, which leave room for a necessary openness to all people, and that common guidance can have variable individual applications. Devotion, sensitivity for the needs of others, appreciation of life experiences as they unfold, recognition of how people may be dissatisfied with these life experiences—all are part of the ethos, call it morality, which would be prominent in these Life Focus Groups. These are only the beginnings of the huge range of psychological issues that ordinary people face every day and are the subject matter of psychological literature. In these meetings, one or more of these principles and perspectives can be portrayed through lectures, poetry, and music and accompanied by opportunities to play out the implications for creating a general morality, the principles guiding anyone's actual life.

7. *Responsibility for one's own behavior*

Suppose you always leave conversations abruptly, come late for appointments, don't send Christmas messages, dominate conversations, and don't return calls. All of these are just part of your normal behavior. You are unaware of any disregard for those who are the recipients of your habitual neglect of normal kindnesses. Are these merely peculiarities of yours with no moral implication, or are they moral deficiencies? You've never even thought about it until one day someone brings it up. Though surprised, you begin to wonder about the morality of your repeated disregard for mutuality.

The need to be idiosyncratic, according to the dictates of your own personal way of life, is foundational to you. But questions pop up. Do you believe that you owe people more personal consideration than you are accustomed to giving? While you have a right to your idiosyncrasies, do you get a free pass vis-à-vis others? Do you want to change your ways to synchronize with others, or do you prefer to continue to live as you already authentically do and take your chances with the world around you? Might you feel more satisfied with your moral character if you recognize how much more responsively you behave in many other situations: you help your students well beyond your professional obligation; you give money anonymously to support important community services; you make breakfast so your wife can sleep late; you pick up your neighbor's kids when they have conflicting commitments?

Thematically framed conversations in Life Focus Groups can cover the complexity of people's moral concerns. Rather than offer authoritarian or indoctrination, these relational messages can tap the diversity of individuated styles. Unanimity of perspective is not expected, and group continuity provides a developmental sense of lessons learned. The recurrent messages over time, more or less integrated, can replace the fast track of moral clarity, as we live with differences in circumstance and values. So our relational messages can energize a creative evolution of the community's perspective, providing a human scale to moral consciousness.

Moral relativity

What is evident is the interface between moral relativity and moral absolutism. To incorporate moral relativity, so basic to the psychotherapy ethos, is a daunting objective, because absolutist morality has a strong foothold in the public mind, which has been dominated by sharp definitions of acceptable behavior. A lie is a lie; cheating on your spouse is cheating on your spouse; being late is being late; no ifs, ands, or buts. The raw truth is that, while a sharp definition given by moral absolutism has its merits, there are equally important and innate reasons for moral relativism.

One reason is the existence of context, a fundamental reality. There is no choice about that, except as we may temporarily ignore this or that part of the context. No behavior occurs by itself. It is embedded in the world that houses it. Morality is no exception. There are societies where polygamy is morally acceptable. Killing in a wartime battle is morally acceptable. Missing a meeting to take care of a parent's health emergency is morally acceptable. It may be morally acceptable to be a whistleblower or to take a planned vacation instead of going to a friend's wedding. Context interferes with absolutism.

A second important factor is *proportion*. Just as the number 2 has a proportional relationship to the number 4, stealing bread has a proportional relationship to murder. Absolutist thinking must take its place with the equally imperative awareness of *proportion*. For example, a man on his deathbed, to satisfy an absolutist principle of honesty, tells his wife the full truth: he has been seeing another woman for the last 10 years. How does this square morally with the importance of compassion for his wife, who suffers from the confession? For him, the need for truthfulness seemed more important than his wife's well-being. Which principle has greater importance: his absolutist need for honesty or his wife's need for a harmonious ending? There is no one answer, but there is some social momentum toward moral relativity. The proportionality of his need for truthfulness on his deathbed and the quality of her continuing life could weigh heavily in favor of his keeping his mouth shut.

There is no absolute blueprint for how people should live their lives. In spite of the widespread belief in moral absolutism, people exercise moral relativity, not as a cop-out from the severity of absolutism but because they have a sense of proportion about what matters. We readily cheer movie heroes who have temporarily gone bad. Those who are appalled about moral relativity because of its ambiguity fail to notice that they make relative choices all the time.

Because of the flexibility of such standards, many people, however, believe moral relativity is a weak foundation for a moral society. Worse, moral relativity is often mistakenly seen as the *absence* of morality. Critics say that society cannot live with approximate perspectives on relational basics. Actually we do so every day. We are hospitable with one another, even when our views conflict. We keep our appointments, even when other compelling interests call. We let gauche remarks pass by without rancor.

Perhaps such loose standards are less supportable when we are addressing issues with larger social consequences, like getting drunk in a bar when you are supposed to be home, getting money on false pretenses, or spreading vicious rumors. The standards within any community—whether a Life Focus Group, a neighborhood, or a nation—may be quite strict, as needed, but they may also be lenient when circumstances warrant. Murder, rape, extortion, racism, slander, and other morally abhorrent behaviors are so toxic that law prohibits them. But these gross moral violations, which arouse our strongest absolutist need for prevention, must not justify a decisive vote for absolutism.

The option of creative judgment is not just an excuse for social violation. It is recognition of actual circumstances and a developmental process. Each age contributes public attention to this process, usually without intent and quite often a quiet testament to the nature of social evolution. Still, because of the inescapable complexity of moral relativity, the management of it is a challenge to the society's aggregate skill. It is also laced with power struggles among people who wish to establish their own sense of morality. Though there is no Utopia, psychotherapy's methods have been grounded in the idea that you can help correct for mistaken context and proportion. These opportunities for exploring the make-up of our morality are a natural accompaniment to psychological explorations. Within the Life Focus Groups, the accentuation of primary life themes is the vehicle for examining both individuality and the common stream of communal well-being.

In conclusion, clear moral standards must be joined by proportion and context. We can eliminate proportion and context only by ignoring it. This fundamental is always lurking in the background ready to incorporate existing circumstance. If, for example, your child violates morality by skipping school and you find out about it, you might not even want to mention it. That does not mean it is okay to miss school. Perhaps you quietly recognize your child needs some disobedience or daring and that a mild transgression is not likely to turn into a major problem. With other children that would not be the case, and some serious talk and mutual strategizing about how to solve the problem may well be in order, perhaps including one or another form of punishment.

We might wonder how a society, in the face of people making their own personal judgments, can tolerate an indeterminate set of standards. Of course, that is an important concern. The judgments of moral relativity are not casual, however. They are part of a communal evolution where people's individual minds play off each other over time. They are not casual judgments but the result of the marination of ideas and feelings as they evolve in the communal mind.

A mysterious consensus is created in this fluid process. It's like basic chemistry; disparate elements come together in an identifiable union, and, for example, hydrogen and oxygen become water.

Chapter 11

Polarities
Self-formation

Carl Sandburg, the American poet, writes about the wolf in himself—the hog also, and the baboon. Then he goes on to say:

> I got a zoo, I got a menagerie, inside my ribs, under my bony head, under my red-valve heart and I got something else: it is a man-child heart, a woman-child heart: it is a father and mother and lover: it came from God Knows Where: it is going to God-Knows-Where—For I am the keeper of the zoo: I say yes and no: I sing and kill and work: I am a pal of the world: I came from the wilderness. ("Wilderness" from *Cornhuskers* [1918])

With all such characters living inside every person, working with any individual, the therapist is doing a form of group therapy. Through speech and behavior, each part of the person gives clues to its existence. The therapist must guide the individual in identifying these parts, letting them speak clearly for themselves, and finding a place for each part in the community of the self. To feel whole in the presence of such internal diversity is a big challenge in the life of anyone. At the same time, the inaccessibility of certain parts for inclusion into the whole is a potential source of disturbance.

This recognition of the integrative requirements of divided personhood was highlighted by Frederick Perls, who emphasized the polar aspects of our lives. He gave major attention to the split represented in his concept of a topdog/underdog split, a key aspect of his early work. For Perls, the topdog was a tyrannical part of a person, the one who dictated how we "should" behave. The underdog sabotaged these admonitions with its own oppositional tricks for not accomplishing these supposedly indispensable behaviors. The key was to integrate the two sides with each other. Instead of the rank dismissal of either part by the other, integration would replace dissonance.

Topdog and underdog are not the only splits in a person. We hold many opposites, like cruelty and kindness, boldness and timidity, and grandiosity and humility. These are also more subtle dualities, all of which contribute to the total behavior. These *multilarities*, representing the many sides of the individual, are present in clusters of potential experience, rather than just in polarities. A peace advocate, for example, might be troubled not only by her polar anger—against an opponent of her views—but also by her need to spend more time at home, by her distaste for many of her associates in the peace movement, by her cynicism, by the frustrations of failure, and even by people commenting on the mole on her upper lip. These elements of her many-sidedness may be as disharmonious with her work in the peace movement as the simple polar opposite. Indeed, it is a primary function of the human brain to pit together into a coherent unity that which might otherwise lie fallow—isolated and dysfunctional.

When looking at polarities or multilarities, the therapist's assumption is that those parts that are disharmonious have poor or little contact with each other, existing instead as segregated elements. This anthropomorphic statement about personality characteristics is not alien to human descriptions. It offers the parts an understandable voice. This brings us to the concept of the empty chair, which invites actual dialogue among these animated parts of a person. As the communication between these "characters" evolves, they are guided to a sharper and more responsive contact, and the parts become better positioned to experience each other in a new light.

A woman named Caroline felt tortured by her indecision about having a baby, and her suffering grew greater with each tick of the biological clock. There were (at least) two sides of her—one wanting a child, the other opposed. These sides, personified in a therapeutically guided dialogue, each had stereotyped attitudes about themselves and about the other side. At the start, their positions were so fixed that a fresh dialogue seemed unlikely. The one who did not want the child was the dominant one, although not so dominant that she had won out. In spite of not having been able to settle the issue, she was certain she was right, and she could eloquently spell out exactly why she didn't want a baby. Her life was going well and she didn't want it disrupted by the needs of a child. She was also convinced that at the age of 35 she ran great risks giving birth, and to add to the burden, her brother had congenital heart troubles, a condition she feared passing on to her baby.

At no time in Caroline's opening statements did this side take into account the needs of the other, whom she saw only as weak, and she got away with it because the side that wanted a child was intimidated and could not think well in the face of the dominating onslaught. She was reduced, not to outright crying, but to dripping from her eyes—a passive, defeated shell. The supposedly superior side maintained her position only by ignoring the sabotaging influence of the side who wanted a baby.

This supposedly weaker side would not, however, give up. That side felt she had little basis for argument, but she did manage to whine her way to a standoff. Whimperingly she would allude to the feeling—sentimentalized—that she might be missing the special pleasures of parenthood, without which there could be no personal maturity. Although she said she wanted a baby, she communicated no strong sense of personal loss. Her feelings seemed like those of a person who has been defeated.

After several exchanges in the dialogue, the side wanting the baby became more clearly aware of her feeling of futility. Then it hit her that she was not saying the things she wanted to say. She proceeded to attack, eloquently pointing out the narcissism of the part that didn't want the baby, pinpointing her cowardly and unnecessary fears, and accusing her of closing her mind to any experiences she could not fully control. At this point, she began to get through. By the time the two sides were finished, they were having a conversation worthy of equals—not a resolution yet, but a sense of one side toughening up to a position of validity and the other softening to a position of warmth. Then, with each side more respectful of the other, Caroline developed a curious freedom about her relationship to babies. When she saw a mother and child wrangling in a supermarket, she was relieved she did not have a baby. But this relief did not mean she *could not* have a baby. On the other side, when she visited her brother's home she played with her infant niece happily for the first time, but she realized this did not mean she *had* to have a baby.

This newfound internal harmony greatly relieved the pressure, but she was not ready for a decision. Then, following this experience, a breakthrough came on another front—perhaps coincidentally, perhaps as a result of her new openness. Her perfectionistic attitudes had also stymied her in her job, where she had been wavering on a crucial but difficult research project. After her mind became loosened in the baby dialogue, she soared on this project and is now practically finished. The question of having a baby was not yet answered, but the change in self-regard could be contagious. New learnings in one arena commonly cross over to provide beneficial effects in others.

Internal dialogue

In creating a dialogue among parts of a person, the prime task is to improve the quality of the contact. The parts, alienated, will not, at first, talk straight with each other. They both know the script but don't know how to change it. They simply play their roles as they have become familiar. Only with a meeting of the minds can each side become valuable to the other, beginning to meet the other's needs.

The reason these alienated parts have become masters of misconnection is that they are afraid they will be harmfully influenced by the other part. And there's plenty to be afraid of. If you don't like to fight, for example, and you talk to the part of you that wants to join a gang, you are in danger. If you're deeply religious, you will shun the atheistic side of you. If you have strong sexual prohibitions, you will be frightened by sexual arousal. The therapist, counteracting these impasses, must recognize the strategies that impede dialogue, such as digression, stonewalling, failing to object when objections are called for, misunderstanding what is being said, or flavorless reactions. Once making connections, the patient may find it exciting to be aggressive, though not necessarily joining a gang. Or the patient may discover a broadened view of religion, though not necessarily going to the extreme of atheism. Or the patient may yield to sexuality without becoming wanton or vulgar. Each part in the dialogue risks taking on aspects of the other. Whereas these parts may have seemed incompatible in the beginning, there are actually fewer incompatibilities than one may had supposed.

Closer to everyday experience, we see these fears represented in the assiduous attention many parents give to their children's selection of friends. If the parents worry about what their children may pick up from certain contacts—drugs, diseases, or antisocial values—they will be wary and upset about some of their kid's contacts. At the same time, young people's lives are broadened and enriched by contact with customs and habits different from their own. Discerning perception is required on the part of both parent and child to distinguish dangerous threats, like drugs, from insignificant ones that may be related to snobbishness, like having friends who eat salami rather that pate.

The greatest sense of danger comes when positions are polarized. Love and hate seem prohibitively antithetical when in their extreme forms—such as lifelong, dedicated commitment versus the wish to murder. Reducing the burden of this contradiction helps make each more accessible. Smiling, for example, does not require undue commitment, and grimacing does not lead to murder. When people incorrectly read intense love and hate into milder feelings, dialogue can help them to make the necessary discrimination.

Inter-relational dialogue

Of course, the need for dialogue is not just among internal aspects of the self. It is also with the world at large. We each need to communicate with many external characters. Some key characters may not be available, such as those who have died, and to a lesser extent people who have moved, those who no longer seem interesting, friends from another time, people met in passing, or even a stranger who bumped you hard in a crowd. Although continued relationship is no longer available, these people may be valid targets for leftover communication. You may, for example, feel that you should have shoved back when the unknown person bumped you and may need to "say something" to that person. With some people who *are* still available, external dialogue could be just too difficult—you might not want to confront an 85-year-old mother who ignored you when you needed her, or a touchy colleague, friend, or boss.

When unfinished communication exists, the relevant outside person can be imagined into availability by seating him or her in the "empty chair." The patient speaks to the chair as though the other person were actually sitting in it.

This option has powerful leverage, broadening the range of people with whom patients can communicate directly in a therapy session.

Novelists constantly provide themselves this opportunity, creating characters in their mind's eye and expanding tension as the characters develop. However, while the novelist's imagined character may have no clear connection to the novelist's actual world, in therapy the person in the empty chair is clearly representing someone with whom the patient has unfinished business.

The imagined presence was put to use in a session with Janine. Janine hated men. She had plenty of reasons. After having been left by her father in childhood and raped in adolescence, she was married to a man she thought was a "horse's ass." In recent years, she had walled herself off from men, because for her there was no middle ground between loving them too much and cutting them out of her life. Nevertheless, she had no problem with me, seeing me more as an exception than a member of the male sex. If she had found me to be one of "them," she would have had the direct opportunity to face one of the hated human beings. Because I was not one of "them," the empty chair gave her a chance to try herself out with man-at-large. I asked her to imagine that the collective "man" was sitting in the chair. She started by vigorously moving the chair backward, setting the distance she wanted. Then she went on to say what she had already told me, "I think most of you are assholes, collectively. Collectively, you treat women pretty shitty."

That was a strong beginning, but the same old words. More substance was needed. The advantage of using the empty chair is that the "man" does not register hurt and walk out. The empty chair exercise allowed Janine to experience her power and her anger, where otherwise both would have remained diluted. The playing out of drama helps us get to the bare bones of any particular experience.

Then, wanting to add substance and unpredictability to the conversation, I asked Janine to sit in the other chair and become the collective man. She expressed dismay and said I was pushing her boundaries pretty hard. I assumed she felt as though she had been asked to join the enemy camp, but I only wanted the conversation to be more palpable. In spite of her reservations, Janine took the other chair. As the collective man, she told Janine, "We only do what you let us get away with." That was a point she hadn't brought up before, so the conversation was getting fresher. Then she returned to her chair and replied, "We don't have your birthright," by which she meant male privilege. She was ready to let it go at that, but the implication of an unfair advantage which women might never overcome required elaboration. I said she seemed to have more to say. So she went on, "You're born with a power that we don't have when we're born, and it takes us a long time to get it. You make damn sure you don't give up much of it either." Now she had gotten across not only men's cultural advantage, but their greed in hanging onto power. She was also making sure men would feel responsible for their greed.

It's apparent that I guided Janine to a more specific dialogue than she might otherwise have created. Like any writer or editor, I had decided the dialogue needed something that she was not giving it. When she did give it more, the additional words fleshed out her introductory statement, which was, "men are collectively assholes" and roused her to a more incisive sense of herself.

Then I asked Janine to move back into the chair of the collective man. When she didn't seem to have anything further to say, I asked her, "What do you, as the collective man, think of Janine's words?" She said, "We can't help it. If we're born with it, we can't help it." This was a lame response, but it was not necessary at this point for the villain to have his best answers available. There was not enough there to deny his arrogance and disregard, which fit Janine's view of the collective man.

She moved back to her own chair and said with a certain sour recognition, "Why should you want to help it?" Then in his chair she said, "We shouldn't want to help it. What did I ever do to you?" In an actual encounter, she might have acceded to this disavowal of responsibility by men, who with easy dismissal would have made her feel she didn't have a leg to stand on. But internally she would have seethed. In the free environment, where her own authorship reigned, she felt bold enough to say, "Just about everything there was to do to me." Again, good editing required her to specify, so I said, "Chapter and verse." "My father, the guy who raped me when I was 16," she went on, "the asshole that I married, who beat me up all the way." Then she said to me, "I don't think he wants to talk about that," gleeful to have cornered these men and their evasive techniques.

This dialogue was a significant advance for Janine. Still, I asked her to find out whether he did want to talk about it and then to move into the other chair and see what he had to say. He said, "I'm really sorry. I didn't do any of those things." She moved back to her own chair and stuck to her guns, saying, "Yes you did!" Seeing her jaw firm up, I asked whether she could feel the sensations in her face. This was important because the feelings would add a sense of reality to her words. She could. I suggested she let those feelings be a part of what she would say. As she concentrated on the feelings in her chin, the words aroused were, "I'd like to punch you out. But I'm tired of being angry."

At this point Janine diverted her eyes from the collective man and looked at me. I directed her back. When she addressed him straight on, it became clear what she had been avoiding. She started to cry, saying in despair, "This is what I guessed. I don't want to cry." I explained that this crying was part of her hurt and accentuated the reality of it. She could go on anyway. But she felt stopped. Because she needed some backing, I asked, "Do your tears stop you from telling him how pissed you are? Speak even though you're crying, even though you're pissed."

We are at a crucial point. At the very moment of experiencing her possibility for expressing herself deeply, she faced the dreaded contradiction between being strong, on the one hand, and crying, which to her meant weakness. She had to find out that she could cry and still have her strength and validity. It would become a wet strength rather than the dry and mechanical strength she saw in men. Then she said, "None of you are ever going to do it to me again. I know that. I know how not to be your victim anymore. And I have as much power as you do." There was no question that she meant every word of it and that she was no longer speaking from a position of weakness or defeat. By this time, her tears no longer felt weak, even to her. But after her harsh words, she felt sad. Even though she didn't want to remain alienated, she was afraid to give up her anger. It seemed to be her protector. Once she recognized she did not, in fact, feel vulnerable, even while sad, she was able to joke and laugh with confidence and the "collective man" disappeared.

Personal essence

So far, we've been looking at an individual who has a variety of characteristics and who expresses these characteristics in relation to the world outside. Now we come to the concept of the "self." First, we must establish the distinction between this world-directed, actual person and the concept of the self. The is a muddy distinction to make. This word "self" is often used as a reference to the person, as in saying, "I did it myself." In this sense the person and the self are the same. But the concept of self also plays an organizational role.

We began by highlighting the multiplicity of personal characteristics we all live with. Now we must address the need to look at the self from the standpoint of *personal identity*. Having a unified recognition of who we are brings us to the identity component of the self. This sense of self can be a vital link to the quality of our existence. Ninety years ago, the one-eyed, pipe-smoking American cartoon strip character Popeye the Sailor Man caught the hearts of a huge readership with the words, "I am what I am, I'm Popeye the sailor man." The unadorned self-respect of this peculiar man always knew who he was and charmed generations of moviegoers and comic strip fans. What's notable about the popularity of Popeye's theme song is that it only mirrors what everyone is already guaranteed—to be what they are. Being who you are is one of the great tautologies, as assured as daytime at noon. There is, after all, nothing else to be.

The catch is that to *be*, which is assured, is different from *knowing,* and it is on this ground that the concept of self enters into the search for personal essence. We recognize characteristics that are representative of who we are to satisfy the need to know who we are. But in the face of a huge variety of experiences, this search for personal identity is an ambitious project. Whether you know what your experiences tell you about your essence is not assured. The best you can do is sense a reality of self that fits best with what you do and feel. To know who you are is to face contradiction. Still, elusive as the self is, searching for it remains compelling. It is represented in the well-known Greek adage, "know thy self so that you may depart in knowledge, wisdom, and love." People through the ages have yearned wistfully to have the answer.

So popular is this wish today that the concept of the self may be the contemporary successor to the venerable "soul" and the more recent construction, the "unconscious." For centuries, the soul served as a guide, designating an individual's essence, as well as representing a person's eternal existence. The unconscious, on the other hand, has been less ambitious, serving as an illumination about unaware influences in how we live our lives. But soul and unconscious both have major shortcomings; each concept is short on clarifying the nature of the person. The soul is nebulous, bypassing the actual nature of the specific person and requiring a mystical trust, which does not usually describe worldly behaviors. The unconscious, on the other hand, *is* specific to each person, offering an unaware but functional directedness of behavior. That functionality is evident, for example, when a person is influenced unconsciously to have catastrophic expectations about troublesome daily activities. The soul, more mystical and general than the unconscious, intones a personal essence, offering a reassuring belief about what we *really* are. The soul seems disembodied and yet eternal. People oriented to their souls try to live as the soul directs them, but the soul does not speak clearly and the interpretations of its mission can be diffuse.

People nowadays do not talk much about souls. Almost none of my patients bring it up. Still, the soul has an indefinable but dear sense of the human spirit. Historically, it has been a great force in people's attempts to understand their deepest natures. It is a lyrical and benevolent representation of our elusive sense of what we are really like.

For a century, the unconscious has largely replaced the soul as a conceptual orientation to what we really are. It does not have the soul's value implications. Instead it has a no-holds-barred dynamic where the id, ego, and superego wrestle for dominion. The unconscious has been far more fruitful than "soul" in explaining otherwise incomprehensible experiences and has been compelling as a source of impelling energy. But it has also been a source of separation between what the person knows about herself and what remains hidden in the unconscious. Though more experience-rooted than the soul, the unconscious maintains only a ghostly link to surface experience and is directed by cryptic motives buried in unreachable filing systems. The unconscious so often contradicts the surface of existence that it becomes easier than ever to be confused about who we *really* are. Popeye would have no part of such complexity.

The self is instead a source of personal guidance and enlightenment. It is faced with the challenge of integrating the variety of life experiences. I may be aggressive, I may be kind, I may be ambitious, I may be facetious, I may be philosophical. How does all this enter into my identity? To summarize these experiences is a daunting need, which we try to do when we create eulogies or classify historical events. People live every day, working, dreaming, expecting, always trying to fit into the world. One may have been a singer who brought happiness to millions or a storyteller who kids listened to with rapt attention. These illuminating summations of a person's existence are keys to self-knowledge, honoring a central part of one's life's repertoire. They keep tabs on what anyone's life is or was about. They are good summations, measuring up to the adage to know thyself. But they are far from the whole story.

Point/counterpoint

The concept of self addresses the interplay among whatever aspects of the person come into focus, crossing the line between surface experience and depth. This interplay takes surface experience at face value, not simply as a substitute for what is obscured. There is no "real" self, hidden by surface experience, but rather a community of selves that vie for ascendancy. An intellectual man, for example, feeling unhappily caught in a studious way of life, gets fed up and says his "real" self is a gardener. Not so. In terms of the interplay among his options, he is talking about two of his selves—the intellectual self and the gardener self—each with its own character.

Therapists considering the population of selves that I propose can learn a lesson from music, where point/counterpoint interaction is a familiar compositional factor. In point/counterpoint, independent musical voices are set against one another. Some are complementary, others dissonant, but all contribute to the integrity and richness of the entire piece of music. In a culture where harmony in music, as in other things, is frequently considered the ideal, anything short of a smooth blending of voices can seem like a blemish that distracts attention. Yet, as musicologist Arthur Bullivant (1983, p. 501) says, "There is no fundamental reason why contrapuntal music should be more difficult to appreciate than harmonic, and the listener who is prepared to forget past prejudices will find the experience infinitely rewarding."

So it is that the self, composed of many voices, harmonious or dissonant, invites the listeners—therapists and patients—to embrace variety and create the unity that lies beneath the complexity of human experience. That some of a person's selves are obscured from attention does not mean that they are more or less real than the manifested self. It means that these selves need to be coordinated with each other. Though these obscured selves may seem close in concept to the unconscious, they are not the same. Each self has an identity of its own, rather than a substitutive role in the person's makeup.

For example, it has been easy for therapists guided by the concept of the unconscious to say that a person who indicates love for his mother "really" hates her in his unconscious mind. What I am proposing, in contrast, is that the selves in the background are counterpoint voices and the aim of wholeness is to honor these voices, each with its own merits. Classes of self, like the intellectual self and the surfer self, are usually recognized by directly observable experiences. They are more easily fleshed out than the misty characterizations of soul and unconscious. These classes of self may be formed by the most intense experiences, like being screamed at or worshipped by one's mother, or by defining statements like, "Whenever the chips are down, you leave." These are shorthand identifications of clusters of actual experiences. Through the naming process, a person may be identified in innumerable forms: an iconoclast, a robber, a singer, a coward, or a noble person. At some point, as the significance of these characteristics evolves, these classes of experience may merit designation as selves.

Let's look at how many different ways we can organize these experiences into selves with which we may identify. At its highest sweep, the self-integrates the events of a lifetime. An epitaph is one example. "Here lies Eric, friend to all; all ways and always." For those who knew Eric, this self-designation may be a fitting summary, and it may even be evocative of many stories in Eric's life. But this epitaph does not encompass the breadth of his life. Eric survived a fall into one of Venice's slippery and polluted canals. He played practical jokes on whoever he thought would sit still for them. He daydreamed whenever he could.

Yet, even though everyone's life has comparable breadth, many people search for a unifying summary of their existence. Joaquim Machado de Assis (1990), a nineteenth-century novelist, recognized this minimalist yearning for one self, the self, when he wrote: "Among civilized people [epitaphs] are an expression of a secret... egoism that leads men... to rescue from death at least a shred of the soul that has passed on" (p. 202).

The urge to rescue a shred of their souls, a fragment that will register their existence, makes many of our patients feel compelled to spend their lives reaching for hints of their true proportions within what they fear is a shapeless existence. Because shapelessness is often seen as fractured identity, they may give their sense of self a premature shape, falling for flawed summations and getting stuck in identification with them. Often they have no idea what's wrong because they don't realize how they have summed themselves up. The concept of the self not only helps recognize this problem but also gives guidance for continuously reconstructing our summary of ourselves.

Even in contrast to the multiform nature of the self, the notion of a single image of who we are remains attractive. In 1994 the *New York Times* reported on a poll in which 1,136 people were asked to say who they are, in one word. Jesse Jackson said he was "somebody." Martina Navratilova said she was "kind." Mario Cuomo called himself a "participant." Margaret Atwood said she was "indescribable." Michael Kinsley said it was a stupid question. Although the *Times* writer recognized the scientific limits of the poll, he believed it "provides a compelling sociological snapshot"

(Barron, 1994). For some people this search for an easy sense of identity is nothing more than grieving over an ancient fragment of themselves. Others try to harmonize their behavior with their most desired qualities.

We see this quest all the time in therapy. Here are two stanzas of a poem written by one of my patients:

> She looked through the veil she had woven
> From threads of her everyday life
> Forming scaffolds she willingly clung to
> In the attempt to reach paradise
> But too close was the weave and the pattern
> It allowed not a breath to escape
> So it caused her to spin in confusion
> And she landed... somewhere... out there in space.

At what threshold do elemental experiences, the "threads of everyday life," qualify as ingredients in the formation of self? A sly remark, a dog growling menacingly, a toy broken, a teacher's smile for a perfect answer, or witnessing an auto accident? Experiences like these can be so transitory or their meanings so blurred or neutralized that they fly below the radar and are not part of our self-formation. Stronger experiences are more likely to register: early brutalization by bullies, marvelous storytelling by an uncle, annual trips to a vacationland, being often told you're lazy, brilliant, mischievous, or rebellious. The therapeutic challenge is to get a fresh view of these incremental influences, which could then coalesce into a new sense of self. But lowering the threshold for new and therapeutic self-formations is difficult when the patient's mind is already made up about what counts.

For example, a patient comes in depressed. His wife left him, and the divorce settlement leaves him feeling financially destitute. Because of economic downturns, his business is slowly going bankrupt. In his mind, he *is* his marriage, his business, his financial predicament. Since his favorite ingredients of self-definition are gone, he no longer knows who he is, perhaps doesn't even care. The fact that he is brilliant, affable, enduring, and kind recedes far into the background. His addiction to the existing self criteria must be dissolved. Therapy must reengage and reconfigure both his sorrows and the multiplicities of his self-possibilities.

Dangers of the classified self

Self-formation must overcome the stagnancy of classification. When we speak, for example, of a "gullible self," as opposed to a person being gullible, we tap into the famous existentialist differentiation between essence and existence.

Essence represents what people characteristically *are*, a parent or a carpenter, compassionate or exploratory. *Existence* refers to actual experience—individualized, unlimited, released from defining classifications. As Rollo May pointed out, existentialism derived its name and its character through its reaction against the Western concern with people's essences. People were cavalierly classified and cataloged (May, Angel, & Ellenberger, 1958). To be defined by one's nationality, family membership, sexual or racial identity, chosen organizations, IQ, career skills, and the like is alien to the boundary-expanding options our culture has come to insist on. The self, therefore, as an enduring classification of one's characteristics, might constrain this need for freedom.

But our patients do suffer from this threat. They are already stuck with narrow classifications of their nature. A primary aim of psychotherapy is to release them from what they already experience as the givens of their lives, to recognize flux in their environment and the versatility of their own powers. The release from these limiting classifications is not inherently a release from classification itself, but rather a call for new, fruitful classifications.

In the early days of existentialism, the restrictive forces of classification were especially evident. Jean-Paul Sartre inspired a revolt against assigning essence status to behavior as the defining factor in forming people's character. Proclaiming "man is nothing else but that which he makes himself" (Sartre, 1948, p. 28), he assigned to people the full and continuing responsibility as agents of their existence. His words were full of bravado and helped stamp personal freedom into the minds of many. But his aphorisms, catchy slogans taken out of context, came back to haunt him. He was misunderstood by people who were eager for philosophical release from constraint.

Sartre never meant his views to be taken as a dismissal of the enduring nature of identity. After the misunderstandings accumulated, he explained that existence precedes essence but does not replace it. Being what we are is joined with carving ourselves out. *Essence* grounds us as human beings who have enduring characteristics, but it's only a partner to the crucial factors of anyone's actual *experience*. But the genie of the primacy of existence was already out of the bottle, and his corrections didn't help much. Given the postwar reformulations of human possibilities and the widespread urge to jettison behavioral and attitudinal fixities, the increased fluidity of values challenged customs. The emphasis on existence rather than essence encouraged people to think they could do or be anything and that social concerns were less pointedly the concerns of individuals.

Fritz Perls, in spite of his innovative designation of enduring internal characters such as topdogs and underdogs, retained a strong anticlassification mindset. As part of this theoretical atmosphere, Gestalt therapy emphasized the action properties of the self. The view, in a nutshell, was that the self was a system of ever-fluid contacts, a process rather than a structure, a result of a continuum of engagement and awareness. As Perls and his colleagues (1951) said, "The self is not... a fixed institution; it exists wherever and whenever there is... interaction. To paraphrase Aristotle, when the thumb is pinched, the self exists in the painful thumb." (p. 373).

This was a key perspective honoring versatility of mind, but at the same time it ignored the self as an enduring composition of characteristics. Even though Perls and colleagues said that the self exists in the painful thumb, the infinite succession of all our experiences was still of greater interest than the abstract self. Misgivings about abstractions and a yearning for greater appreciation of the uniqueness of each experience permeated nonpsychology circles as well.

One of the many voices warning against the petrification that occurs in classifying experience was the novelist Joyce Cary (1961), who observed that if you tell a child the name of a bird, he loses the bird. The concern was warranted, but it's also apparent that there is an equal but opposite truth: If you know the name of the bird, its history, and its habits, you may get to know the bird better.

Given these opposite considerations—losing the bird and getting to know it better—it is evident that the principles that win out in any method, the ones that come to be a method's major theme, relegate counterpoints to the background. So the classification of experience—the naming of the bird—lost out temporarily to the simple actuality of the bird. Though this configurational counterpoint of classification could enrich the person's sense of self much like harmonic undercurrents deepen primary musical themes, many people could not integrate them. In music, as I've said, disparate voices can resonate simultaneously in the listener's ear, but the verbal mind easily narrows in on a main theme, avoiding contrapuntal intricacy.

Trying to live with the existential credo of personal freedom caused many therapists to give only background importance to the enduring and identifying characteristics in a person's life. My wife, Miriam, and I took a step toward the classificatory experience through our concept of the I-boundaries (Polster & Polster, 1974). Through this concept, we proposed that the quality of continuing experience was highest when the individual's range of acceptable self was not threatened by the prospective new experience. For example, if my sense of acceptable self does not include crying, anger, assertiveness, or submission, I will be careful not to engage with others in a way that might bring forth these behaviors; or if I do engage, it will likely be awkward and have reduced benefit.

We named and described some large classes—essences—of these I-boundaries: value boundaries, expressive boundaries, body boundaries, familiarity boundaries, and exposure boundaries. Each boundary delineated parameters of the self, of that sense of what it is to be "me." Within these boundaries, this feeling of being "me" was so compelling that to rend the boundaries would be disturbing. Thus we concluded that these boundaries comprised the range of experiences wherein each person's self was recognizable and acceptable.

Yet, dangers notwithstanding, classifications must be given greater attention even when they collide with the individuality so highly prized in psychotherapeutic circles. Over years of being oriented to individuality, psychotherapists have increased their skills in fostering stronger, more personalized behavior in their patients, and they have guided them to new levels of individual personal awareness. They often did this instead of seeing the enduring community of people and institutions as a key support for an enduring sense of self. Now, when the isolations in our society are of greater concern, it has become important to recognize that therapy's emphasis on personal accomplishments has overshadowed the durable qualities of belonging. These durable qualities must be accommodated to maintain context, continuity, dependability, and coherent change.

Shared identities are brought into unforgettable relief by an infinite range of simple experiences, such as "a candle lit at a ritual, the flap of a flag, or the odor of onions and thyme sautéing in olive oil" (Moerman, 1993, p. 96). More than a sentimental crutch or a nostalgic rush, these stimulations of our self-realizations enable us to drink in the special assurances that group identification provides.

These assurances may be empty if the individual fails to participate with the depth that is called for. Those most absorbed in the group to which they belong will most readily recognize the self that is reflected in membership of a group of friends; or a worker proud of his company's productions; or a member of a beloved family; or even a participant in a square-dancing group, a bowling club, or a stamp collectors' society. These associations are self-clarifying only to the extent that one's current life experiences fit the membership. In full identity with the group, membership may create a brightened self, recognizable and refreshing. This brightness must be maintained continually by the fluctuations and experiences of the individual's actual behavior.

Membership in an enduring community offers a major reference point, a guide to a sense of self through the generous opportunity to tell about personal accomplishments. One is continually challenged to create congruence between self and community as well as between self and continuing personal experience. The self is therefore defined by this continuing exploration, which results in advances in such functions as assertiveness, goal-directedness, confidence, affection, and receptivity—all of which are important for friendships, business success, entertainment opportunities, good sex, and a happy marriage.

All these personal functions, the enhancement of which has been the core purpose of therapy, have also been crucial to the formation of self, constituting the substance of what one's life is about. We must ask, therefore, whether it is sufficient for a person to reach experiential goals if she has not also increased her awareness of who it was who reached them.

Chapter 12

Resistance

The common view of resistance sees it as the refusal to do what some external source demands. The French Resistance Movement during World War II was driven by the refusal of some French people to yield to Nazi governance. An example more relevant to the psychotherapist is the person who refuses to work in his father's company because he needs time to discover what career he wants to create. Another example is resistance to an idea, like dictatorship or accumulation of wealth or federal taxation policies. While these examples all represent the refusal to submit to outside pressure, they are different from what most psychotherapists mean when they speak of resistance. In psychotherapy we refer to resistance when the authority is *internalized* and no longer actually in power. The patient is caught in a personal dilemma, troubled with a compelling need to resist an inner facsimile of the old authoritative pressure, long gone but still exercising control. He becomes stunted in his choice-making, often betraying his own self-interest.

This adaptation of the meaning of resistance was a cornerstone of psychoanalysis and other theories that emphasized authoritarian supremacy, plugged into the patient's mind, leading to self-suppression, canceling important life opportunities. Because of this internalized suppression, the individual person may well, for example, be unwilling to do her homework even though she wants a college degree; refuse to accept other people's opinions even though she needs stimulating conversation; refrain from laughing because that would be too lighthearted. Life is filled with such mistakes, and it is a fundamental task of all people, and surely those in therapeutic work, to resolve these entrapments.

If it weren't for such resistance, people *would,* after all, enjoy themselves at picnics. They would succeed at work, cry when they're sad, play with their children, have orgasms when sexually engaged, and so on. Traditionally, resistance implies that people are not doing what they "should" be doing, like visiting a friend, doing homework, or writing a song. Any illogical interference to moving in these directions has been blamed on resistance, a stubborn, self-defeating influence, alien to the person's rightful behavior. According to this view, the barrier must be removed, so that the "right" goal may be reached. Hence, the resisting force is seen as a saboteur and, in fact, as an agent not of the self but rather of the antiself. It surely seems that way when, for example, one person insists on obedience, even when independent behavior would be in his best interest. A strange psychological alchemy takes over and won't let anything happen that even suggests disobedience. When in obeying he fails to do what is obviously the right thing, we want to obliterate the power of the pernicious effects of invisible authority, leaving the individual free to be the person he could or should be.

To expand this concept, Gestalt therapy introduced the idea of "creative resistance," which told us that people resisting can turn their resistance into desirable characteristics. For example, refusing to obey a parent may lead to the freedom to invent. Indeed, there is more to people than their thwarting or yielding nature. Each of us is composed of a panorama of events and understandings, all of which make their marks in the formation of our lives. Therapy needs to reach beyond negative consequences and recognize the creative effects that may accompany inhibitory pressures.

We see that this self-inhibiting behavior or feeling is not just a dumb barrier to be removed, but a potentially creative force for managing a dissonant world. For example, a child learns to inhibit his crying after discovering that it brings unwelcome reactions from his parents. Because his arena of action is restricted to the environment he can navigate, he takes conditions as he finds them and does the best accommodation he can, including the end of crying. Later on, he becomes less limited, ranging farther from home, developing a new sense of his nature. Now, it becomes apparent that there was a serendipitous learning process. He unhooks himself from the previously learned, no longer useful messages.

The person who stopped crying because of the pain it brought when his parents spanked him, left him, surrounded him, or hollered at him, has done more than just block his crying. Through perceiving his parents, he has thereby extended his sensitivity. He has discovered what life can be like when crying is an unacceptable alternative. He may have become toughened and durable. He may have developed tenderness about the needs of others. He may have expanded his powers to assimilate sensation without having to release it. On the other hand, he may also have developed a cold nature so as not to be tempted to cry or developed a chronic whine or a thousand other unpleasant characteristics. In any case, the concept of creative resistance takes the person as he is and accentuates what exists so it becomes an energized part of his character rather than a depersonalized dead weight.

Labeling the unwillingness to cry as merely resistant would be misleading. To remove the resistance in order to return to the purity of crying is futile because the person who has resisted has learned new things. There is no way to return. Every step in the re-organization of the mind becomes part of a new formation of the individual's makeup. He does not become the old person plus a resistance that is removable. He is a developing person.

Gestalt therapy has sent a message not of resistance but instead has emphasized the relationship among the disparate parts of the person. These are disconnected from each other because of the seeming incompatibility of their characteristics, which actually have the possibility of becoming integrated. We saw this in the previous chapter regarding the role of polarities, and we must now further apply the idea of re-integration to the full range of personal characteristics that have become alienated from one other.

Therapy without resistance

No need or characteristic of the individual exists alone; its counterpart is also present. The union of these aspects is complicated by the large range of internal realities that may not be peacefully achieved. We have already examined this struggle in the examination of the Gestalt concern with polarities. Each faction in this scenario wants to dominate, and each is also subordinate to the individual's need for internal unity.

The neighborhood tough guy may, for example, also have a soft side that once plagued his existence. Showing his soft side may have gotten him into trouble, or he may have internalized standards of his childhood and views his periodic moments of softness as threats to his self-esteem. So, in the interest of survival, as he sees it, he covers over and subdues his soft responsiveness. He got the message of *toughness* early on and forgot what he reflexively wiped out of existence.

The therapist must be alert to the surfacing of polarities, which often requires sensitive attention. For example, a moistness appears around the tough guy's eyes, or perhaps just a flicker across his eyes, a swelling in his lips, or a relaxation of his wrist. At first, the disowned soft side would be easy to disregard; he has been doing it for so long. Even if the person is willing to engage the two parts of himself in dialogue, there would at first be a poor quality of interaction, including mutual disregard, scorn, low energy involvement, and a sense of the futility of any interactions; what could they have to say to each other? The therapist, however, contributes her observations and brings to the patient's awareness the chronic discounting and stand-off. The patient is intrigued, and then vitality enters into the dialogue. The disputants address each other more vigorously, each insisting on recognition for its contribution to the totality of the individual's experience. Gradually the acknowledgment comes, that each does something to define the person in full dimensionality. Rather than becoming a one-dimensional tough guy stereotype, he can become, for example, a compassionate tough guy, a tender but outspoken professional, or any of a number of other variants. He is free to invent for himself all the possible permutations of being tough *and* soft. When this happens, he is whole and more open to doing what had once seemed unlikely and troublesome.

Given this broadened perspective on the diminishment of personal function, it's worth looking at the therapeutic factors that carry the therapy method beyond the concept of resistance into a broad scope of the troubles evident in personal dysfunction. Here are a number of those considerations.

From dissonance to unity

In the last chapter, we saw that a person is a composition of characteristics that can be dissonant and that call for integration. The same is true not only of polarities but of the full range of dissonant characteristics. In fact, this is a holistic imperative: When a person's characteristics seem incompatible, they are still actually quite available for integration. At first, it seems they are incompatible because each aspect is vying for acceptance. But we can achieve empowering and fulfilling behavior and feeling through the addition, rather than subtraction, of one part, even when it seems destructive to the whole. This integration gives validity to a broad range of dissonant aspects of the person, creating a fresh scenario.

A therapeutic fairy tale will illustrate. Frank says he is unable to enjoy himself at family picnics. He feels neurotic and dull. Rather than seek a guiding authoritative source for this idea, one that disapproves of his behavior, we look instead for the variety of personal expressions that accompany Frank's complaint, the absence of pleasure at picnics. We see that while he is talking, his face is screwed up in a painful expression, part of the unfolding configuration of his experience. The therapist suggests that Frank attend to his face. Frank agrees, and when he focuses on his face, he is surprised to notice tension there. As he stays with this sensation, he begins to feel warmth developing in the tense area and then he experiences a slight movement. "It's an involuntary grimace," he says. As he concentrates on the grimace, the tightness grows, bordering on pain. The therapist suggests he make a sound that might fit the tension and movement, and Frank screws his face up and grunts several times. When asked what making that sound feels like, he says it's like wanting to have a bowel movement but can't quite get it out. He feels weird about this fantasy, but he also feels some relief from the tension. He actually likes making the sound but is embarrassed and blushes as he speaks.

"Suppose," says the therapist, "that you just make the sound, setting aside any meaning it may have for you." Frank makes the sound again, and this time his hands begin to move slightly in rhythm with the sound. Asked to notice his hands joining in, Frank says, in surprise, that they're giving a beat to the sound and he then begins to snap his fingers. Soon, laughing, he says, "This is incredible fun," and goes into lively song. Finally, he's overcome by hilarity, falls to the floor saying this is more fun than shitting. And unlike shitting, he can do this publicly. He is aware of absorbed internal excitement and of being carefree. There is little concern about defecating or any other mistake that free expression might lead him into. The original feeling of prohibition is gone. Bowel movements are not the paradigm of action, and he feels whole. No villains, only characters in this story.

This illustration took seriously the simple aspects of the person that were part of the story. The process of moving from each aspect to the next had the natural amplifying powers of life's flow and moved him on to climax and closure. In the stalemate between fear of defecating and the fun of rhythmic pleasure was a surprising newfound freedom. This altered his stuckness by revealing a fresh fertility in his makeup, transforming struggle into creation. Such ingredients, in this instance focusing on the tension in his face, grunting, snapping his fingers, and singing, changed the chemistry of his personhood, forming a new configuration. *What is, is. One thing follows another.*

Instead of trying to reach particular goals or meanings, the psychotherapist following these precepts focuses on what's actually present. This offers a large range of possibilities. The patient's beguiling voice, dramatic story, contradictory statements, perspiration, glazed eyes, flaccid posture, unfounded optimism, and so on, ad infinitum. The therapist's own attitude, imagery, sensations, and so on are also fair game. From this range the therapist chooses a particular move forward, one that invites the patient's unfolding of thoughts and feelings. When the therapist helps the patient enter the flow of what is actually happening, a resuscitative process is started that enlivens even simple events.

The experiment

A key companion of this integrative process is the "experiment," which offers an opportunity for the patient to safely practice facing certain interpersonal challenges. It is a representative of the motto "we learn by doing" and allows a free-wheeling opportunity for patients to behave with more feeling in this experimental situation than they might in their everyday lives. It has the effect of keeping the person in an action mode rather than trying to figure out what past experience has caused current behavior. The "experiment" has been called a "safe emergency" because of the expertise and guidance of the therapist. That solid support and leadership make the experience safe, even though the content might otherwise feel prohibitively risky.

While safety is provided by the benign emotional climate, there remains a felt emergency. The patient is facing an uncertain consequence because the therapeutic sweep enters them into areas that were until now out of bounds and laden with fear. Laura, for example, while turning away, refers to her grandmother. This might be easily passed over, but the therapist senses significance. In fact, Laura had been traumatized by her grandmother's death and had learned to manage intimate relationships coolly. By now it was just part of her familiar style. The shock she had experienced at her grandmother's death became real again. A further amplification came when the therapist asked her to play the role of her grandmother. Laura then remembered Grandmother sitting like a sparrow, with her head tilted to one side. Laura tilts her head, assuming her grandmother's posture, and looks at the therapist with the same undemanding, loving expression she remembers her grandmother had. Only now she feels what it's like to *be* such a loving person. She blushes with the animation brought on by the easy affection. Grandmother was like a star in the heavens beaming out from the deep reaches of the universe, but now she's no longer an everyday part of existence. Now in this experiment, the grandmother returns to life within Laura's own skin, a hint of what Laura has left behind.

While there was safety assured in this therapeutic exchange, the risk of mourning existed. Laura's mourning had been set aside when Grandmother died. Now, she discovered that she was actually beyond mourning and was ready to assimilate Grandmother's basic warmth. Feeling this warmth, she realized her spouse, children, and colleagues needed her. However, on those occasions when she couldn't give them what they needed, she felt unlovable, and then she couldn't love them either. The therapist says, "Be your grandmother and tell these people about you." Still playing her grandmother, Laura tells about how, as a child, she wanted to know everything and was constantly coming to her grandmother with stories about new discoveries she had made. Laura's spouse, in fantasied dialogue, responds by saying that's just what he loves about Laura and what he's been missing. To Laura's children, Grandmother tells how Laura could always make up games and toys out of the most unlikely materials, a wooden crate, an old quilt. Then the therapist asks Laura to respond as her children. Turning to the imagined Laura, they observe the fact that she never just plays with them and would she please, please, and who cares about dinner. Laura, realizing what she has dismissed from her own adult function, is inspired to become again what she had once been, supporting herself now that the support of her grandmother is gone. Instead of a mournful resignation about her coldness, Laura transcends her immobilization and restores warmth.

This is only one illustration of the consequences of re-creating grandmother. The improvisational possibilities are endless. The action is open-ended, transcending accustomed modes for dealing with memories, fears, or sadness, and moving the individual into untried and unpredictable directions. In the improvisational cycle played out in the experiment, the patient was moved to fresh ways of being. As I have said elsewhere,

> The patient in therapy... may tremble, agonize, laugh, cry, and experience much else within the narrow compass of the therapy environment. He is traversing uncharted areas of experience which have a reality all their own and within which he has no guarantee of successful completion. Once again she confronts the forces that previously steered her into dangerous territory and the return trip

(may) become as hazardous as he had reflexively feared. The therapist is her mentor and companion, helping to keep in balance the safety and emergency aspects of the experience, providing suggestion, orientation, and support. By following and encouraging the natural development of the individual's guiding themes through their own directions into completion, the therapist and patient become collaborators in the creation of a drama which is written as the drama unfolds. (Polster & Polster, 1973)

Thus we see that the concept of resistance has served well in our examination of unfulfilled behavior. It reveals ways people aren't behaving in their own best interests. So describing the drama of dissonant experiences within the person, each aspect with its own merits, helps restore harmony, as internal struggle becomes a stepping-stone to personal revelation. It's evident that not only is resistance useful as a guide to understanding the disruption of personal function, but it also leads to valuing the integration of dissonant aspects of the person. What is divided becomes one.

Psychological detective

During the age of resistance, the psychological detective was a primary prototype, representing the uncovering of the hidden. Many of us are fascinated by following clues until we find a hidden ingredient. The temptations of psychotherapeutic detection are supported by the fact that we often *can* discover that which is already there. Mother bakes a pie. Child hopes it's a pecan pie. It is covered, though. Child lifts the cover and sees a pecan pie. The excitement radiates in the child, a new delight. But the pie *was* already there. Only the discovery is new.

It's difficult to transcend the magnetism of uncovering and replace it with creativity. Creativity is the development of something that never existed before, like what a mother experiences when she bakes a pecan pie. Though she may have a lifetime of experiences with pecan pie, this new one never existed before, and her pleasure comes from the process of creation and the freshness of experiencing an altogether new pie. So too in therapy do we discover what is developed anew. In the earlier illustration, Frank was unable to have fun at family picnics, and then he did something that at first was reminiscent of defecating. But this was replaced by a pleasurably fluid and musical movement. We followed his sequence of experiences, which culminated unpredictably in a lively song. There are also "uncovering" aspects in the experience, and looking for the hidden is not wrong. But it is more rewarding to follow the freshly unfolding process than to view it as uncovering something previously obscured. I would rather bake a pie than look for one, though I never turn one down when I find it.

Immediacy of function

The emphasis on immediacy is another methodological advance that also overshadows the role of resistance.

For example, the woman who looks around the room while talking seems preoccupied and not engaged. When the therapist suggests that she notice how her eyes wander and that she say what she sees, this may represent inordinate curiosity, which, when acknowledged, results in a lively, visual experience. Although the original inclination of the therapist may be to consider looking around the room as irrelevant to the current process, a mere deflection, a change in priorities may lead to the discovery that looking around the room is primary and talking to the therapist secondary. A basic propellant to change is the acceptance—even accentuation—of existing experience, believing that such full acknowledgment will, in itself, propel the individual into an unpredictable but beneficial progression of experience. This step-by-step process is a partner to the experiment. It is faithful to the existing readiness of the patient. No great leap of insight is required nor is there a harsh confrontation.

This flow of experiences is easily integrated, step by step. Gradualism builds in drama, with the fresh experience of each moment building into a crescendo of meaning. A major barrier to the development of this flow is impatience, as the thoughts and feelings expressed may not seem important enough. It is a key therapeutic function to affirm the value of the seemingly unimportant. This can be accomplished by a selective process, which keeps the conversational development close enough to importance that, when added to the magnetism of the therapy atmosphere, will come closest to affirming the importance of the single event. If I, as therapist, say to the patient that his words could use some added color and that I would ask that he sing them, he will likely find that important, even if it might otherwise seem irrelevant. I have credit in his bank, so he goes with the request. It turns out to transform a boring observation into a colorful understanding and deeper connection with me. This attention to the small contributors to the flow of experience builds up a crescendo of importance as each new moment opens people to the courage to face what is next, and the safety of doing so. As this builds into climactic affirmation, the trip has been one of relative safety, so the alarm bells of nextness are softened and what often had been called resistance is a much lessened force.

New climate

Even in the early psychoanalytic accentuation of resistance, there was a larger process in which the analysis of resistance was secondary to the fertility of the therapeutic encounter. The sessions included freedom of speech, absorbed listening, and open-minded acceptance of the forbidden.

This receptivity to a natural flow of mind softened the internal dissonances that plagued the otherwise beleaguered patient.

This setting—individual or group—is well known as benign, composed of people who commonly benefit from secure communication. They are not likely to be adjudicated, ostracized, flunked, ridiculed, or otherwise pilloried as a result of their actions or words.

People are, therefore, not crowded by the complex, causative requirements of the world out there. The climate is usually one of live and let live; there is a subtle optimism that the puerile, the confusing, the disgusting, the frightening, and their like, will soon turn the corner and become vibrant, touching, revealing of inner beauty, and restorative. Consequently, there is less need for people to interrupt themselves with resistance. When one believes that what is happening will turn out well, even if presently painful or problematic, acceptance is easier. Each individual may discover an expansion of psychological space within which to function.

The new community is, of course, not Eden. People do get angry with each other, misunderstand each other, trick each other, walk out on each other, and shower a whole range of kindred brimstone on their co-sufferers. Usually these mutual disturbances are dealt with skillfully and with an understanding of life's unruly happenings. Because of the shared exploratory climate, the extended time opportunities, and the presence of a therapist who is commissioned to mind the store, these dissonances can be grist for the mill of growth.

Personhood

Many excellent therapists offer a clear sense of presence. They are empathic, well-schooled in a large range of human experience, radiant, and absorbed. They can be tough or tender, deep, serious, or funny. They are capable of great absorption with another person's storyline and open to facing the dragons of the mind. Yes, these are extravagant expectations, but they serve as guidelines to understanding the therapist's role. If patients spend intimate time with such a person, some of it will rub off on them. Patients then absorb a new way of perceiving, articulating, and considering. They learn new perspectives and recognize alternatives to whatever is happening. They engage in a new partnership of feeling and experience with someone who knows how to accept, frustrate, and arouse. They meet surprise and adventure, and hopefully, they imbibe a respect for what it is to be a human being.

In the face of such awesome characteristics, we may well wonder whether humility is also included. Fortunately, it's not necessary that the therapist be such a marvel as we might wish. What is more important than the inventory of desirable characteristics is the fact that the therapist is, after all, a human being. As one, he or she affects one. Once when a patient wanted me to refer his 14-year-old son to a therapist, he specified that he wanted it to be someone by whom he would like his son to be influenced. That's not a bad question to ask. The therapist's personhood ranks high along with techniques and knowledge. A kind person will affect others through his kindness, a demanding person through her demands, a person interested in power through his forcefulness. What is important, however, is that the therapist not be required to hide these characteristics or interests (especially when they organically appear). However, she must also be tuned in to the consequences of her characteristics in order to serve the well-being of the patient. The therapist's influence is indispensable and unavoidable, and if the exercise of it risks putting inappropriate demands on the patient, this only reminds us there is no guarantee of a good job. Permitting the influence to appear does not free the therapist of the requirement for exercising a transcendent artistry that unites her own personhood respectfully with the authentic personal needs of the patient.

People's personal needs include the expansion of the range of experience that their identity will allow. They will commonly express only those that do not threaten their sense that they are still themselves. It's important that they learn to experience aspects of themselves they formerly obliterated as too threatening. The narcissist feels endangered by having to listen to others. The macho man feels terrorized by his impotence. The chronically supportive person feels engulfed by disquieting rage. All of them have narrowed their self-definition by refusing to accept alienated parts of themselves. The whining person, the saboteur, the leech, the ogre, all may be exiles from awareness, now calling for their right to be heard. Malaise ensues because the risk of reappearance by these characteristics causes unbearable disturbance for the individual's self-image. When new behavior in stimulating therapeutic relationship happens, previously unacceptable characteristics can be reflexively assimilated. Given a new voice, individuals may discover themselves to be quite different in actuality from what they feared they might become. These alienated parts have found a home. The patient's sense of self expands, encompassing new possibilities in behavior and feeling, setting limits based on present experience, not just past trauma.

Sharpening contact

The seven basic contact functions are talking, moving, seeing, hearing, touching, tasting, and smelling (Polster & Polster, 1973). These are going on all the time, and the improvement of the quality of these forms of contact can involve quite simple practices, following specific deficiencies as they are observed in the therapeutic session. In focusing on these functions, the Gestalt therapist seeks to improve such qualities as clarity, timing, directness, and flexibility.

The patient may, for example, talk too loudly, too abstractly, or too distractedly, or exhibit many other manifestations of poor contact. All of the contact functions have been subjected to erosive deterioration by cultural prohibitions. Growing up is a lengthy process of learning what not to see, touch, say, or do. Many people have overlooked their own contact functions for so long that, although dismayed about their lives, they have little awareness of the simple, but far-reaching, deficit. Gestalt therapists are oriented toward these interruptions and deficiencies; they must develop a safecracker's sensitivity to what is missing as well as to what is too much.

In working with a man who speaks incessant gobbledygook, the therapist may ask him to limit himself to simple declarative statements. Or the therapist may respond to the circumvented meaning. Or the therapist might ask a verbally stingy woman to add a few words to her sentence once she thinks she has completed it. Or the therapist may ask a monotonal man to sing his words. Following this tack, therapists will frequently meet with objections, but if the procedure fits, they won't have to work through so-called resistance; they can just do the thing and see what happens. When the request is not far out of line, people are surprisingly accommodating to trying out the therapist's instruction. As the patient warms to her task she may discover a new clarity, a pungent sense of humor, or an affection that endures through the expression of criticism. When the patient begins to respect the liveliness accompanying her critical faculty, she is on the road to magnifying her diminished zest. The original dread of herself as a tyrannical critic may evolve into the discovery of her genuine perceptual powers and the zing of not soft-pedaling them.

Goal setting

It's only natural for people to look ahead in any process and set goals. This is true for both therapist and patient. If not for the inspiration of personal goals, there would be no therapy in the first place. People want to get better in specific ways. The task of the therapist is to bracket off these goals so in order function in continuingly present experience—even though at heart he is wanting the patient to give up alcoholism, improve relationships with people, find good work, say goodbye to dead parents, and so forth. The difficulty of coordinating goals with immediate process is not unique to psychotherapy. A home-run hitter in baseball will tell you he cannot focus on hitting a home run. He must attend to the ball and to his own swing. Great novelists do not foreclose their own surprise at how their characters develop. Psychotherapists also must tune in and remain faithful to what matters in the unfolding situation.

Tight therapeutic sequences

I have described tight therapeutic sequences extensively in chapter 8. Now, I just want to point out their relevance to a diminished role of resistance in the therapeutic repertoire. What is relevant here is that the tight therapeutic sequences depend on immediate short steps in the movement of the patient's communication. This gradualism makes it easy for patients to say yes to the process. This simple fluidity lowers patients' sense of danger, diminishing their need to resist this manageable sequence. Such sequentiality builds into a storyline that can be assimilated while maintaining faithfulness to the organically unfolding process. It brings the person closer and closer to feelings and behavior that were previously feared. The resulting storyline has its own drama, developed with a lowered need to thwart the process. This means that the sharp attention to each moment is undemanding while relying on the person's own timing to reach new understanding, inspiration, ideas, memories, and behavior potentials.

Conclusion

The extensive attention given to the idea of a therapy without resistance might well be interpreted to mean that therapy is a free ride, one which can achieve results without actually facing problems. Not at all. Therapy's very existence is a response to people whose minds have been beleaguered with contradiction, shame, failure, confusion, and all the other manifestations of troubled living. Nor does this examination exclude the fact that the origins of the trouble do not come entirely from the external world. Rather they reside in the contradictions between one's basic needs and the hospitality of the world to accommodate these needs. Psychotherapy deals with the registration and integration of life's complexities.

Chapter 13

Public trust

Psychotherapy's social importance has gone far beyond that of giving help to people needing to solve specific problems. Instead by its advocacy of individuality, its accentuation of relational bonding, its emphasis on free expression, and its description of common states of mind, it has met a larger need in modern society. It has provided an encyclopedic range of writings and lectures that populate our libraries, bookstores, and universities. For more than 100 years, these communications have multiplied, evoking a community-wide interest in self-examination, moving society into the Age of the Psyche. Nowadays, when there is a mass shooting, we ask why the mental health system can't prevent this, and we seek public comment by psychologists. When a marriage goes bad, we talk of suppressed anger or excessive dependency or self-centeredness. When a person feels troubled and the response is, "You should talk to someone," we know they mean a psychotherapist. When an employee gets fired, we may say he was too bossy or too rebellious or too meek. Hardly anything we do these days is free of speculation about motives, conflicts, and identities.

People analyze movies to find the psychological message. They form groups of like-minded people, including categories such as single mothers or ornithologists or alcoholics or even those with the name of Smith. A large body of empathy is publicly and privately expressed for the downtrodden or the misunderstood, recorded in popular books, magazines, newspapers, and television. There is substantial consciousness about people trying to become the best people they can become.

The silent momentum of this century-old expansion of psychotherapeutic understanding and application appears in the wake of the continuingly dominant role of religion, whose hold on the cultural mind remains unarguably huge. Despite a gnawing image of spoiling the joy of living and sponsoring a number of archaic beliefs, the influence of religion continues to be strong. That is a pivotal reality and will help to point the way for psychotherapy to engage the population at large with its perspectives, building a public trust in its offerings.

There is good reason to recognize the enduring powers of the belief in an everlasting supernatural guidance. Without going into a detailed examination of the historic motivations for this belief, we can assuredly recognize that in one form or another, it has been here a long time and probably will continue to be. Elsewhere, (Polster, 2015) I have examined some innate characteristics of people for whom a belief in the supernatural is a magnet. The supernatural will probably continue to exercise its influence on society. But what is more pertinent is to recognize that religion is not the only game in town. The amount of attention devoted to other responses to understanding the nature of living and the directions we set into our lives has become so large that it merits recognition as a major cultural force.

Yes, indeed. Psychotherapy's palette of ideas represents an alternative to the Western religious systems of orientation and guidance. Psychotherapy is explicitly awakened to the integration of diverse human experiences rather than to a universalist credo. Rather than give priority to uniformity of behavior, psychotherapy envisions the successful merger of anyone's individuated personal circumstance with communally prescribed priorities as a hallmark of an inclusive mind. Such recognition of the compatibility of the individual and the universal is so fundamental to a beckoning society that a successful management of the two merits a high level of social trust.

Belief in the universal and the supernatural, as we see it in the Western religions, is no casual reality. It will undoubtedly be present in the Life Focus Groups. Secularity notwithstanding, it is humanly compelling, perhaps irresistible, for people to want to understand a universe by speculations and beliefs that rise beyond the missing facts. People have a natural extrapolative function that strives to tease out beliefs about an invisible world or the ultimate nature of existence. That is common, even among those dedicated to the perspectives of psychotherapy. Many people in the Life Focus Groups will have such spiritual interests, and these represent their legitimate need. Indeed, this reach into the seemingly unknowable is often quite exciting and illuminating. However, in these groups this does not create dogma. Our focus is on the broader landscape of more directly observed aspects of society itself.

Psychotherapy's prospects for public trust need to be achieved in its own thematic and procedural way. To expand the social impact of therapy's distinctive style and repertoire, I suggest that the trust so vital to its social application can be expanded by satisfying a triad of conditions: Conceptualization, Continuity, and Community. Psychotherapy has made prodigious contributions to the conceptualization of our human existence, but has fallen short on the other components of this triad: continuity and community. Let's take a look.

Conceptualization

Conceptualization refers to the large body of perspectives and procedures that psychology and its antecedents have been exploring from ancient times to the present. In this book, I have given voice to some of these principles and procedures from the standpoint of Gestalt therapy, but these represent only a small part of the contributions of psychology. Furthermore, other fields of study, notably philosophy, literature, and religion, have joined in taking large strides in understanding the human experience. Our sense of life is surely interwoven with the offerings of the Greeks, Shakespeare, Rousseau, and Nietzsche, as well as Galileo, Newton, and Einstein. While these expansions of the mind's horizons have provided bountiful years of enlightenment, we may well experience ourselves as recipients of the baton of human progression, participants in the magnetism of a growing perspective and absorbing action.

Psychological perspectives have themselves contributed substantially, expanding the cultural interest in the nature of our lives. These explorations have been voluminous and are beyond the scope of this chapter. They include insights concerning common human experiences such as sibling rivalry, hormonal dysfunction, symbolism, competition, and shame. We have explored the nature of ambition, love, embarrassment, empathy, and the innumerable accompanying conditions of living. While the resulting understandings are by no means clear-cut, they are the indispensable instruments for further exploration of the place of people in this complex universe.

How do we cull a meaningful message from the countless ideas already communicated? How do we frame a sense about the nature of our lives? How do we make this transformation from academic and clinical purposes to those of palpable guidance of everyday people? All of this is well under way, and progress is evident in, among other places, the various forms of life focus groups. These include mindfulness groups, self-help groups, men's groups, women's groups, 12-step groups, religious and relational groups, Seligman's internet and military explorations, civic groups, compassion groups, and social media groups.

Let's take a look at listening as one conceptual theme that was examined at a Life Focus Group. Listening is an example of a commonly unnoticed force in relationships. It is a springboard for continuity, ensuring that what I say will faithfully connect with what you say. This connection provides grace to conversation and a union between otherwise separated people. As with all basic functions, there are roadblocks to listening. The urgency to speak may cause me to be more occupied with waiting my turn than with listening to you. Or I may be afraid of what I hear—what it might stimulate in me, such as anger, submission, or opposition. Or I may become confused about the meaning of what I hear. Or I might feel put down or accused or invited to something I don't want. In the distracting silence of partial listening, continuity is interrupted and life becomes choppier than it would be in a more harmonious listening.

Here is an example from a Life Focus Group meeting in which listening was the subject of exploration: One person in a sub-group, Tom, spoke about the intrusions he feels in everyday life, bemoaning the fact that intimacy of conversation is so rare for him. He became most aware of its absence only after a power blackout. The loss of electricity created a metaphorical blank space, making him more clearly aware of listening as a phenomenon in its own right, as well as a call for response. While this accentuation of his listening led him to the practical effect of conversing intimately, the contrast with his normal experience made him all the more appreciative of the vitality of listening. Then he said, "This is so cozy and it's romantic and wonderful. But why must we wait until the electricity goes out?"

While listening intently to these observations, a second person, Phil, influenced by the way he heard the observation about electricity, responded with his own experience of listening by telling about a personal memory. It was just an ordinary story, but in the high focus of this meeting, it had strong emotional resonance. He said, "When my two sons were smaller, we'd go into the bedroom at night just when they were going to bed, turn out the light, and they would say, 'Tell us a make-up story, Daddy.' They listened and then I would just start spinning this story. It's the phrase that the story always started out with: Once upon a time, in a place far, far away. You know, we would just journey to this far-away place, you know like all these stories do. They just listened. It was just incredible. The absolute greatest of pleasures."

He felt deeply about this, because he had been more than ordinarily moved by what he heard from Tom. The immersion he felt upon hearing the first person's candlelight experience impelled him into his own, idiomatic pathway, with his memory tapped, love for his children registered. When he listened to the teller of the electricity outage story, he felt the spirit of it and it reminded him of his fairyland of pleasure and the marvel of his children listening to him, enraptured as they listen, listen, listen. The same words, heard with a more common half-hearted listening, might have passed by with little effect. Instead, each person in this conversation experienced an affirming mutuality amplified by the entire plenary group addressing the same issue.

A further affirmation of the relational importance of listening is the work of the actor. For him, listening is a basic instrument that steers him into the believability of his own words. To listen well and be authentically affected by what he hears contrasts with the pretense commonly attributed to acting. He is inspirited by having heard the other character and also by having that character listen to what he says. It is probably true that some actors can "pretend" and speak their lines from memory. But good acting is more than pretense. Alan Alda explained,

> When I started out as an actor, I thought, "Here's what I have to say; how shall I say it?" On M*A*S*H, I began to understand that what I do in the scene is not as important as what happens between me and the other person. And listening is what lets it happen. It's almost always the other person who causes you to say what you say next. You don't have to figure out how you'll say it. You have to listen so simply; so

innocently, that the other person brings about a change in you that makes you say it and informs the way you say it." (Quoted in Taylor Willingham "Listening is Key to Acting" [texasforums.wordpress.com, no longer available])

Listening is just one example of the bountiful range of themes people face every day that highlight personal perspective. The stimulation provided by the Life Focus Group magnifies personal reality. Such an evocative setting is a contrast with just living, where themes might pass people by as unremarked phenomena. Such themes as compassion, ambition, laughter, gift giving, and many others call out for a level of attention that is often absent. Each of life's basic themes arouses intimate storylines, revisiting the experiences of each person.

The recognition and understanding of these themes are part of the material that the field of psychology has long been exploring. While these thematic guidelines are illuminating, a next step for conceptualization is to create pithy insights. Psychotherapy has some offerings, as I show below, but they are all vulnerable to the complexities of the real world and the insufficiency of shorthand language. In the everyday world, shorthand language gets center stage and there is little room for expanded examination or communal exploration. Nevertheless, the real world is pivotal for shaping the mind, which seeks a quick read.

Still, the everyday people around us arouse and nourish us in an ongoing continuity. While we feel our individuality, there is also a surge to union, which is evident in the Life Focus Groups but is dimmed by the more manifest individuality that guides each person. Such separateness is mitigated, though, in some mysterious neuronal dynamic pointed to a union of people. This impulse to union goes on, often silently, unnoticed by many because they live in a world where the most evident reality is that self and other are distinctly separate. The boundaries between people, commonly felt, may fade in special circumstances, such as in the instruments in a great orchestra playing together, or in an audience entranced with an orator, or in a conversation where each remark builds seamlessly on the preceding one. In the search for union, it is restorative for the Life Focus Group to provide exercises inviting people to pay attention to the experience of listening and to how it affects the coherence of their conversational relationship.

Perhaps psychotherapy needs more pithy guidelines than many of its themes offer. There are some illuminating attempts. For example, Gestalt therapy's widely influential advisory to live our lives in the "here and now" caught the attention of the populace, reminding us that the moment-to-moment experience should be recovered from the befuddling complexities of past and present, there and then. While the aphoristic here and now represented a necessary emphasis on immediacy, the larger theoretical Gestalt picture included the entire background of anyone's immediate existence. It is this coordination of immediacy and context that is crucial for good living.

Another popularly recognized observation was created during the heyday of transactional analysis, which coined the concept "I'm O.K., you're O.K." This represented an affirmation of the acceptability of people as they are. This was an important message, but it left out obvious exceptions, where people were clearly not at all O.K.

Another more recent example is that of the team of Harville Hendrix and Helen Hunt (Hendrix & Hunt, 2015). In advising marital couples, they make three lively points: 1) Conflict is growth trying to happen; 2) It's not him, it's you; and 3) A laugh a day keeps the divorce lawyer away. These are sharp guides, clarifying to many, but, of course, the contradictions are also there. A laugh a day may not keep the lawyer away, and it may cause you to ignore what should be faced. Hendrix and Hunt, of course, elaborate these maxims with detailed illustration, but the maxims themselves are short and don't only lead to growth; they may also squash it. For example, it may not be as much you as the other. But the easily assimilated aphorisms have turned out to be a safe stimulant for public understanding. The beauty of successful slogans is that, while they are all plagued with contradiction, they may hit the social communication mark by getting the intended message across while the contradictions remain inactive in the background. That is what is often felt about the Beatitude that tells us that the meek shall inherit the earth. It gets across the equality of people, whatever their social status, but it may not be seen as an advocacy for meekness. What a successful slogan can do is provide a general perspective that sweeps into the public mind as a rallying point around which people can organize their lives.

Although psychotherapists have not generally encapsulated their ideas in commonly understandable terms, the material for wise prescription has been there since the beginning. Some of the observations offered by major theoretical contributors have expressed perspectives comparable to the homilies of religion, providing distinct social potential if reframed only slightly. For example, Freud said, "We are so made, that we can only derive intense enjoyment from a contrast and only very little from a state of things." He is implying that we should pay attention to life's diversity, rather than to favor a fixed standard set by other people. Pavlov said, "Don't become a mere recorder of facts, but try to penetrate the mystery of their origin." This tells us not to narrow ourselves with simple facts but to welcome the mystery of their context. Erik Erikson said, "There is in every child at every stage a new miracle of vigorous unfolding." He is telling us to recognize the exceptional flow of life, one miracle after another. William James said, "The greatest discovery of my generation is that human beings can alter their lives by altering their attitudes of mind." This is a reminder that if we think anew and feel anew, we invite the new. These were all wise observations that were read by many, especially in the professional ranks, but they were stated for a rational rather than inspirational purpose. Though people did not leave whistling the tunes, the music is there. While these psychological assertions don't ring bells, they do reveal key aspects of the human condition, parallel to the illuminations provided by religious maxims.

Psychotherapy has created its own pathways to public understanding, and its future expansions will come in its own forms. As I have said, much of this has already happened and will continue to unfold as psychotherapy attends more pointedly beyond its clinical purpose by addressing such quintessentially common issues as conflict, desire, relationships, imagination, and loyalty. The Life Focus Groups personalize these messages, each of which is pivotal for public acceptance, within a communal structure.

While psychotherapy maxims are people-friendly and lubricate interrelationships, they are often either ignored or held so strictly that many people fail the test. Generally, therapists do not want to give pronouncements about required behavior. People should not feel doomed if they don't measure up. Still, there are certain positions that, wary of absolutism, they have individualized to fit the life of the specific person. Pay attention; be faithful to what you perceive; develop empathy; join up with your surroundings, human and otherwise; keep plugging away at your purposes; find a place where you feel belonging; get the best education that fits your needs, and so forth. There are a huge number of such psychologically familiar perspectives, widely accepted as fundamental to human well-being. While offering no utopian expectations, psychotherapy has offered a corrective process for illumination. However, such messages may often be pithy slogans, illuminating but narrow. They must be filled out with storyline, each person having the opportunity to say where the instruction fits into their actual experience and how these maxims have concretely served to affirm their lives. This fleshing-out process is addressed in detail in chapter 6 on Life Focus Groups.

Nevertheless, it must also be said that, no matter how strongly people want unity, they don't have to have it. Dissonance has its own majesty and is functional in its own right. Dissonance can be a relief from union, a veiled opportunity to create new harmonies, perhaps as rebellion, perhaps to solve a puzzle, or just as part of the unruliness of events. It is a signal for an advance in conceptualization.

Community

Religion has shown the way to communal accessibility, even indispensability. Through the creation of the congregation, large or small, it has provided a vehicle for people to gather together and create a picture of basic behaviors and feelings. Each congregation has a life of its own, functioning beyond the attendance of any specific members. The housing for the congregation is usually a familiar edifice, with which the practices of the group are identified. Indeed, when one walks into a church, a synagogue, or a mosque, one enters a sanctuary, invited to leave the ordinary stream of life and reach out for the eternal and mysterious. Sometimes the housing serves as a glorification, symbolized by monumental architecture that helps to enlarge people's experiences and gives them a head start in communal dedication and inspiration. This can also be felt in the greater intimacy of small-scale settings. In either case, the communal sensibility is grounded in people joining together, converging their individual needs with a communal awareness, further amplified with music, historically important stories, and a universal affirmation of personal acceptability.

In the Life Focus Groups people talk to each other about key aspects of their lives. This practice contrasts with religion's supernatural guidance and targets themes that populate our minds but usually receive only glancing attention. The sharpness of attention in the Life Focus Groups, as well as the simultaneity of communal responses to these themes, amplifies individual personal awareness. Further, the joined examination of these themes fosters microcosmic implications. That is, the experiences of the group represent more than what people feel individually, as they serve as a spin-off from the model of the larger society, lighting up not only individual experiences, but life itself. Music and its companions, visual and verbal art forms, add an arousing entertainment value. While entertainment is often dismissed as lighthearted and evasive of depth, it is a hidden factor in biblical stories, revelatory novels, and fruitful conversation. Such experiences as beauty, helplessness, tragedy, and personal success and endurance receive a boost in awareness of life's range of happenings. The communal option for psychotherapy has been blunted by its historical emphasis on privacy. But nowadays, the communal exploration of intimate experiences is no longer widely prohibited by a professional insistence on privacy. Over years of conducting therapy sessions in front of large conferences, I've seen that many of the people I've worked with have been more inspired than inhibited by the presence of a benign and lively audience. The exploratory atmosphere of the Life Focus Group is designed to keep interpersonal reciprocation open, and the resulting resonance encourages a high level of trust, and when safely shepherded all these factors help to connect us to each other more deeply. The engagement also provides the widely overlooked benefits of witnessing, which involves empathy of the listeners to the unfolding stories, fostering an appreciation of others and heightening the impact of everyone's experience. Since people are naturally interwoven, there is a great potential for pleasure. These explorations also address other compelling needs, such as the need for moral guidance, a story to live by, and a place of assured acceptance. It is within this enlarged and lyrical landscape that a contemporary public momentum can move psychotherapy beyond the mere clinical remediation of what has gone wrong in an individual's life.

Throughout this book a primary purpose has been to characterize the functions and relationships that are inherent to the creation of trust within the Life Focus Groups. As important as examining what has gone wrong, people must also be directed to the commonalities and wonders of what actually happens in their lives. Hence, the mission becomes less a matter of "fixing" people than igniting them to incorporate the vast human landscape into their lives.

The trust that is created has two faces. One offers standards and procedures, many of which are described in this book, and are based on actual happenings. The other is a symbolic trust. From the symbolic position, trust is grounded in a powerful belief system, sometimes mistily defined and sometimes commonly understood. Trust is attained not only because of benefits but by dedication to a general belief system. For example, a symbolic trust may be felt about family and may override the actual facts about discordant values, insensitive punishment, infertile conversations, and so on. For many people, the family symbolizes a special mindset for intimacy, and this is not up for continued assessment. Family is family, and to know it allows its desirability to survive beyond specific conflict, disappointment, or even personal violation. So it is also for many, multiplied exponentially, with the concept of God, in whom symbolic trust is felt to be supreme, whether benefits are felt or not.

Symbolic trust, so embedded in interpersonal attachment, is further enhanced by the sense of connectedness of people with each other. While it is an exaggeration to think of people as indivisible from each other, there is, nevertheless, a strong sense of "we" that guides much of human relationship. Forgiveness is easier when a "we" is operative. Indeed, we are not alone, because we are we. While it is important not to diminish a fundamental individuality of people, it is also true that connectedness is compelling. So compelling in fact, that it borders on indivisibility. Experiences of seeming indivisibility happen only under extraordinary circumstances, such as in deep meditation and profound religious experience, orgiastic sexuality, heroic courage, hallucinations, and sudden awakenings from sleep. Their importance stretches even further than that of these exceptional events. They serve as a beacon into the more common experiences of connectedness, serving as a microscope, alerting people for lesser but vital realizations of relationship and its accompanying sense of belonging. Though I may not experience my spouse, my friend, my church, my profession, or my country as indivisible from me, the union creates a sense of unquestioned identity. Most of us are quite satisfied to feel this "we" aspect of living without experiencing the fullest merger that devotees and monks describe.

Only in special forms of concentration or in the presence of special talent or inspiration does one experience revelatory oneness. It is on the road toward the unreachable where we find ourselves in the highly reachable pleasures of connectedness, in that place of interacting with others—an everyday happening that is personally nourishing. A telephone call from a dear friend, a birthday celebration, visiting a childhood home, these are samples of palpable connectedness. This sense of "we" is prominent in the

Life Focus Group, which fosters a communal vitality, a palpable example of the poetry of connectedness.

Can psychotherapy induce a symbolic trust that meets the need for heightened communal engagement? The answer is partially given historically. People are masters of symbols. They create them quite generously, giving abstract importance to political parties, corporate brands, and heroic personages, as well as mother and the flag. So it is not unrealistic that a movement like the Life Focus Groups may develop symbolic powers of its own, associated with practical trust about receiving an enlightening perspective, nourishing procedures, and vitality of relationship.

Continuity

Psychotherapy has been bounded by its concept of "terminated therapy" and its attention to acute problems. It is true that during the flush of long-term therapy, the process often lasts a few years, but even then, the sign of a successful therapy was that it would become finished. Nowadays, even long-term therapy has been dramatically reduced by insurance-oriented time limits.

The Life Focus Group is a vehicle for changing that time limit by its indefinite extension of the group's duration, potentially meeting for a lifetime. This expansion makes sense, given a change in purpose from solving specific problems to the everlasting need for connection, orientation, and guidance. Many groups already meet for indefinite periods of time. Two Life Focus Groups that I lead have been meeting for about 25 years, though their membership has changed. Not surprisingly, when group members speak about the trust they experience, it is based not only on the content of the meetings but also on the enduring nature of the setting, the relationships, and the group itself. It takes time for ideas, empathy, and familiarity to get full registration. As one group member said, in speaking of her trust of the group to accept whatever she was revealing, "I think that open expression has something to do with longevity too. It's being known over a long time. I don't think I would have that sense of 'no danger' in any group that was new to me. I don't think I'm wired like that."

While the trust in these groups increases with continuity, one must also ask whether this increased level of trust creates a risk of dependency. Therapy, after all, has commonly been seen as no more than a way station to living well. The capability to be independent has been measured by freedom from continued guidance. Indeed, it is true that dependency is a risk. What must be recognized, though, is the pleasure and affirmation of a lengthy relationship. A person who misses the neighborhood she moved away from; the person who would faithfully attend her book club meetings; the person who has had a long marriage: these people may well have soaked in the beauty of their experiences. Yet they can also live independently of these experiences. They find these sources of personal grounding to be a support rather than an interference with their independence.

This integrative requirement is a phenomenon with which we all live, incorporating contradiction. Combining such potentially dissonant characteristics as trust and dependency is not only common but inevitable. For example, if people are forthright, they may also become insensitive. If people are kind, they may also be gullible. If they are inventive, they may also be chaotic. Plainly there is a natural downside to any desirable characteristic, which is to say, anything that can be done can be overdone. So, though dependency may, indeed, result from continuity, the risk is counteracted by security, inspiration, and practical insights into everyday living.

In an enduring Life Focus Group, this challenge for integration could also be explored, just as many other life themes are. The group design allows for vigilant attention to the role of any theme in any member's life. It would surely be absurd to exclude a continuity of life exploration because it encourages trust. Given the benevolent effects of trust, it is better to deal with the potential pitfalls in trusting than to wipe out the continuity that fosters it. Continuity is an important basis of trust, and this trust can help expand the benefits of psychotherapy in our culture.

The triad of conceptualization, community, and continuity are, indeed, key factors in psychotherapy's development of a public trust. In the long run, this trust must take its place in the momentum that a social ethos inspires. The ideas of monogamy, democracy, women's rights, abolition of slavery, and religious freedom represent only a few of the social progressions that occurred when the time was ripe. This is an elusive process, but the signs of psychology's expanded impact on society are so broadly evident, as I have tried to show, that it promises to continue its expansion into the orientation and guidance of people at large. The chemistry of progress creates an insistent pathway.

There is now ample precedence for this to happen—for trust and connection to grow and thrive among the members of Life Focus Groups and the movement within which they are embedded. These perspectives and activities are on the edge of a new ethos. They can transform psychotherapy from a privately remedial and secular experience to one that kindles a new level of public awareness and an accessibility that would be dependably available on a lifelong basis.

Author's note

Segments of my previous books are included verbatim in the current book, with permission of the publishers. They are:

Beyond Therapy
A Population of Selves
Twelve Therapists
Every Person's Life is Worth a Novel
Gestalt Therapy Integrated

Also vital for the current book is *Uncommon Ground*, published by Zeig, Tucker, and Theissen, Inc. in 2006. While no verbatim segments appear in the current book, the writing of *Uncommon Ground* was important in the development of my perspective enunciated in the current book.

Bibliography

Alda, Alan. (2006). Quoted in Willingham. T., "Listening is key to acting." http://texasforums.wordpress.com/author/texas forums.

Barron, J. (1994). "In Just A Word, Who Are You?" *New York Times*, Nov 14, pp. B1, B4.

Beisser, A. (1970). The paradoxical theory of change. In J. Fagan & I.L. Shepherd (Eds.), *Gestalt therapy now*. New York: Harper & Row, pp. 77–80.

Buber, M. (1955). *Between man and man*. Boston: Beacon, p. 6.

Bullivant, A. (1983). In D. Arnold (Ed.), *New Oxford companion to music*. New York: Oxford University Press, p. 501.

Cary, J. (1961). *Art and reality: Ways of the creative process*. New York: Doubleday.

Csikszentmihalyi, M. (1990). *Flow*. New York: Harper Perennial, p. 54.

Damasio, A. (1999). *The feeling of what happens*. New York: Harcourt, pp. 27–29.

Dawkins, R. (2006). *The God delusion*. New York: Bantam.

Eiseley, L. (1975). *All the strange hours*. New York: Scribner's, p. 3.

Estrup, L. (2010). *Flying without wings: Life with Arnold Bessier*. Film available through LivEstrup.com.

Elliot, T.S. (1943). *Four quartets*. New York: Harcourt Brace Jovanovich.

Hendrix, H., & Hunt, H. (2015). *Making marriage special*. Nevada City: Harmony.

Hunter, J.D. (2000). *The death of character*. New York: Basic Books.

Johnson, Deborah Liv, (1995). "Tanzania." Across the White Plains. CD: Mojave Sun Records.

Kierkegaard, S. (2011). *Purity of heart is to will one thing*. New York: Harper Collins.

Machado de Assis, J. (1990). *Epitaph of a small winner*. New York: Noonday Press, p. 202.

May, R., Angel, E., & Ellenberger, H. (1958). *Existence*. New York: Basic Books.

Moerman, M. (1993). *Ariadne's thread and Indra's net: Reflections on ethnography, ethnicity, identity, culture and interaction. Research on Language and Social Interaction*, 26(1), 85–98.

Newberg, A., & Waldman, M. (2009). *How God changes your brain: Breakthrough findings from a leading neuroscientist.* New York: Ballantine Books.

Paltin, C. (2014). Personal communication.

Perls, F.S. (1947). *Ego, hunger and aggression.* London: Allen & Unwin, p. 21.

Perls, F., Hefferline, R., & Goodman, P. (1951). *Gestalt therapy.* New York: Julian Press, p. 90, p. 373.

Polster, E. (2015). *Beyond therapy.* New York: Routledge.

Polster, E. (2006). *Uncommon Ground.* Zeig, Tucker & Theissen, Inc.

Polster, E. (1995). A population of selves. San Francisco: Jossey-Bass.

Polster, E. (1987). *Every person's life is worth a novel.* New York: W.W. Norton, pp. 4–96.

Polster, E., & Polster, M. (1974). *Gestalt therapy integrated.* New York: Random House.

Polster, E. (1972). Stolen by gypsies. In A. Burton & Associates (Eds.), *Twelve therapists.* San Francisco: Jossey-Bass.

Proust, M. (1924). *Remembrance of things past.* New York: Random House, 124–126. Quoted by Sandel, M. (2010). *Justice.* New York: Farrar, Straus, & Giroux.

Kennedy, R. (2010). Quoted by Sandel, M. *Justice.* New York: Farrar, Straus, & Giroux.

Sarton, M. (1966). *Private Mythology.* Norton.

Sartre, J.P. (1964). *Nausea.* New York: New Directions.

Sartre, J.P. (1948). *Existentialism and humanism.* London, Methuen, p. 28.

Schlesinger, A. (1992). *The disunity of America.* New York: W.W, Norton.

Siegel, D. (1999). *The developing mind.* New York: Guilford. p. 305.

Smith, A. (1965). *Wealth of nations.* (first published 1776). New York: Modern Library.

Stegner, W. (1993). *Where the bluebird sings in the lemonade springs.* New York: Penguin Books.

Woolf, V. (1927). *To the Lighthouse.* London: Hogarth Press, p. 47.

Yapko, M. (2009). *Depression is contagious.* New York: Free Press.

Afterword

Margherita Spagnuolo Lobb[1]

Having come to the end of this book, so expertly introduced by Scott Churchill, a leading American scholar of academic phenomenology, I would like to return the compliment with which Erving placed this book in my hands by contextualizing it within the framework of his thought, which has been so significant for the development of Gestalt therapy.

I would like to start by saying a few words on our relationship, before outlining the trajectory his publications have taken and the novel insights they have brought to psychotherapy, and paying tribute to Erving's generative style, in keeping with the "hermeneutic circle" triggered by Goodman in the foundational work *Gestalt Therapy*.

Our relationship

I first met Erving Polster when I was 23 years old. A fledgling psychologist, I went to train in psychotherapy under him and Miriam on the advice of a lecturer of mine, Prof. Herbert Franta. It was 1980, and after publishing *Gestalt Therapy Integrated* in 1973, they had moved from Cleveland to La Jolla in California. That book was a seminal work, enthusiastically hailed everywhere by Gestaltists eager for a new reference text for their instruction. Although it was an academic work (Erving taught in the Department of Psychiatry at the University of California, San Diego), it was easily comprehensible and open to the various currents in Gestalt therapy and psychology emerging at the time. Thus it was welcomed favorably by many who felt frustrated by the opacity of the foundational text (*Gestalt Therapy*, by Perls, Hefferline, and Goodman, 1951), by the theoretical gap left by the founding group with their refusal to write other books, and by the antitheoretical stance taken by Perls in his later life. The book thus responded to a need for new tools for teaching Gestalt therapy.

My training in San Diego, California, was a dream come true for me. It was an unforgettable experience, one that left a deep mark on me, perhaps in part because of my tender age (Erving likes to joke that he needed my father's permission to accept my enrollment in his post-graduate program), in part for the new language I was learning to live with, and in part for the "crazy" Californian lifestyle that was a real eye-opener for me. Today I understand that what I learned from "father Erving" and "mother Miriam" was to develop my aesthetic sense and ability to grasp what is taking shape and emerging from the present moment, an ecstasy toward the blooming of a flower, toward the desire for something better that springs from the tear of a client. I owe my inner Gestalt sensibility to them, as can be grasped from the title of my book *The Now-for-Next in Psychotherapy*[2] and its contents. Drawing clearly on one of Erving's recurring themes, it seeks to merge the phenomenological and aesthetic perspective of the Polsters with the teachings of Isadore From (my therapist) on the phenomenological field and those of Daniel Stern (my mentor) on primary relationships.

Today I am proud and almost overwhelmed to receive this book from Erving, a testament of sorts, to be published as part of the Gestalt Therapy Book Series, edited by the Istituto di Gestalt HCC, Italy. With much the same sense of awe I felt at 23 years of age, it is like receiving a gift too great for me, and I can only hope to make good use of it. That it should be the first book of the new series published by Routledge is certainly a promising sign.

Themes in his published works to date

Erving Polster is one of the world's most esteemed psychotherapists, an author of major importance for Gestalt therapy.

After the publication of the ground-breaking work *Gestalt Therapy Integrated*, written with his wife Miriam, Polster published *Every Person's Life Is Worth a Novel* (Norton, 1987), in which he speaks of the enchantment that comes from every person's life, and where, interestingly, he connects the function of therapy with the discovery and sustainment of that enchantment. Here, the definition of neurosis no longer revolves around the repression of unacceptable experiences (as in the tradition of psychodynamics), or the disowning of parts of the self (as stated in Perls, 1969), but turns on the concealing of our being interested/interesting, which in practice means neglecting an interest in, or aesthetic propensity for, our own vitality. Remaining within the phenomenological framework of the making of experience in the here and now, he sheds a highly original aesthetic light on Gestalt therapy work through the concepts of interest, curiosity, and love, both in the therapist and the client. It is a perspective that enables integrity to be restored even in borderline situations of great suffering for the client—situations neglected by humanistic psychotherapies at the time of their inception, which later would come to emerge in clinical practice.

According to Polster, experiencing the enchantment of our lives is possible when we "consciously lean into nextness" (Polster, 1987, p. 46), as it is in that passage of the now-for-next that we find the freshness to develop our life stories with vitality and a sense of belonging.

In the book *A Population of Selves: A Therapeutic Exploration of Personal Diversity* (Jossey-Bass, 1995), Polster proposes a definition of the complexity of the self through the concept of connectedness (which builds on the concept of the now-for-next). Every part of the self is interconnected, for which experience proves to be unitary, despite the complexity of its diversification. It could be said that in this book, Polster redefines the concept of organismic self-regulation, so dear to humanistic psychotherapies, to make it less simplistic by incorporating the concept of complexity into it.

In the book *From the Radical Center. The Heart of Gestalt Therapy*, authored together with Miriam (GIC Press, 1999), they define the quality of contact (p. 37), in what they call the "attention triad," a combination of three processes: concentration, fascination, and curiosity. These comprise a practical description of what we mean by "being fully present at the contact boundary." Developing the crucial theme already set out in '87, that being interested/interesting is a quality of good contact, they provide a phenomenological description of awareness. Awareness is not consciousness; it has the meaning of the Greek word "Karis": to be totally present here and now, in the reality of this very time and space, with the harmony that comes from the organism being focused on only one thing. (We would say at the contact boundary; Aristotle would say "in the finger that hurts."). Awareness is the quality that characterizes contact and makes the self a unique and unified experience of body, mind, and soul.

The clinical use of the concept of interest here implies two remarkable aspects. The first aspect is that the therapist's feeling of interest in the therapeutic setting is a barometer of the quality of contact with the client. The second is that fluctuations of interest in the therapeutic relationship can be a guideline for the therapist to understand the flowing of the client's energy involved in contact making and therefore can improve the therapeutic process. Usually the therapist's interest is captured by the vibration that she feels in the therapeutic field, and the vibration is transmitted by the client's contact making, which includes a drama made of wishes and fears at the same time.

As a matter of fact, in the experience of interest, many basic principles of our approach are included: the human essence of "being-with"; the freshness of being open to novelties; and the deliberateness that emerges at the contact boundary as creative adjustment of organism/environment field. In other words, interest is what confirms our aliveness, in terms of energy, of meaningfulness, of relationality.

In the book *Uncommon Ground. Harmonizing Psychotherapy and Community to Enhance Everyday Living* (Zeig, Tucker & Theisen, Inc., 2006), Polster builds on an idea that appeared in *Gestalt Therapy Integrated*, which is that psychotherapy should be applied to common people—a psychotherapy that embraces all the population in its entirety, because "therapy is too good to be limited to the sick." He proposes *Life Focus Communities* as a methodology for large groups, with the aim of fostering in individuals a sense of belonging and of continuity, both fundamental ingredients for people to feel connected in social communities. Anyone who knows the foundational work *Gestalt Therapy* (Perls, Hefferline, Goodman, 1951) will recognize in Polster's commitment to social communities the social activism that animated Goodman and the founding group, and which ever since has remained strong in all Gestalt therapists (especially among our colleagues at the New York Institute for Gestalt Therapy), as expressed in their support for minorities across all social periods and geographic regions. Even if Polster makes no explicit reference to the foundational text, his idea that therapy cannot be limited to the individual echoes in all of us, because the organism/environment field is such a fundamental concept for Gestalt therapists. Indeed, Fritz Perls connected his insights on the development of aggressiveness in infants and criticism of psychoanalysis with the need for society to recognize the power of rebellion in its members. The unity of the individual and society is key for us.

The concept of Life Focus Communities features again in *Beyond Therapy. Igniting Life Focus Community Movements* (Transaction Publishers, 2015), an important thread in Polster's works, up to this book.

Thus we see how Polster has continued to focus on certain fundamental concepts throughout his life, changing the framework repeatedly to bring out new aspects. Those concepts can be summed up as enchantment, the now-for-next, and life focus groups. Even though they take us back to classical themes in psychotherapy, such as narrative, metaphor, and healing stories, they nevertheless contain a revolutionary originality for psychotherapy in their use of aesthetic phenomenological knowledge, which in this book is applied to large groups. Erving captures the heart of Gestalt therapy, that of staying with an experience as it evolves, of being guided by one's senses in understanding the profoundness of the other, and of the organism/environment unity that guides social life. However, he adds a connection with the transcendental that is quite peculiar, in that it is not esoteric but generated by the senses, as it is by staying focused on the here and now of contact with the other that we can reach a third reality, one that transcends us, wherein lies true change. That seems to me a foundational insight not only from the perspective of therapy, but also anthropology.

The innovative proposal of this book

Polster's thought falls within the scope of humanistic psychotherapies, which in the Fifties affirmed the dialogical value of the therapeutic relationship, overcoming the medical model and considering the therapist a "journey companion" for the client. For clients know the way out of their suffering. They are fundamentally healthy by nature, they just need to be accompanied wisely on their road to self-knowledge. When Polster says that therapy is too good to be limited to the sick, he makes another epistemological leap to imply that therapy *should not* be limited to the individual, but addressed to large groups and social communities.

His leitmotif strikes me as profoundly aesthetic and phenomenological, in its focus on experience in the making and the deliberateness that orients people in contact between them (the now-for-next), as well as on the self-regulatory effect that has at the community level (Life Focus Communities). To grasp experience in the making, Polster uses decisively aesthetic concepts, such as enchantment, in particular. Grasping the enchantment of events does not simply imply ecstasy. At the clinical level it also implies recognizing and feeling recognized in relational processes—whether bodily, cognitive, or emotional—in which spontaneity is stifled and there is suffering. Aesthetic knowledge allows us to access the invisible of the here and now (as Scott Churchill so clearly highlights in his preface) and to act at an unexpectedly deep level of therapy (see Spagnuolo Lobb, 2013). If we apply that concept to contact between individuals in groups, if we all recognize the reaching-toward in us and in others, a spark of magic occurs, as mutual recognition and heightened awareness at our contact boundary opens us to perceiving what transcends us as individuals and to entering another reality—a wave through the group, a faith that goes beyond individual limits, which drives true change in people.

This book pivots on the concept of enchantment, something that is "commonly seen when large numbers of people are moved by union with others, all pointing toward a common human experience" (as stated in the introduction). From the Gestalt therapy perspective of the now-for-next (the phenomenological reaching for the immediate future), Polster brings us to the perspective of enchantment, a phenomenon of communal ecstasy (from the Greek *ékstasis*, to come out of oneself) made possible by the sharing of an experience that, although human, transcends individuals. It is the triumph of the overcoming of individualism, where the author appears to affirm that only this experience of widespread human unity generates change.

It is an innovative insight and proposal for therapeutic change, one of great impact on our human and social values. In the Fifties, Beisser (1971) introduced a concept that would become crucial for humanistic therapies and for Gestalt therapy in particular, that of paradoxical change, while in those same years, Watzlawick (1967) distinguished first-order (superficial) change from second-order (authentic) change. Gestalt therapy took up those breakthroughs and put into focus the concept of co-created change as betweenness in action. Taking a fresh look at humanistic culture through the lens of what we might call a *field* perspective, Polster explains that change concerns communal feeling, a third reality that is created when a group of people are together. It is communal experience that creates change and growth. Just think of the social and political import of that concept, as well as the new light it throws on evolutionary theories.

Polster invites even the great Western religious systems to shift toward a field view: "This communal orientation and the accompanying guidance is a departure from the western religions in its understandings about life, its techniques for personal enlightenment, and its development of a new morality".

I find the three aptitudes on which Polster appears to base his conviction quite striking—an opening toward the invisible (toward mystery), achieved through an aesthetic and ecstatic attitude; the communal movement that occurs in community processes; and the overcoming of the narcissistic attitude in favor of a more holistic view that transcends the individual.

As he says in his introduction:

> These and other explorations into communal extensions of private therapy showed that the whole of its story is larger than its enhancement of the individual and their personal freedom. It also incorporates a broad perspective on the nature of living and the interest in the eternally elusive mysteries.

I have always found Erving's way of being open to mystery (his "enchantment" as he calls it) touching. I see it in the smile he gives when someone is about to discover something or when he challenges a person, expecting them to understand. This opening to mystery is indicative of both his intelligence and his humbleness. His intelligence makes him capable of both humor and Gestalt intuition, putting together the various details related by a client to restore the original brightness to a pallid figure. Instead of boasting about his intelligence, he has always placed it at the service of the other, waiting for him like one waits for a friend, or for a teammate to pass her the ball. What I have known as a personal trait of Erving's (his ability to ask simple questions, like Saint Augustine wondering why the sea could not be emptied into a bucket) in this book becomes a harmony of theory and practice, of opening up toward the mystery of diversity and of the humbleness that lies in being enchanted by life. It offers not just insights into the relational needs of people, but a pathway toward therapeutic and human maturity, which is enchanting.

Here, the aesthetic curiosity about human relationships that has always distinguished Erving adds force to a new perspective, in which change is generated by the possibility of feeling the magic of being together, by the enchantment that is created between people united by a common experience. This concept is very much in line with contemporary studies in Gestalt therapy, as it is a change not in the contact boundary between two individuals, but one generated in and by the field, encompassing those he calls "forever elusive mysteries." As he says, "This will require transforming psychotherapy's emphatic individualism to a communal belonging and enlightenment."

After the deeper rooting and innovative developments humanistic therapies found in Erving's previous works, here they find in this book fresh nourishment to reflect on community change. As human relationship professionals, we can look beyond individual processes and extend our gaze to take in mutual recognition and exchanges and that yearning for a common objective that transcends individuality. It seems to me an epistemological step forward, one that is necessary in a world in which a pandemic has made us realize how interconnected we are biologically and how nobody can save themselves on their own. So even in the realm of human relationships, we need to shift the focus from the organism/environment contact process (which pivots on the dyadic relationship) to the community process, understood as a communal movement toward a common objective.

Observing the group process rather than the individual process allows us to draw much greater strength than that which is created in the dyadic relationship, while enabling us to move past the narcissistic perspective, notoriously based on the sense of guilt at not being enough for the other and on the anger/disappointment at not receiving the exclusive love of the other. A community perspective deflects us from the anxiety of not feeling good enough for the other and from the anger aroused by not being recognized by him, with such suffering instead viewed from the broader outlook of the community, bringing our image of ourselves back into perspective and entrusting it to the support of our peers (Spagnuolo Lobb, 2018).

An enchantment that elicits enchantment. Erving's style

Putting aside the contents of this book, I am struck by the evocative power of the author's literary style. While reading through the pages, I felt inspired, and it made me want to write, too, to engage with Erving on the ideas that his words stimulated in me. This book generates action in the reader, not introjection. Far from being a showcase of his ideas, Erving evokes in the reader a desire to contribute through contact with him. His way of relating and narrating has therapeutic value in itself.

Just as *Gestalt Therapy*—our "bible" as such—was written with the intent of not being introjective, but rather of generating ideas (see Perls et al., 1994), it must be said that my teacher has reached the heights of writing a profoundly Gestaltist book, one that gives rise to movement and experience in the reader, rather than stagnant introjects. The reader, absorbed by the Gadamerian hermeneutic circle, will only be transformed by the contents of the book if she gives herself up completely to the reading experience—"to understand the book he must have the "Gestaltist" mentality, and to acquire it he must understand the book" (Perls et al., 1994). It is the great principle of experience, the heart of phenomenology and aesthetic knowledge, that Erving embodies, ultimately, in this book.

I have studied Polster's works in depth—I have even translated some into Italian—and I can testify to how each and every time it has been an experience of understanding human relationships through my own transformation. In this way, this new and compelling book restores the connection between therapy and life.

Notes

1 Psy. D., Director of Istituto di Gestalt HCC Italy (Milan, Siracuse, Palermo), post graduate School of Psychotherapy recognized by the Italian Ministry for University and Research.
2 Spagnuolo Lobb M. (2013), *The Now-for-Next in Psychotherapy. Gestalt Therapy Recounted in Post-Modern Society,* Syracuse: Istituto di Gestalt HCC Italy Publ. Co., www.gestaltitaly.com.

References

Beisser, A. (1971). The paradoxical theory of change. In J. Fagan & I. L. Shepherd (Eds.) *Gestalt therapy now.* New York, NY: Harper Colophon Books.
Perls, F., Hefferline, R., & Goodman, P. (1951/1994). *Gestalt therapy: Excitement and growth in the human personality.* Highland, NY: Gestalt Journal Press.
Polster, E. (1987). *Every person's life is worth a novel.* New York, NY: W.W. Norton & Co.
Polster, E. (1995). *A population of selves: A therapeutic exploration of personal diversity.* San Francisco: Jossey-Bass Publishers.
Polster, E. (2006). *Uncommon ground. Harmonizing psychotherapy and community to enhance everyday living.* Phoenix, AZ: Zeig, Tucker & Theisen, Inc.
Polster, E. (2015). *Beyond therapy: Igniting life focus community movements.* New Brunswick, New Jersey: Transaction Publishers.
Polster, E., & Polster, M. (1973). *Gestalt therapy integrated. Contours of theory and practice.* New York, NY: Vintage Books.
Polster, E., & Polster, M. (1999). *From the radical center. The heart of Gestalt therapy.* Cleveland: GIC Press.
Spagnuolo, L. M. (2013). *The now-for-next in psychotherapy. Gestalt therapy recounted in post-modern society.* Siracusa. Italy: Istituto di Gestalt HCC Italy Publ. Co., www.gestaltitaly.com.
Spagnuolo, L. M. (2018). Aesthetic relational knowledge of the field: A revised concept of awareness in Gestalt therapy and contemporary psychiatry. *Gestalt Review, 22*(1), 50–68. DOI: 10.5325/gestaltreview.22.1.0050.
Watzlawick, P., Beavin, J. H., & Jackson, D. D. (1967). *Pragmatics of human communication.* New York, NY: Norton.

Index

abstractions 21, 67, 87, 127
"accessibly hidden" concept 41–4, xi; defined 41; enhanced realization 44; in everyday life scenario 41–2; in non-business scenario 42–3
Adams, John 65
adrenalin 13
afterlife 27
aggressiveness 88, 158
Alda, Alan 144–5
ambition 27, 143
anal stage 4
anti-gay morality 108
Aristotle 127
artists 32
attention: curiosity 20–1; enchantment 23; fascination 18–20; here-and-now concept 46; narrowing of 46
attention triad 157
authentic change 159
authority 107
awareness: composite 83–4; continuum 85; and figure/ground formation 38; focalized 80–1; fundamentals of 80–92; ingredient 84; and insight 81, 82; loose therapeutic sequences 90–2; and meaning 81–3, ix–x; phenomenological description of 157; role of 80; stream of 85; tight therapeutic sequences 84–90

Barton, Anthony viii
behaviors: authority as base in controlling 107; communal 75, 76, 77, 147; and contagion 77; current 36; and current events 36; and experiences 36; home 3; homosexual 36; and morality 104, 106, 109; morally abhorrent 113; and multilarities 115–16; neighborhood 3–4; past experiences and 133; personalized 128; required 147; responsibility for one's 111–12; school 3; self-inhibiting 130; and unconscious 35; unfulfilled 135
"being-with" 157
Beisser, Arnold 40, 63, 159
beliefs 142
belonging 68–79; and communities 72–3; and conformity 68; congregation 74–5; ethos 75–9; and societal aura 68–72
Beyond Therapy. Igniting Life Focus Community Movements (Polster) 158
birth 27
book clubs 71
brain: as anticipation machine 86; primary function 116; scans 97; specialized functions 97
breathing 12, 13, 83
Buber, Martin 97
Buddha x
Buddhist meditation 16–7
Bullivant, Arthur 123

Cary, Joyce 127
Case Western Reserve University 4
castration anxiety 4
change 159; paradoxical theory of 40
chaos 91
Chaplin, Charlie 32
childhood experiences 83
churches 10

Index

Churchill, Scott 155, 159, viii–xi
client-therapist relationship: concept of interest in 157; morality in 105; transference in 96
co-created change 159
communal conversational vitality 27
communal ecstasy 159
communities 72–3; belonging to 72–3; membership in 128; and public trust 147–50
compartmentalization 45
competition 143
composite awareness 83–4; *see also* awareness
concentration: act versus object of 12; as agents of misery or happiness 13; communal implications 21–2; as a contentless form of energy 13; as core concept of Gestalt therapy 11; and curiosity 20–1; and enchantment 23–34; and fascination 18–20; fundamentals of 11–22; simplicity in 12, 14
conceptualization 142–7
conferences 10
conflicts 76
conformity 68, 76, 77, 79; *see also* belonging
congregation 62, 74–5, 147; *see also* belonging
contact boundary: amplification of contacts 96–103; common contacts 100–3; defined 93; fundamentals of 93–103; I-thou relationship 97–100; morality 104–14
contacts: amplification of 96–103; common 100–3; functions of 138–9; importance in therapy sessions 93–6; I-thou relationship 97–100; poor 138–9; versus relationships 93; sharpening 138–9; technical 100–1; transference 96; value-free function of 93
contagion 77
content, supremacy of 16–7
continuity 91–2, 150–1; of concentration 12; congregational 74; group 15; in tightened therapeutic sequences 85–6
contradiction 72
Cornhuskers 115
courage 61
creative resistance 130

creativity 41, 58, 135
crying 130
Csikszentmihalyi, Mihaly 86, x
Cuomo, Mario 124
curiosity 20–1
cynicism 19

Damaso, Antonio 14
Dawkins, Richard 75
death 27
"The Death of a Psychiatrist (for Volta Hall)," 99
depression 77
depth 28–33
depth dimension 82
depth psychology x
dialect 77
disobedience 104, 114, 130
dissociation 45
dissonance 132–3; functions of 147; in groups 109; replacing with integration 115; and resistance 137; resolving 114
distractions 12
divorce 27
dread 65
drugs 77

Eiseley, Loren 53, x
ékstasis 159
élan 13
Emerson, Ralph Waldo 69
empathy 143; in artistic experience 32; communal 30; group 63, 141, 150; of listeners 148; momentary 20; in moral dilemmas 109; and morality 104; and social networking 72
empty chair concept 116; inter-relational dialogue in 118–19
enchantment 23–34, 156, 159, 161; defined 23; and depth 28–33; examples of 23; in exploration of life experiences 25; versus familiar pleasures 31; and lightness 28–33; and microcosm 26–7; occurrence of 23; in religious experience 33; transcendence of nature's laws in 23; in wedding 33
enhanced realization 44
entertainment 32
Erikson, Erik 146
ethos 75–9, 91
events: in Gestalt therapy 11–2; in psychotherapy 11

Every Person's Life Is Worth a Novel (Polster) 156
excitement 13
existence 126; and enchantment 26, 32; versus essence 125–6; and I-thou relationship 97; soul as representation of 122; summary of 123, 124; and synaptic experiences 8; two-world 9
existentialism 126
experience(s): artistic 32; and behaviors 36; childhood 83; depth at the surface 83; diversity of 37; elusiveness of troublesome 51–2; enchantment in exploration of 25; flow of 86; fluidity of 35–6; lyrical attraction of 27; as an occurrence in time 46; pathological 56; pleasant, staying with 40–1; present 47–8; and primal familiarity 1–2; religious 34; superficiality/depth dimension of 82; surface 38, 80, 122, 123; synaptic 8; veil covering the interiors of 14

Facebook 71
Fagan, Joen viii
fascination 11, 18–20
Faulkner, Robert 53, x
fetus 98
field perspective 159
figure/ground: "accessibly hidden" concept 41–4; basic process 35–44; belonging 68–79; flow of mind 37–41; fluidity of experiences in 35–6; formation as basic dynamic of awareness 38; happenings in 35; here-and-now emphasis 45–9; life focus groups 56–67; mutuality of 37; overview x–xi; storytelling 49–55
films 27, 63
first-order (superficial) change 159
fluidity: defined x; of experiences 35–6; figure/ground resonance at root of 35–6; lowering sense of danger with 140; of moment-to-moment experience 84–6; releasing 90
Flying without Wings: Life with Arnold Bessier (film) 63
focus: engaging in 25; esthetic and relational pleasure from 14–5; excesses and distortions in 26; guidance in enhancement of 26; and microcosm 26
folk music 65

Franta, Herbert 155
freedom of speech 136
French Resistance Movement 129
Freud, Sigmund 11, 56, 58, 146
From, Isadore 7, 156
From the Radical Center. The Heart of Gestalt Therapy (Polster and Polster) 157

generosity 61, 65, 66
genital stage 4
geographical displacement 27
Gestalt Institute of Cleveland 7
Gestalt therapy 5–7, 11, viii–ix; versus Buddhist meditation 16–7; creative resistance in 130; events in 11–2; ground in 82; here-and-now approach in 46–7; immediacy of experience in 41; intention of 17; sharpened/expanded awareness in 80; and transference 96; without resistance 131–5
Gestalt Therapy: Excitement and Growth in the Human Personality (Perls, Hefferline and Goodman) 155, 157, viii
Gestalt Therapy Integrated (Polster and Polster) 155, 156, viii
goal setting 139
God 27, 63, 71
Goodman, Paul 7, 155, 157, viii
gradualism 53, 136, 139–40
grandmother, death of 133–4
gratitude 61; expressing and receiving 108–9
grimace 132
gross national product (GNP) 70
ground 82
group therapy 21, 22, 115
group(s) 10; continuity 15; conversations 15; formations 16; growth 9; individual therapy in presence of 62–3; plenary 60–1; process 22
growth 8; adversarial component of 76; and conflict 76; time for 64
growth centers 10
growth groups 9
Guernica (painting) 32
gullible self 126
gypsies 1, 10n1

Hall, Cavin 4
happenings 35; as agents of misery or happiness 13; distractions from 12; and diversity of experiences 37

hate 92
Hefferline, Ralph 155, 157, viii
Hendrix, Harville 146
here-and-now concept 45–9;
  effectiveness of 46; narrowing of attention in 46
hilarity 27
holism 45, x
home behavior 3; *see also* behaviors
homosexuality 4, 36, 107–8
hormonal dysfunction 143
housing projects 10
"human interest" stories 71
Hunt, Helen 146
Hunter, James Davison 104
husband-wife relationships 29, 54, 105–6, 110–11, 146

I-boundaries 127
I-it relationship 97
immediacy 136; "accessibly hidden" concept 41; deflection from 38; of expression 16; of function 136; and Gestalt therapy 41, 47, 82; limits of 41; and meaningfulness 15; restoration of 36
immediacy of experience 41; *see also* experience(s)
inaccessibility 19
incongruities 5
individuality 68–9
ingredient awareness 84; *see also* awareness
inner experiences 80; *see also* experience(s)
insights 81, 82
integration 132–3; of experiences 21, 46, 142; failures of 79; of personhood 17; replacing dissonance with 115, 135; spatio-temporal 86–7
interest, clinical use of 157
intermarriage 73
internal dialogue 117–18
Internet 72
inter-relational dialogue 118–21
"invisible hand" 69
I-thou relationship 97–100; *see also* contact boundary

Jackson, Jesse 124
James, William 146
jealousy 27

Johnson, Deborah Liv 60
Joyce, James 53, x

Kafka, Franz 53, x
Kempler, Walter viii
Kennedy, Robert 70
Kierkegaard, Søren 45, x
kindness 64
Kinsley, Michael 124

lectures 66
lesbians 28, 111
letting go 40
libido 13
life: inspiration for 13; and self 14
life focus: engaging in 25; excesses and distortions in 26; guidance in enhancement of 26; and microcosm 26
life focus communities 158–9
life focus groups 15, 43, 56–67, x; characteristics of 26–7; communities 148; concept of home in 98–9; and congregation 74; continuity of 150–1; design options for 62–7; enchantment in 27; ethos 75–9, 91; figure/ground concept 56–67; films in 63; individual therapy in presence of group 62–3; listening in 143–5; music 65–6; observations in 58–9, 61; personalization of messages in 147; perspective makers 66–7; practice programs 63–5; purpose of 56; reporting to plenary group 60–1; session introduction 58–9; stories 43–4, 106; subgroup demonstration 57–8; subgroups 59–60; theme consolidation 61–2; theme introduction 57; trust in 148–9
lightheartedness 28, 30
lightness 28–33
listening 143–5
Lobb, Margherita 155–61
loose therapeutic sequences 90–2; *see also* tight therapeutic sequences
loss of interest 20
love 27, 29, 65, 72, 143; and depth of experience 82; fear of falling in 38–9; and hate 92; inability to 28–9, 134; manifestation of 91–2; mother's 21; and narcissism 161; romantic 23, 29; wanting 29
lyrical attraction 27

Machado de Assis, Joaquim 124
mantra 12
marital couples 29, 54, 146
marriage 27
mass shooting 141
May, Rollo 126
Me Generation 26
Mead, Margaret 69
meaning: and awareness 81–3, ix–x; horizontal dimension of 81; vertical dimension of 81–2
meaningfulness 15
meditation 63–4
meditation music 65
meditators 12; brain scans of 97
memories, repressed 82–3
men's groups 71
mental pictures 53–4
Merleau-Ponty, Maurice ix
microcosm 26–7
mindfulness programs 71
mind(s): "accessibly hidden" regions of 41–4; flow of 37–41; union of 97–8
mirror neurons 75
misunderstanding 27
moral absolutism 112–13
moral dilemmas, accepting 109
moral relativity 112–14
moral values 27
morality 104–11; absence of 113; biting the hand that feeds you 110–11; context 114; gratitude 108–9; moral dilemmas, accepting 109; moral effect of key people 109–10; nonverbal 109; old 107–8; proportion 113–14; in psychotherapy 104–5; responsibility for one's behavior 111–12; righting a wrong 110; "shoulds" in 107–12
mother-daughter relationship 102–3
motherhood 116–17
multilarities 115–16
music 27, 65–6
mutuality 75; and belonging 22; in congregation 74; and convergence 22; ethos 77; of figure and ground 37; and gratitude 108; group 75; inter-relational 75; and morality 109, 112

narcissism 117
Nausea (Sartre) 50
Navratilova, Martina 124
Nazis 129

neighborhood behavior 3–4; see also behaviors
networking 71–2
neurosis 156
neurotransmitters 13
new climate 9
New York Times 124
Newberg, Andrew 97
nextness 88
non-interpretive movements 39
nonverbal acts 8
nonverbal morality 109
novelists 119
novelty 40; expectation of 43
now-for-next 159
The Now-for-Next in Psychotherapy (Lobb) 155

Obama, Michelle 28
observations, in life focus groups 58–9
old morality 107–8
optimism 65
oral stage 4
otherness 93, 96
other-world experiences 3; see also experience(s)

Paltin, Caroline 78
parent-child relationships 47–8
parents, dialogue with 47–9
patients: concentration of 12; unyielding characteristics of 20
Pavlov, Ivan 146
peace advocates 116
Perls, Frederick "Fritz" 5–6, 11, 22, 46, 85, 115, 126–7, 155, 157, ix, viii
Perls, Laura 7
personal identity 121
personal improvement 25
personal loss 27
personhood 137–8
perspective makers 66–7
phallic stage 4
phenomenology 7, 82, x
phenomenon 21; belonging 68; enchantment 23; lightheartedness 26; listening 144; microcosm 26; mutuality 75; networking 71–2; otherness 93, 96; "should" 107; tight therapeutic sequences 84; transference 96
Picasso, Pablo 32
pleasures 22, 31

plenary groups 60–1, 66
poetry 27
point/counterpoint 123–5
polarities 115–28; internal dialogue 117–18; inter-relational dialogue 118–21; and multilarities 115–16; personal essence in 121–3; point/counterpoint 123–5; surfacing of 131
Polster, Erving 155, 156–61, viii–xi
Polster, Miriam 64, 127, 155, 156, 157, viii
A Population of Selves: A Therapeutic Exploration of Personal Diversity (Polster) 156
populist psychotherapy 8
porn 105
prayer 63
present experiences 47–8
primal familiarity 4; characteristics of 1; conditions for fostering 9; and experiences 1–2; in focus groups 57
process groups 22
Proust, Marcel 53, x
psychoanalysis 4, 24, 61; cryptic unconscious in 82; enlightenment aspects of 56; versus Gestalt therapy 11; and resistance 129
psychological detective 135–40; contacts 138–9; goal setting 139; immediacy 136; in new climate 136–7; and personhood 137–8
psychological regimes 104
psychosexual stages 4
psychotherapy: access in ix; anticipatory excitement in 32–3; communal option for 148; enchantment in 23–4, 31; goals of 36; group designation 74; individuality in 68–9; intention of 17; populist 8; primary aim of 126; public trust in 141–51; search for meaning of events in 11; social importance of 141; without resistance 131–5
puberty 27
public trust 141–51; in communities 147–50; conceptualization of 142–7; and continuity 150–1

Rabelaisian self 19
relational groups 71
religion 27
religious experiences 34; *see also* experience(s)

religious organizations 71
repressed memories 82–3
resistance 129–40; and contacts 138–9; creative 130; defined 129; and disobedience 130; dissonance to unity 132–3; examples of 129; experiment 133–5; and goal setting 139; immediacy 136; and integration 132–3; in new climate 136–7; psychological detective 135–40; therapy without 131–5; and tight therapeutic sequences 139–40
responsibility 88
Romeo and Juliet 73
Rose, Charlie 69

safe emergency 133
Sandburg, Carl 115
Sandel, M. 70
Sarton, May 99–100
Sartre, Jean Paul 50, 126, x
school behavior 3; *see also* behaviors
second-order (authentic) change 159
self 14; classification of 125–8; gullible 126; and personal identity 121; Rabelaisian 19; as source personal guidance and enlightenment 122; as successor to soul 122; superior 19; superior versus klutz 18–9
self-help groups 71
self-image 107–8
self-inhibiting behaviors 130; *see also* behaviors
self-realization 24, 128
self-recrimination 87
sensory-motor beings 8
sequential inevitability 86, 89
sermons 66
sex 29
sexual relationships 54
shame 143
shared identities 128
Shepherd. Irma Lee viii
sibling rivalry 143
Siegel, Daniel J. 86–7
Smith, Adam 68–9
social networking 72
soul 122
speech, freedom of 136
spirit 13
Stegner, Wallace 69–70
Stern, Daniel 156

stimulus 36
storytelling 16, 49–55; details in 53–4; difficulty in 53; elusiveness of troublesome experiences in 51–2; mental pictures in 53–4; variation in 51; vitality of 50–1
subgroups, in life focus groups 57–8, 59–60, 66
superficial change 159
superficiality 82
superiority 19
supernatural, belief in 141–2
surface experience 38, 80, 122, 123; see also experience(s)
survival 72
symbolism 9, 143
synaptic experiences 8; see also experience(s)

taboos, loosening of 10
"Tanzania" (song) 59–60
technical contacts 100–1
terminated therapy 150
therapeutic sequences: loose 90–2; tight 84–90, 139–40
therapies: access in ix; anticipatory excitement in 32–3; communal option for 148; enchantment in 23–4, 24, 31; goals of 36; group designation 74; individuality in 68–9; intention of 17; populist 8; primary aim of 126; public trust in 141–51; search for meaning of events in 11; social importance of 141; without resistance 131–5
therapists: concentrated attention of 12; and curiosity 20–1; curiosity of 21; fascination by 18; here-and-now experience 45; loss of interest 20; personhood of 137–8
therapy groups 74; continuity 15; conversations in 15, 16; formations 16
Thoreau, Henry 69
tight therapeutic sequences 84–90; events in 84–5; illustration of 87–90; and moment-to-moment process 85–6; and resistance 139–40; role of 85;
and sequential inevitability 86, 89; see also loose therapeutic sequences
To the Lighthouse (Woolf) 91
topdog 115
toughness 131
town meetings 10
tragedies 72
transactional analysis 146
transference 96; see also contact boundary
trust 147–50
two-world existence 5, 9

Uncommon Ground. Harmonizing Psychotherapy and Community to Enhance Everyday Living (Polster) 157
unconscious 35; conscious/unconscious split 38; cryptic 82; versus focalized awareness 80; interpreting nature of 38–9; psychoanalytic view of 38; and soul 122
underdog 115
union 97–8
universities 10

verbal presentations 66
vital 13
vitality: communal conversational 27; of original events 50–1

Waldman, Mark 97
Watzlawick, P. 159
wedding 33
Weisz, Paul 7
welfare agencies 10
Whitman, Walt 69
will 13
withdrawal 88
women's groups 71
Woolf, Virginia 91

Yapko, M. 77

Zinker, Joseph viii

Printed in the United States
By Bookmasters